P9-ASN-438

WITHDRAWN

DATING METHODS IN ARCHAEOLOGY

JOSEPH W. MICHELS

The Pennsylvania State University

CARL A. RUDISILL LIBRARY
LENOIR RHYNE COLLEGE

SEMINAR PRESS   New York   San Francisco   London

A Subsidiary of Harcourt Brace Jovanovich, Publishers

913.031
M58 d
106470
Sept. 1978

COPYRIGHT © 1973, BY SEMINAR PRESS, INC.
ALL RIGHTS RESERVED.
NO PART OF THIS PUBLICATION MAY BE REPRODUCED OR
TRANSMITTED IN ANY FORM OR BY ANY MEANS, ELECTRONIC
OR MECHANICAL, INCLUDING PHOTOCOPY, RECORDING, OR ANY
INFORMATION STORAGE AND RETRIEVAL SYSTEM, WITHOUT
PERMISSION IN WRITING FROM THE PUBLISHER.

SEMINAR PRESS, INC.
111 Fifth Avenue, New York, New York 10003

United Kingdom Edition published by
SEMINAR PRESS LIMITED
24/28 Oval Road, London NW1

LIBRARY OF CONGRESS CATALOG CARD NUMBER: 72-84274

PRINTED IN THE UNITED STATES OF AMERICA

To Gabriele

Contents

Chapter Three. Basic Units of Analysis in Archaeology

Part Two

METHODS OF RELATIVE DATING

Chapter Four. Sequence Dating through Stratigraphic Analysis

Chapter Five. Sequence Dating through Seriation

Chapter Six. Cross-Dating

Part Three

METHODS OF CHRONOMETRIC DATING

Chapter Seven. Dendrochronology

Chapter Eight. **Archaeomagnetic Dating: Paleoorientation and Paleointensity**

Chapter Nine. **Radiocarbon Dating**

Chapter Ten. **Potassium–Argon Dating**

Chapter Eleven. **Fission-Track Dating**

Chapter Twelve. **Thermoluminescence Dating of Pottery**

Chapter Thirteen. **Obsidian Hydration Dating**

Preface

As an undergraduate studying archaeology, some years back, I often marveled at the way the excavated remains of prehistoric communities were understood to belong to a particular period in the past. The time depth of human prehistory seemed staggering. Professors would refer to a given culture as being "relatively young: only 6000 years old," when I had trouble comprehending the interval of time that separated the twentieth century from the era of the Old Testament! How could anyone be sure about anything that was supposed to have taken place 6000 years ago; including the idea that it actually did take place then rather than some other time? My professors would try to explain the methods of dating but I could not seem to shake off the feeling of unfathomable mystery that lie behind their judgments of archaeological time. It took a long time for this feeling to disappear, and I suspect that this feeling had something to do with my subsequent professional interest in the problems of dating.

I have written this book with the intent of dispelling this aura of mystery for future students of archaeology. In my own studies of dating methods I recognized two recurring aspects of uncertainty that contributed to the sense of mystery that I sought to dispel. One was my ignorance of the actual procedures and instrumentation involved in a particular dating method, and the other was my difficulty in understanding the extent to which the results were accurate and reliable.

In order to clarify dating procedures, therefore, I have chosen to regard *methodology* in its most literal sense in preparing the chapters that describe dating methods. With recipe-like detail I attempt to guide the reader through the steps that lead from sample recovery to determination of age. An effort is made to familiarize the reader with the *hardware* that is utilized during the course of dating. Although the descriptions of method are somewhat detailed there is no attempt to make this a technical laboratory manual. For readers interested in going further into any specific technique each chapter ends with a comprehensive list of readings.

Questions of accuracy and reliability are often more difficult to answer satisfactorily than questions of method. All of the dating techniques described have been the object of various criticisms. I have attempted to review those aspects of each method that have suffered significant criticism; always with the aim of putting such criticism into perspective.

One of the first notions that the reader must abandon, in order to secure a proper perspective, is the idea that our calendrical time scale, with its calibration by years, months, weeks, and days, is an appropriate model for passing judgment on the value of all time scales. The Christian calendar, like all calendar systems, is qualitatively different from all other dating systems currently in use by historical scientists. It was devised by the subjects of history themselves. In societies that employed calendars there was a consciousness of history and a desire to record it that impelled men to devise methods of defining precise temporal relationships between events *as they occurred.* This consciousness of history must not be confused with a consciousness of seasonality or autobiographical consciousness. It is fair to conjecture that all human societies were conscious of the recurring cycle of seasons and had developed unformalized systems of reckoning time accurate enough for planning out those activities that related to subsistence. Similarly, all individuals perceive their own existence as a time-dependent phenomenon. Concepts of *past, present, and future,* therefore, are part and parcel of human existence. The important difference lies in the meaning of past and future for a given society.

Subsistence needs, even when they include the need to know the proper time for planting and harvesting, seldom require a knowledge of time greater than the annual cycle of seasons. Within this cycle the calibration may need to be very specific or very general. Nature, however, provides very adequate temporal cues that can be used by man to regulate his subsistence activities. Temperature, rainfall, plant growth, the duration of daylight, animal behavior—all of these can serve man just as well as a formalized calendar in determining when he should plant, harvest, rotate field plots, set out fish traps, or move his family to a good berry-picking area.

It is in the context of religious behavior that we find the earliest impetus to the construction of formal calendar systems. Often these early calendars were designed to delineate significant episodes in the agricultural cycle of a society. However the underlying strategy was not to guide the farmer but rather to guide the priest. Calendars were used to regulate ritual behavior; including rituals which were designed to ensure the success of the agricultural venture. Preoccupation by priests with the causality of ritual motivated them to chronicle the sequence of natural events that were concomitant with the progress of the growing season. In this way a corpus of careful observations of periodic astronomical events was compiled. A number of these events were recognized to be cyclical such as the phases of the moon, the Earth's orbit around the sun, the heliacal rising of the planet Venus as the Morning Star. Such cycles, 28 days, 365 days, and 584 days, respectively, served as time scales.

Time scales are a product of dating systems. The system of dating in common use among societies with recorded histories involves careful observation of periodic astronomical events. Our own time scale, the Christian calendar, is based on the Earth's orbit around the sun, the phases of the moon, and the rotation of the Earth on its axis in relationship to the sun. These events provide the basis for our concepts of the *year*, the *month* and the *day* respectively. All of these events are cyclical and can only be differentiated by a system of counting. Thus we count the number of days in a month, the number of months in a year, and the number of years that have elapsed since some arbitrary point in the past such as the birth of Christ. The Maya had, in addition to a solar and lunar calendar, a Venus calendar with a cycle of 584 days based on the interval of time between the heliacal rising of the planet as the Morning Star. They also had a system of differentiating repetitive cycles called the *long count*. This amounted to a consecutive tally of days from a zero point projected far back into the past.

The historical scientist will make use of a society's calendar if possible but more often than not he will be obliged to turn to some other dating system or combination of dating systems either because there was no recorded history or because the history of a society extends back in time beyond the threshold of literacy. In judging such alternative dating systems the historical scientist is concerned not so much with how closely the resulting time scales approximate the Christian calendar but rather with how adequately they delineate significant change in the culture history of a society. A time scale that can accurately delineate millenia, but not centuries or decades, should be judged favorably when it is applied to the culture history of a society that undergoes little significant change during submillenial episodes. Such a time scale would be entirely unacceptable, however, for societies such as our own that undergo significant change almost every 20 years. It is in this spirit, then, that a comparison of dating systems and their respective time scales should be made.

PART ONE

TIME AS A DIMENSION
OF ARCHAEOLOGY

○

CHAPTER ONE

The New Archaeology

The decade of the 1960s witnessed a revolution in archaeology (Martin 1971). The archaeologist, impatient with his meager contributions to the mainstream of ethnological enquiry, yearned to escape the confining role of culture historian. During these past ten years, he has become an ethnologist in his own right, one who specializes in the study of time-dependent cultural processes. This revolution has been facilitated by new developments in dating.

Archaeology is anthropology to the extent that it is not simply history—not simply the chronicling of events. Yet without control over the temporal sequencing of events, archaeology is in poor shape to contribute to the mainstream of cultural anthropology. It is through the study of cultural processes that archaeology remains a vital discipline of the behavioral sciences (Clarke 1968). This is the quandary that archaeology has had to suffer during most of its lifetime. Dating has always been its "Achilles' heel."

The past decade witnessed technological breakthroughs that will eventually lead to the routinization of chronological analysis. Included here are such innovations as computer-assisted component discrimination, cross-dating, and seriation. In addition, we have improved techniques of radioactive isotope dating, dendrochronology, archeomagnetic dating, and obsidian hydration dating. They illustrate the contributions of the biological, physical, chemical, and mathematical sciences that began to coalesce during the 1960s into a comprehensive inventory of dating techniques (Figure 1).

In the past, the underlying strategy of data collection and analysis

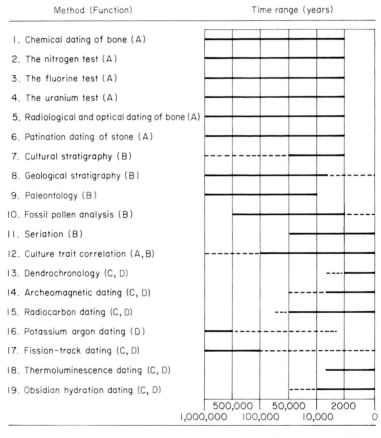

Figure 1. *Summary of dating methods. The principle dating functions are as follows: A, evaluation of intracomponent associations; B, relative dating of components; C, chronometric dating of artifacts; D, chronometric dating of components.*

in archaeology was heavily influenced by the aim of securing some measure of satisfactory control over the arrangement of events in time. The anxiety of the discipline with regard to dating is illustrated by such past practices as wholesale reliance upon stratigraphic trenching, the selective recovery of only those artifacts that were time markers, preoccupation with monumental architecture and its associated fine arts, artifact typologies of form but not function, and the publication of reports that devoted hundreds of pages of text and a profusion of illustrations to the documentation of chronology while almost completely ignoring a consideration of human behavior. Happily, that era has come to a close.

New Trends in Archaeological Field Work

What the impact of routine dating will be on the strategy of archaeology can already be glimpsed by a consideration of some of the new trends as they contrast with more traditional appraoches. Perhaps the most dramatic shift is the current emphasis on a *regional approach* in archaeological research (Struever 1968). Instead of searching for a single site that can be dated conveniently, the archaeologist conducts a systematic survey of a moderately large geographical area and selects a number of sites for excavation that collectively represent the range of variation—cultural, chronological, and ecological—for the region. The regional approach is untenable if the archaeologist has little confidence in his ability to temporally order the components of these many sites, or if the effort required in dating merely one of the sites exhausts the financial and man-hour resources of the project. Both of these liabilities were common prior to the 1960s, and the archaeologist tended to limit himself to the excavation of a single site that stood a good chance of being successfully dated and appeared to be culturally representative of the region.

Normally, the excavation of such a site would be exhaustive. Numerous seasons of field work would be devoted to the task, and the laboratory work would spread over years as stratigraphic profiles were painstakingly prepared, elaborate typologies of artifact style constructed, and high-quality illustrations made of all datable artifacts and features. The descriptive monograph might appear in print 5 or 10 years later, and might contain a few paragraphs that could be considered *behavioral*. Such a strategy limited the number of sites a single archaeologist could hope to study completely during a professional lifetime.

The most serious objection to this earlier strategy, however, was that the behaviorally significant units of analysis—the community and the society—very often received only scant attention. Sites were repositories of data needed to elucidate historical sequences of local culture. Once the sequence was established for a given region, archaeological interest waned. This seldom happened, however, since the task of constructing a reliable sequence was formidable, given the few techniques for dating available to the earlier researcher. As a result, multiple projects within the same region—always seeking the same kind of information—occupied specialists for generations.

The way in which a single site is approached for excavation also has changed. Earlier, the archaeologist, focusing on dating needs, selected phases of building construction, stratified middens, tombs, and datable artifacts as the object of excavation. Today, the archaeologist searches for the archaeological evidence needed in reconstructing demographic, political, social, and economic systems. This search involves a comprehensive mapping of large areas of a site. We seek to record the location of civic centers, residential neighborhoods, craft barrios, agricultural fields, or, as in the case of nonagricultural communities, activity areas on living floors.

The accumulation of such information usually involves the excavation of a representative sample of the site area. As a consequence, a good portion of time and money goes into the recovery of information that assumes the existence of an adequate chronology without necessarily contributing to its determination. To justify this course of field work, the archaeologist must be confident that, in the course of recovering information directly relevant to the solution of problems of behavior, he will recover some data that is susceptible to dating. Such confidence is bred on the awareness that, given the wide range of dating techniques now available, one or more will be applicable to the data at hand. Happily, the demands for excavation controls are very stringent when the objective is to reconstruct behavior, for such controls are assumed by many dating methods.

The converse, however, is not always true. Controls necessary for dating purposes do not always satisfy criteria for successful behavioral reconstruction. Take, for example, the stratigraphic-trench approach to site excavation. The trench may yield chronologically significant discontinuities in soil deposition, or in phases of building construction, but it may not permit interpretation of the activities conducted at that locality at any given time, or it may fail to supply sufficient clues as to the function of a particular building.

Obviously, some sites are excavated simply because they are there and because they are in danger of being destroyed. These are the tragic cases. University, state, and federal museums are filled to the brim with old collections excavated because of salvage needs but left unanalyzed or only partially analyzed because the traditional chronological controls were inadequate. The significance of the site thus is placed sufficiently in question that archaeologists are hard put to justify the expenditure of effort needed to conduct ethnological inquiries with the material. So long as it is true that less effort is needed to conduct a fresh excavation of a new site than to date an old, existing site collection, these collections will continue to gather dust in museum storage rooms. New dating techniques, especially thermoluminescence and obsidian hydration dating, where dating is performed on the artifacts themselves, may shift the balance of effort and encourage students to attempt the analysis of these older site collections.

New Trends in Artifact Analysis

Many different kinds of artifacts exhibit noticeable variation in form, materials, embellishment, and quality of workmanship. Such artifacts traditionally have received most attention in laboratory analysis since such variation is often a very sensitive and reliable key to the dating of archaeological components. At first glance, such selectivity does not seem particularly inappropriate, especially if the assemblages being examined contain large quantities of such artifacts. The archaeology of complex societies is a case in point. When the investigator is faced with monumental architecture, sculpture, ornamental vases, prestige goods made from precious materials, and quite explicit art styles, it *seems* appropriate to pay less attention to the more mundane implements such as stone tools, utilitarian vessels, and the waste products of various crafts. Under such conditions, thorough analysis of only 10% of an artifact assemblage can result in a full-length descriptive monograph. Such selectivity becomes a clear distortion, however, when applied to the material culture of simpler societies. The result, which has been called the *fossile directeur* approach to culture taxonomy (Sackett 1966: 359) is best exemplified by such expressions as *hand axe culture* or *microlith culture*. Such expressions can still be heard *occasionally* in discussions of Paleolithic archaeology. The assemblages of simpler societies may exhibit noticeable variation of form, material, and quality of workmanship in only a handful of cases, often less than 2 or 3% of a collection.

Obviously, such a selective analysis, although contributing important chronological controls, fails as a satisfactory strategy for achieving the ethnographic reconstruction of a once-living community. Today, such a strategy is out of favor. True, taxonomically sensitive artifacts continue to undergo intensive study as a vehicle for dating, but the total artifact inventory now is being examined from the standpoint of function and activity. This is because artifacts contribute important clues concerning various behavioral subsystems of a culture. The present-day strategy of artifact analysis reflects this fact. The functional classification of artifacts often is given priority over stylistic classification, and no artifact receives simply stylistic analysis. One methodological innovation associated with this shift in orientation is the growing interest in the use of controlled experiments for interpreting the function of an artifact. Considerable effort currently is being spent in designing experiments that permit the archaeologist, for example, to identify the type of task that can account for a particular wear pattern on a stone tool.

It is not my intention to leave the reader with the impression that old archaeology is bad archaeology. On the contrary, like all sciences, archaeology is a progressive undertaking. What has gone before is indispensable to what is taking place now. Indeed, several of our most widely applicable methods of dating have undergone progressive refinement over a period of time certainly equal to that of the history of the discipline itself. I wish merely to underscore my opinion that new developments in dating have played an important role in enabling the archaeologist to focus upon the ethnology of the past.

READINGS

Clarke, D. L.
    1968   *Analytical archaeology.* Methuen, London.
Martin, P. S.
    1971   The Revolution in archaeology. *American Antiquity* **36**, No. 1: 1–8.
Sackett, J. R.
    1966   Quantitative analysis of Upper Paleolithic stone tools. *American Anthropologist* **68**, No. 2, 356–394.
Struever, S.
    1968   Problems, methods, and organization: A disparity in the growth of archaeology. In *Anthropological archaeology in the Americas*, edited by B. Meggers. Washington, D.C.: Anthropological Society of Washington.

CHAPTER TWO

Dating Objectives in Archaeology

The Dimension of Time

The first observation we need to make about time is that it is a continuum—a continuum that we sense as a succession of events. Our points of reference are those events we view as in some sense marking a change in the state of things. Change is a chronological landmark for the archaeologist (Chang 1967). Change permits us to divide the continuum of time into discrete temporal segments, or periods.

These temporal segments are units of time within which no significant change occurs or, at least, changes that do occur are not significant enough to upset the overall arrangements of a culture and therefore can be structurally tolerated. Such a period of time is treated as a synchronic segment—as a period within which all temporal points are regarded as contemporaneous. What is the meaningfully tolerable range of archaeological contemporaneity? One scholar has answered this by declaring that absolute numbers of years matter little other than as a comparative attribute: What must be considered is whether generalizations concerning behavior and style can be applied validly to the entirety of the period in question (Chang 1967). Here, of course, the important point is: What aspect of a culture is being studied? If the archaeologist is interested in investigating the evolution of political systems in a given culture area, he may regard changes in ceramic style, or even possibly in economic behavior, as being within tolerable limits of constancy and therefore not cause for further subdivision of the time continuum. On the other hand, minute changes in the political affairs of an area may, in the mind of the investigator, justify subdivisions each of which is a mere fraction of the temporal continuum. The criterion brought to bear on the question of what is a stationary state from the standpoint of culture inevitably varies to some extent from one investigator to another. The strategies of dating are intimately tied in with how an investigator answers that question with respect to his own data and his own analytic objectives.

Regrettably, all too often the methods of dating available to the archaeologist in a particular circumstance limit the range of precision with which the time continuum can be subdivided. In such cases, the archaeologist has to make do with synchronic segments that comprise an undesirable amount of cultural realignment. Such temporal segments are routinely referred to in the literature as *periods of transition*. In the archaeology of complex societies it may happen that virtually no period can be safely treated as a stationary state. On the other hand, in the study of Lower Paleolithic cultures of Europe, archaeologists often are hard pressed to identify behaviorally significant discontinuities that can serve to justify the delineation of synchronic segments.

Of course, the more we know about a culture, the more anxious we are to improve the diachronic study of its underlying processes. This results in increased incentive to acquire greater and greater precision in the delineation of synchronic segments.

Dating Objectives

All efforts at dating appear to fall within one or more of three underlying strategies: *periodization*, determination of relative age, and absolute or *chronometric* dating.

Periodization

Time is a continuum that can be delineated into temporal segments in accordance with the objectives of the archaeologist and within the limits of his technical capability. The process by which the archaeologist accomplishes the delineation of synchronic segments is termed *periodization.*

Consider the following hypothetical case. An archaeologist investigates a particular geographic subregion. During his investigation, he excavates six archaeological sites designated 1 through 6. Excavation of Site 1 reveals the remains of adobe dwellings, agricultural products such as maize, grinding implements for the production of flour, ceramic vessels, and fired clay figurines. Site 2 is a rock shelter site. In the shelter he discovers the butchered remains of a number of large mammals, fire hearths, chipped stone artifacts, projectile points, and some bone tools. Site 3 is a shell-midden site located on the bank of a river. Excavation of the shell mound reveals quantities of mollusks, fish vertebrae, and bird and land mammal bones. The artifacts consist of various chipped stone tools, small projectile points, a few ground stone celts, and quantities of soapstone vessel fragments. In addition, he finds a variety of personal ornaments, such as beads and pendants made from soapstone, shell, bone, or exotic types of stone.

Site 4 reveals a complex of artifacts that closely resembles that of Site 1. Site 5 resembles Site 3; it also is a shell-midden site, and contains a similar inventory of archaeological and ecological specimens. Site 6, although not a rock shelter, yields an assemblage of artifacts and other remains remarkably similar to the assemblage of Site 2.

In reviewing the results of these excavations, he observes that it is possible to group the sites into three classes. He assigns sites to a class on the basis of the subsistence activities and the nature of the community's technology, as these can be inferred from the archaeological record. Class A incudes Sites 1 and 4 and consists of communities that practice farming, possess permanent dwellings, and exhibit a technology of seed grinding and ceramic industry. Class B includes Sites 2 and 6 and consists of communities that inhabit temporary encampments, hunt large mammals, and possess a well-developed lithic industry. Class C includes Sites 3 and 5, communities that occupy river-bank sites and base their subsistence on the exploitation of a wide range of locally available plant and animal resources.

The technologies associated with this class include the manufacture of shell artifacts and soapstone vessels. The presence of personal ornaments manufactured from locally unavailable materials suggests the existence of trading networks connecting widely separated communities.

The following question then arises: Do these three classes of sites constitute contemporaneous microenvironmental variants of a single culture or do they constitute three different cultures of differing age? If the site classes do not share any specific trait resemblances, yet the sites themselves are all found in reasonable proximity to one another, with no natural obstacles to contact between, it is fair to hypothesize that the classes represent three different periods in the culture history of the area.

A periodization of the archaeological resources of our geographic subregion now has been completed. It has been done, first, by constructing site classes through a consideration of the archaeological evidence internal to the sites. Second, by proposing the working hypothesis that these classes represent discrete and contrasting temporal segments of the time continuum because the alternative hypothesis, that these are contemporaneous site classes, appears less plausible. This kind of periodization is done routinely by all archaeologists. No determination has been made, however, as to which of these classes is younger or older, nor has there been any determination as to the actual age of any of these sites, or the cultures they represent.

Relative Dating

Relative dating, the second objective of time control, is concerned with ascertaining the correct order of events. We can illustrate what is meant by proceeding further with our hypothetical case. Our hypothetical archaeologist is interested in determining, first, the validity of the working hypothesis, and, second, the relative age of the three cultures if the hypothesis, in fact, does turn out to be valid. In order to do this, he searches for sites that will permit him to use one of the methods of relative dating, such as stratigraphy. He locates two sites, Site 7 and Site 8. Excavation of these sites yields the following information.

Site 7 resembles Sites 1 and 4 in its upper levels. Considerable quantities of burnt adobe fragments and pottery sherds are found. Underlying these upper levels, however, he notices a soil zone that contains virtually no pottery or adobe fragments. Instead, he discovers modest quantities of soapstone vessel fragments, some chipped stone tools, and substantial quantities of mollusk shell. At Site 8, on the other hand, the upper levels are full of mollusk shell, and he recognizes an immediate resemblance between these upper levels and Sites 3 and 5. There are numerous fragments of soapstone vessels, some beads made of soapstone, three ground stone celts, and a collection of miscellaneous chipped stone artifacts. As in Site 7, however, excavation reveals an underlying soil zone that has very little shell, no soapstone artifacts or sherds, and no celts. In their place, he discovers the bones of large mammals, stone projectile points, numerous well-made chipped stone tools, and some bone artifacts.

By comparison with our previously classified site collections, he can establish that the upper portion of Site 7 is a Class A component, whereas the underlying stratum of Site 7 is a Class C component. Similarly, the upper, shell-midden portion of Site 8 is a Class C component, whereas the underlying stratum of Site 8 is a Class B component. (The term *component* is defined in Chapter Three.) By applying the geological principle of superposition, which affirms that underlying strata are older than those that lie above them, he can conclude from the evidence of Site 7 that Class A sites are younger than Class C sites. Similarly, from the evidence of Site 8, he can conclude that Class C sites are younger than Class B sites. By logical extension, therefore, he also can conclude that among the three classes of sites in his area of study, Class A sites are the most recent, Class B sites are the oldest, and Class C sites are intermediate in age.

The archaeologist thus has completed the initial phase of relative dating for his hypothetical subregion. He has established the validity of his working hypothesis—that the three classes of sites do represent different temporal segments of the time continuum. He also has established the relative age of the three classes. It is now appropriate for him to refer to his site classes as *cultures*, which means that he has delineated an aggregate of communities that share a common heritage of learned behavior and a common natural environment. Collectively, these communities represent an enduring tradition, not merely a moment in time. Finally, the configuration of cultural traits by which each class was defined is distinctive, and temporally and geographically bounded.

Relative dating, however, does not cease with the chronological ordering or discrete culture traditions or periods. Within each period there may be smaller discernible periods, and the sites themselves have not yet been relatively dated on an individual basis with respect to each other. This may not be critical for certain lines of enquiry, such as trait-by-trait comparisons of the three periods. However, if for example, our hypothetical archaeologist wished to study the processes of culture change within one of the three periods, it would be necessary for him to attempt to subdivide that period further. Even without knowing how much time, from a quantitative standpoint, is involved in the historical episodes represented by such subdivisions, he at least will be able to observe valid culture historical trends that may reveal the underlying processes of change. Before illustrating this second stage of relative dating, let us consider our final dating objective, *chronometric dating*.

Chronometric Dating

The term *chronometric dating* refers to quantitative measurements of time with respect to a given scale. It is synonymous with the more traditional term *absolute dating*, but is gaining favor among dating specalists who regard it as a more appropriate term.

The *scale*, or standard of measurement, used in chronometric dating is our calendar year. Measurements of time intervals between events or between an event and the present are expressed in numbers of years that have elapsed between the two temporal points. Therefore, chronometric dating allows us to do two different but related things. We can quantify time, and we can *date* events by reference to the Christian Calendar.

In Part Three of this book a number of chronometric dating techniques are discussed. All of them are based on natural phenomena that undergo progressive change at uniform rates through time. By knowing the rate of change and the amount of change, the number of years that have elapsed since the process of change began can be computed. Working back from the present, the investigator can ascertain the date upon which the process was initiated. There are many complications associated with correlating measured changes in natural phenomena with our calendar system. These complications are discussed in the chapters dealing with specific techniques.

Chronometric dating can perhaps be best illustrated by continuing with our hypothetical case. Let us assume that during the course of excavations at Sites 1 through 8, our hypothetical archaeologist collected samples of charcoal from fire hearths that were uncovered.

One sample each from Sites 1 through 6, and two samples—one from each component—from Sites 7 and 8, were sent to a radiocarbon dating laboratory. Two months later, he received the following report:

Site number	Radiocarbon date
1	500 B.C. ± 125
2	9,000 B.C. ± 350
3	4,000 B.C. ± 250
4	100 A.D. ± 100
5	2,500 B.C. ± 180
6	7,000 B.C. ± 320
7a (upper zone)	1,000 B.C. ± 150
7b (lower zone)	6,000 B.C. ± 300
8a (upper zone)	3,000 B.C. ± 180
8b (lower zone)	11,000 B.C. ± 550

With this data, he can begin to measure the temporal dimensions of the three cultures he has defined. Figure 2 illustrates the kind of chronometric scale made possible by the series of radiocarbon dates.

In studying the local culture chronology, he notes several interesting features. First, the radiocarbon dates of the three cultures do not overlap significantly, even when the standard error of the radiocarbon dates is considered. This demands interpretation. Does it mean that the three cultures represent intrusion of a new population after short periods of abandonment? Or does it simply indicate that our sample of sites dated is insufficient, and that additional data will demonstrate local population continuity through the presence of *transitional-period* sites? Is it some combination of these factors, or some other unsuspected factor?

Another feature that he can observe is that Cultures C and B are of approximately equal duration, whereas Culture A is significantly briefer. What does this mean in terms of the rates and processes of cultural evolution? Do Cultures C and B exhibit more variability than Culture A? Will additional data demonstrate that Culture A persists for another thousand years, or that Culture B extends considerably farther back into the past?

Still another line of questioning provoked by such a chronology has to do with the reasons why substantial culture change occurs at those points in time represented by the juncture of Cultures B and C, and the juncture of Cultures C and A. Was it due to major ecological shifts in the environment, local invention of new subsistence techniques, or contact with other cultures?

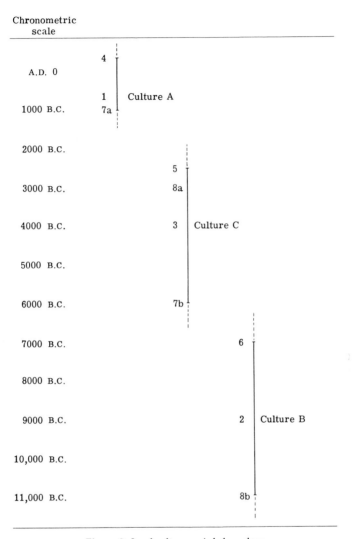

Figure 2. *Local culture-period chronology.*

In raising such questions, we see that knowledge of absolute chronology opens up new avenues of inquiry that otherwise may have been unsuspected or unmanageable. Such chronicling, then, is not merely an end in itself, but a preliminary step to a more adequate behavioral analysis.

Phasing

We have carried our hypothetical case through the three stages of chronological analysis—periodization, relative dating, and chronometric dating—and thereby have established a local chronology of broadly defined cultural periods. We have not completed our study, however, for each of these cultures constitutes an extended temporal segment within which more specific chronological subdivisions may be usefully established. These subdivisions represent a different level of cultural variation, but one which actually may prove more valuable in analyzing cultural process.

Let us continue with our hypothetical case. Assume now that our hypothetical archaeologist has discovered four new sites (9, 10, 11, 12), all of which can be classified as belonging to *Culture A* based on the technological and subsistence criteria previously discussed. Upon studying the pottery of the seven *Culture A* sites (1, 4, 7, 9, 10, 11, 12), he notices that there is variation among the site collections with respect to vessel shape, decorative technique, paste, and temper, and other stylistic and technical considerations associated with the manufacture of pottery. Using these attributes as a guide, he discovers that the seven sites can be grouped into three classes:

Class 1: Sites 7, 11;
Class 2: Sites 1, 9, 12;
Class 3: Sites 4, 10.

Examination of the members of each class reveals that the three radiocarbon-dated sites (1, 4, 7) fall into different classes. This strongly suggests that the groupings represent distinctive temporal segments of the *Culture A* time range.

Ceramic complexes that are chronologically diagnostic are often used to define *ceramic phases*. The concept of a phase is discussed in the next chapter. In this context a ceramic phase is the chronological subdivision of a culture period. With the evidence in his possession, he may propose that Culture A be subdivided into three ceramically defined phases (Table 1): Phase 1, Phase 2, and Phase 3. Phase 1 is earliest since it contains members of Class 1, one of which (Site 7a) has a radiocarbon date of 1000 B.C. Phase 2 is intermediate in age, consisting of the members of Class 2, one of whose members (Site 1) has a radiocarbon date of 500 B.C. Phase 3 is most recent, for it consists of the members of Class 3, one of which (Site 4) has been radiocarbon dated at A.D. 100.

TABLE 1
Local Ceramic-Phase Sequence

Chronometric scale	Cultural period	Phase	Site number
A.D. 100		Phase 1	4, 10
B.C. 500	Culture A	Phase 2	1, 9, 12
B.C. 1000		Phase 3	7a, 11

Seriation

An archaeological phase is intended to serve as minimal tax-onomic class for purposes of identifying site components. Compo-nents assigned to a given phase are regarded analytically as contem-poraneous and as culturally homogeneous. We are, however, aware that even the most minimal period concepts, such as the *phase*, con-stitute extended temporal segments, and that individual site compo-nents very likely will comprise discrete episodes within the temporal segment. We also know that the proposition that member components are culturally homogeneous is a fiction at very specific levels of com-parison. For these reasons, it is often desirable to observe culture change within the duration of a single phase. Here the object is to view change in the context of a community-by-community set of com-parisons. The *site component* is the archaeological equivalent of a *com-munity* or one of its constituent parts. An important dating strategy, then, is to chronologically order individual phase components in a relative age series—early to late. The process by which such orderings are accomplished is called *seriation*. It is a special case of relative dating, and full discussion of seriation is provided in Part Two, Chap-ter Five. Component seriation represents a maximal level of control in delineating the temporal continuum, and is seldom achieved except in areas that have been the object of study for many years.

Again we perhaps can best illustrate seriation by reference to our hypothetical case. The archaeologist has established that Sites 1, 9, and 12 belong to Phase B. This was based on the fact that they shared a common ceramic complex. Let us suppose that this ceramic complex can be summarized as consisting of three pottery types (X, Y, and Z). All three sites exhibit vessel fragments that represent all three pottery types, and it is for this reason that he viewed them as sharing a common ceramic complex. Pottery types are usually defined on the basis of traits that are susceptible to fluctuations in popularity among the artisans who design and manufacture ceramic vessels. The term *style*, as we understand it in the context of modern dress fashions, is used to refer to such traits. They may include anything from vessel shape to decorative motifs. The important point to be made about such traits is that they undergo a history of progressively greater popularity followed by a history of progressively diminished popularity. If we apply this knowledge to pottery types, it would seem probable that as one pottery type was achieving popularity, another type would be declining in popularity. Operationally then, the relative prominence of specific pottery types within a component assemblage could be used to indicate one *moment* in the life history of several pottery styles or types. By ordering a group of these *moments* in such a way as to approximate the popularity model given above for each

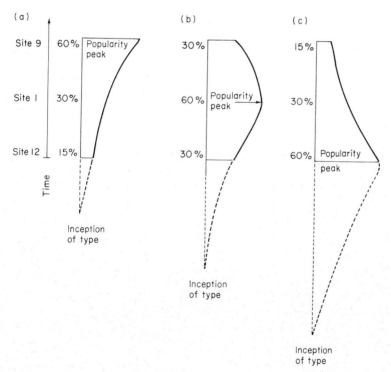

Figure 3. *Ceramic seriation of Phase B sites: (a) Type X; (b) Type Y; (c) Type Z.*

pottery style, the relative chronological sequence for that set of *communities* would be established.

Suppose our hypothetical archaeologist determined that the pottery of Site 1 consisted of 30% type X, 60% type Y, and 30% type Z; the pottery of Site 9 consisted of 60% type X, 30% Y, and 15% type Z; and the pottery of Site 12 consisted of 15% type X, 30% type Y, and 60% type Z. The ordering given in Figure 3 would conform to the popularity model with respect to each pottery type. Such a seriation of Phase 2 sites enables the archaeologist to study short-term cultural processes within the phase.

Summary

The strategy of dating in archaeology involves periodization, relative dating, and chronometric dating. One moves logically from one to the other of these objectives in the course of analyzing field data. From the standpoint of time, the archaeologist is moving from the delineation of temporal segments to their relative position, and finally to their measurement in terms of a standard scale. This logical sequence is repeated, however, and begins with each successful attempt to delineate smaller and smaller temporal segments. Time is a continuum that is structured by events, and dating is our effort at chronicling these events. The more accurate and the more specific our chronicle, the more fruitful will be our search for explanations of cultural change.

READING

Chang, K. C.
   1967   *Rethinking archaeology.* New York: Random House.

CHAPTER THREE

Basic Units of Analysis in Archaeology

Basic Units

Some time ago, Willey and Phillips (1959:18) attempted to define the basic units of analysis in archaeology, and to organize them into a coherent system. By in large, their efforts continue to prove workable as a terminological scheme, and we will adopt their definitions for the purpose of this text.

According to Willey and Phillips, a fundamental characteristic of all archaeological unit formulations is that they are arrived at by combining three sorts of data: formal content, distribution in geographical space, and duration in time.

The Site

A *site* is the smallest unit of space dealt with by archaeologists. Its physical limits may vary from a few square yards to several miles. The term *site* is intended to pertain to a single unit of settlement, which may be anything from a small camp to a large city, or to the locus of some specific group activity, such as a stone quarry or a hunting blind. Any site, however, may constitute the locus of repeated episodes of human activity, and as such they often pose considerable problems in analysis.

The Locality

The *locality* refers to the space that might be utilized by a local group living together or in multiple settlements. It would embrace the entirety of a local group's primary ecological niche; extending as far perhaps as a man could reasonably travel during a day's round of activities. It is entirely likely that a locality would include a number of sites, representing special activity loci as well as residence loci. Geographically, a locality is often a particularly favorable segment of a minor physiographic subdivision, for example, a section of shore line, a section of river valley, or a hill-top mesa.

The Region

The *region* is a considerably larger unit of geographical space that is often likely to coincide with minor physiographic subdivisions, such as river valleys, intermontane basins, or marine littorals. A region usually accommodates multiple local communities or groups that bear strong cultural resemblances to one another due to sustained interaction.

The Phase

The *phase* is a cultural episode in the history of a locality or a region. A phase is defined on the basis of diagnostic trait complexes that distinguish it from other phases that follow or precede it. The episode is a relatively brief interval of time when good archaeological controls are present.

The Component

The *component* is the manifestation of any given phase at a specific site. Sites containing the residue of a single episode of habitation or other group activity are referred to as *single component* sites. A site with more than one episode of occupation is referred to as a *multicomponent* site.

The Local Sequence

A *local sequence* is a chronological series of phases within the geographical limits of a locality. Establishing the local sequence is one of the most important dating objectives of the archaeologist. It involves both periodization and relative dating.

The Regional Sequence

A *regional sequence* is a chronological series of phases within the geographical limits of a region. It is not, however, merely a local sequence with larger spatial dimensions. Localities are regarded as containing culturally homogeneous human groupings. The region, on the other hand, consists of a number of local groups that, although strongly resembling one another culturally, are often recognizably different. In such a case, multiple local sequences are transformed into a single regional sequence through interphase correlation.

Methods of Component Segregation

Components are the basic building blocks of chronology in archaeology. All dating is the dating of components. Segregating individual components for the purpose of analysis, including dating, is a vital preliminary task in archaeological research.

It is always desirable to discover circumstances in which components are actually segregated physically. Only under such conditions are the components useful in formulating phase definitions for a locality, or in dating such phases. Once a satisfactory definition of the local sequence of phases has been established, the diagnostic complexes of traits, serving to define each phase, can be used to recognize the presence or absence of specific phases in the artifact assemblage of a *mixed* multicomponent site. In the latter case, however, components are merely recognized; their constituent artifact assemblages and features remain unsegregated.

Segregation of Components by Stratigraphy

When a piece of ground is selected by a community as their locus of living and working, a history of continuous disturbance begins. First comes the preparation of platforms for activities and for housing, involving the leveling off of some areas. Structures usually require supporting elements that may be imbedded in the soil. Whether the materials used in construction are perishable or imperishable, there is a likelihood that over the years they will come into disrepair and renovation will be required. Renovation may take the form of extending the structures by the addition of new rooms, or may involve reinforcing older rooms, resurfacing old floors, adding new roofs, and so on. Sooner or later, it is likely that the structure will have to be abandoned because it has reached a point of such disrepair that renovation is not economical. This may involve simply the construction of a new dwelling a few meters away, allowing the old dwelling to simply deteriorate and collapse out of neglect, or it may involve deliberate destruction of the old dwelling, leveling a new surface on top of the rubble, and erecting a new structure. Sometimes nature may precipitate this sequence of events. A severe flood or fire may destroy a structure. In addition, the mobility patterns of the community may involve periodic abandonment of a piece of ground in pursuit of subsistence, so that dwellings designed only for temporary use predictably will deteriorate rather rapidly. The piece of ground itself, however, may be reoccupied by a community on a regular basis over the years, each time involving the erection of new temporary dwellings by the families involved.

A second source of disturbance are the activities that members of the community routinely engage in during the course of living. Foodstuffs are brought to the site. They are processed for consumption, and in the course of this processing, large quantities of discarded waste materials are produced. Nonedible portions of animal carcasses, nuts, seeds, and vegetables are discarded in the immediate vicinity of the dwelling and rapidly decompose to form new soils. Various craft activities also take place that involve the production of considerable waste: wood working, stone working, hide working, pottery making, basketry. In addition, the implements utilized by the community break, get lost under foot, or are simply discarded after a specific task: knives, scrapers, choppers, boiling stones, pottery vessles, cordage, netting, basketry. All of these objects mix with the garbage and debris to form what we call *midden deposits*. The midden deposits tend by their very nature to be rich, friable soils that are easily disturbed by the kinds of activities that produced them in the first place, and by other activities such as burial, food storage, recreation, and routine traffic.

We can magnify this picture considerably by imagining the effect on a piece of ground brought about by the presence of a village or town, where the sequence of events is multiplied, and new activities are added. Thus, in many different ways, the piece of ground upon which human activity has taken place has suffered repeated alteration, and it is by correctly interpreting the evidence of alteration that we may hope to isolate components.

In practice the segregation of the strata or layers, which represent the successive phases in the local sequence at a site, is one of the principal tasks of the excavator, and will occupy the major portion of his time. The task is one that involves considerable experience and patience. During the many years of stratigraphic excavation, archaeology has developed an inventory of many different techniques and has exploited many different technologies in its attempt to render the delineation of strata more convenient and more accurate (see Part Two, Chapter Four, on sequence dating by stratigraphy).

Differences in the color, texture, and relative moisture of superimposed soils often serve as indicators of different strata. Such differences, however, are not always easy to discern, and archaeologists have experimented with different lighting conditions and different scraping techniques, as well as with the use of advanced photographic techniques, such as ultraviolet and infrared light photography.

Even after individual strata have been delineated, a problem of interpretation continues to challenge the archaeologist. Does a certain stratum represent a discrete component, or is it simply one of several strata that collectively constitute a single component? It will often be found that certain strata cease toward one end or both in such a fashion that the underlying layers unite to clasp them and hold them within a uniform mass, as if in suspension. Another phenomenon likely to occur is a succession of layers that join up laterally, like fingers extended from the palm of the hand. Both of these conditions signal contemporaneous strata. Such strata therefore comprise but a single component.

Such phenomena should be clearly distinguished from strata that actually represent physical boundaries between components. A good case in point would be a succession of strata that represent intermittent occupation with time gaps between occupational episodes. In such cases, the soil at the point of juncture between any two components may be a layer of wind-blown or waterborne sand, or a layer of decomposed foliage. In rock shelters, collapsed roofing often serves to segregate two components. Thus, any judgment regarding the significance of delineated strata also rests upon considerable study, even after the strata have been recognized.

Stratigraphic Recording Procedures

Every archaeological site reveals a sufficiently different depositional history that the idiosyncracies of each must become known. The initial excavation of a site therefore usually involves trenching or some other tactic designed to expose vertical profiles of the site deposit. The profiles are examined very carefully, and the archaeologist attempts to discern layers of deposit that are distinguishable from one another on the basis of soil color, soil composition, or the kinds of artifacts or faunal remains that such layers contain. As the archaeologist perceives lines of partition between such layers, he attempts to identify such lines by inserting nails or some other tagging device along them so that, should the lighting or moisture conditions change, he will not lose control over the lines of partition previously recognized. Very often the tagging operation goes on for several days, each segment of the vertical profile reexamined at different times, under different conditions of lighting and scraping, in order to ensure that as much depositional detail as possible can be discovered and tagged. Once the profile has been examined and the lines of partition separating the depositional layers marked by some method, the resulting stratigraphy is transcribed on paper. Scaled graph paper is normally used for this purpose. The recording of stratigraphy involves the use of measuring tapes, vertical plumb bobs, and line levels. These instruments aid the recorder in converting the stratigraphic pattern into a metric notation for accurate drawing onto the scaled graph paper.

Sir Mortimer Wheeler aptly has pointed out one of the principal problems involved with recording stratigraphic profiles (1956: 76), and that is the failure to differentiate graphically strata that represent discrete components. Wheeler illustrates the problem with three diagrams (Figure 4). In Figure 4a individual strata are delineated, but virtually no information is provided with which we can evaluate the composition or significance of the units. Such a profile would be useful in associating artifacts but could be made even more useful as Figure 4b indicates. In Figure 4b a set of notational symbols have been employed to contrast individual layers. According to Wheeler,

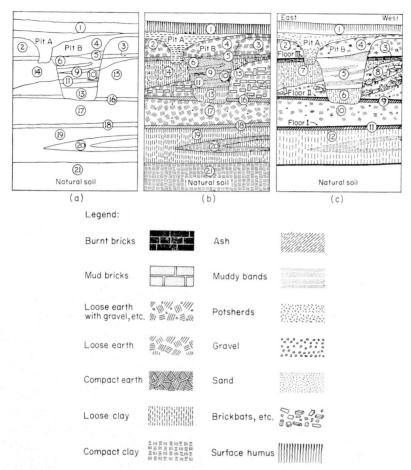

Figure 4. *Recording stratigraphic profiles: (a) undifferentiated section; (b) section unintelligently differentiated; (c) section intelligently differentiated. The key to the symbols for (c) is given in the legend. (From Wheeler, Sir M. "Archaeology from the Earth," Figs. 12, 13. Oxford: Clarendon Press, 1956.)*

the effort represented in Figure 4b also is unsatisfactory, however, for it fails in two respects. First, the general evenness of tone throughout the profile suggests that the recorder may not have fully understood the culture historical implications of the stratigraphy, and second, the recorder failed to indicate in his drawings the location of features, diagnostic artifacts, and other culturally significant items. Figure 4c represents a correction of these deficiencies. In this diagram the building material, floors, pits, and other items of behavioral significance are clearly recorded, in addition to a more effective utilization of graphic depositional symbols.

Habitation Mounds

Many communities are remarkably stable over long periods of time. Such communities generally are characterized by an agricultural economy, and out of a recognition of the enduring nature of their occupation invest considerable labor in the construction of permanent or semipermanent dwellings. In many parts of the world the most common material out of which such structures are made is sun-dried mud bricks or sun-dried mud plaster (wattle and daub). Mud-brick or wattle-and-daub structures seldom endure more than 10 or 20 years, and upon collapse tend to produce an undifferentiated mass of new soil.

Communities normally consist of dozens of such dwellings, and under conditions of tight clustering the resultant periodic destruction and rebuilding will cause a gradual heightening of the level of the ground upon which the village is built. Often, when catastrophic fire or warfare causes the systematic destruction of a large number of dwellings in a single mud village, the entire village site may be releveled, the new ground surface being somewhat higher than the previous ground surface due to the mantle of redeposited building material. Over a period of many centuries a town or village may have witnessed a number of such episodes of large-scale reconstruction, and contemporary occupants may find themselves occupying the summit of an artificial hill.

The excavator thus is confronted with a stratified accumulation of architectural remains. Circumstances, however, may serve to disrupt the symmetry and to complicate the stratification of habitation mounds. To illustrate such possibilities, and at the same time to point out the prevailing sequence of developments in Mesopotamian mounds, Lloyd (1963) provides the model given in Figure 5. This diagram represents the habitation of a village community with a static population. The superimposed remains of five principal occupations have gradually created a small artificial hill. As the site of the village rose in level, the building space on the summit became more and more restricted by the sloping sides of the mound. After the inhabitants of the fifth settlement had departed, the ruins of their houses were molded by the weather to form the peak of a symmetrical tumulus. Vegetation started to grow upon it, and soon all traces of occupation disappeared beneath a shallow mantle of humus soil.

The second and third diagrams in Figure 5 both illustrate cases where the focus of occupation has shifted. In Figure 5b, a small mound has been formed in a manner similar to Figure 5a. From this point onward, however, occupation has continued, not on the summit of the mound, since that had become inadequate, but terraced into its sloping flank and spreading over an extended area of new ground beneath. Further rebuilding therefore caused the mound to extend

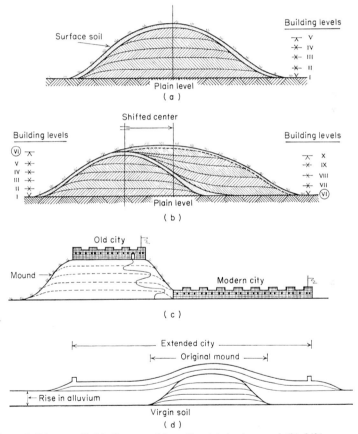

Figure 5. *Diagram of habitation mound formation: (a) simple mound; (b) shifting occupation; (c) increased population; (d) rising alluvium. (From Lloyd, S. "Mounds of the Near East," Fig. 1. Edinburgh, Scotland: Edinburgh Univ. Press, 1963. Reproduced by permission.)*

its coverage in that direction without any increase in its maximum height. Figure 5b illustrates a sequence of events that can create a typical feature in stratification: Traces of the same occupation (Level VI in the diagram) are to be found near the summit of the original mound, and at the plain level in the extended sector at the same time. In Figure 5c, the process of extending the settlement to accommodate an increasing population has taken a much simpler course, and the resulting phenomenon is one seen most frequently throughout the Near East. The fourth and last diagram, Figure 5d, represents a situation that can occur in riverine areas. Here, as the occupation level of the mound rose, windborne dust and the silt deposited by irrigation water or floods caused the surrounding alluvium to rise simultaneously. Soon, the remnants of the earliest settlement were buried deeply beneath the contemporary level of the surrounding plain. Meanwhile, an increase in the population necessitated an outward extension of the city over the accumulated alluvium. Now the foundations of the central buildings rest directly upon the summit of the ancient mound, whereas those in the extended area are built at almost the same level on ground never before occupied. A final alternative mentioned by Lloyd is the case where the actual height of the mound has made habitation at its summit impracticable, and the village grows up in a ring around its base.

Mound Excavation

The central problem in excavating habitational mounds is to record and interrelate the surviving architectural remains. Two techniques are basic to the task of interrelating architectural remains: wall tracing and floor stripping. Wall tracing enables the archaeologist to link up rooms of a multiroom building, and to discern the pattern of community settlement in general. Floor stripping secures discrete component assemblages with stratigraphic significance.

Wall tracing involves several excavation tactics. First, the surface of the ground must be scraped until the upper portions of wall stubs can be discerned clearly in the floor of the excavation unit. The excavator will be alert to subtle differences in the color and texture of the soil in order to identify the presence of wall stubs. Once a segment of a wall stub is detected, scraping at that approximate level may be extended in an effort to follow the wall and recover the entire outline of a room or of a multiroom structure. If the wall stubs are irregular in height, it may not be feasible to follow them through scraping activities, and a second tactic is then employed. A short trench is cut perpendicular to the axis of the wall stub, and the wall face is approached through trenching. Once the surface of the wall is detected with trenching, a trench parallel with the wall can be excavated and the interface between the wall and the external wall fill can be separated with the blade of a knife or some other excavating tool. This trenching is continued until the entire building is outlined. Once the structures are delineated by the detection and unearthing of wall outlines, the inner contents of rooms are carefully stripped down with the objective of detecting superimposed floors, often at intervals of only a few inches. Each of these floors must be removed in turn and the artifacts associated with them carefully segregated.

Platform Mounds

In contrast to mounds that form through the gradual accumulation of structural and habitational debris, platform mounds are deliberately constructed as a base for a temple or elite residence building. Platform mounds are quite common in many areas of the New World. The largest, by far, is the *Temple of the Sun* at Teotihuacán, Central Mexico, built during the Classic period of Mesoamerican civilization. These mounds, usually in the form of a truncated pyramid, are constructed by the piling up of endless basketfulls of earth and stone. When a desired size is achieved, the exterior is shaped and finished with a mud or limestone plaster,or with dressed stone. The general form is interrupted by the construction of stairways, balustrades, terraces, cornices, and other architectural embellishments. The platform supports a building made of variable materials: pole and thatch, wattle and daub, limestone, or adobe.

The stratigraphic analysis of artifacts in such mounds is extremely difficult since the very act of construction involves redeposition of nearby cultural remains as part of the fill. To isolate discrete component assemblages, then, involves differentiating between fill and primary-deposition units, such as the artifact remains located on the floor of the temple or elite household. As in the case of habitation mounds, floor stripping can be an important technique for isolating component assemblages. This is especially true for the floors of earlier buildings that subsequently were covered over by the construction of a newer and larger platform. Another important element in the stratigraphic analysis of platform mounds is the common practice of burying the dead in or under such mounds. Such burials usually represent important individuals who are commonly buried with lavish offerings. Identifying which building phase is associated with which burial and using the component assemblage of the burial for dating purposes is often a successful tactic. In some instances, the architectural finish of platform mounds or technique of construction is sufficiently stylized that phasing can be performed on the mounds themselves. Local sequences then can be worked out by examining the superimposition of platforms of varying design and construction.

Testing for Stratigraphy in Midden Deposits

Archaeologists are often handicapped by their inability to test the chronological integrity of the midden deposits that they excavate. Most use excavation procedures and controls designed to preserve some measure of chronologically significant artifact or feature association. All such controls and procedures are based on the geological principle of superposition, which states that younger units of deposition overlie older units of deposition in a serial order. Geologists recognize the fact that there are a number of natural forces, such as erosion and faulting, that can disturb or obliterate the order or integrity of such superimposed units. Detecting and explaining such disturbances is an important aspect of historical geology.

The archaeologist, while making use of the principle of superposition, is often unable to make use of the geologist's techniques for detecting disturbance. The problem of detecting and evaluating such a disturbance is especially acute in midden archaeology, where no architectural clues are available.

A stratified deposit is one in which the deposition units have superposition and also exhibit contrasting cultural contents. Midden deposits often are excavated by means of artificial vertical units, largely because of the absence of any observable clues that point to natural physical partitions in the deposit. This method also is used in those cases where the physical partitions are so gross or so unsystematic that intrastrata partitioning by means of artificial levels is required. More often than not, the cultural contents of the arbitrary deposition units will contrast. They therefore appear to be stratified as well as superimposed, permitting the archaeologist to assume that the order of deposition of the units accurately reflects the order of cultural succession.

The problem, then, is to untangle the features that may contribute to confusion in stratigraphic analysis. For midden deposits, the following three features should be distinguished:

(1) superposition of the deposition units;
(2) artifact mixing;
(3) the net stratigraphic value of the deposition units.

The *net stratigraphic value* is the concept used to refer to the degree to which the superimposed subdivisions of the midden deposit selected accurately reflect the order of cultural succession. Tests of superposition and artifact mixing will contribute information that can be used to measure the degree to which contrasts in cultural content between deposition units represent valid stratigraphy.

Obsidian hydration dating can contribute to a solution of the unknowns of mixing and also to the determination of net stratigraphic value (Michels 1969). The procedure to be described can be applied to any site which has a sufficient quantity of worked obsidian.

Measuring the rim of hydration on a number of obsidian artifacts from each unit of deposition is the first step. For sites excavated by arbitrary levels, a sample of obsidian artifacts from each level should be measured. The more artifacts measured per deposition unit, the more accurate and reliable the test findings will be.

The second step is to plot on a three-dimensional scatter diagram the frequency distribution of artifact hydration-rim values against the deposition units from which the artifacts were recovered. Figure 6 is a scatter diagram of the total artifact sample dated from the Mammoth Junction site, Mono County, California. The vertical axis of the scatter diagram represents the thickness of the hydration rim. The maximum thickness (thus, maximum age) is located at the bottom of the axis, and intervals of reduced thickness are expressed by the micron values progressing toward the top. The horizontal axis of the scatter diagram represents the deposition units. The deepest units are located at the juncture of these two axes, and progressively shallower units are arranged toward the outer end. All of the scatter diagrams presented will conform to this format. In this case, a range of 1–8 microns (1–8 μm) is represented on the vertical axis. The deposition units at this site were arbitrary 6-inch levels running to a depth of 60 inches. There are thus ten deposition units represented.

The first observation to be made is that mixture is clearly present in all deposition units. This can be seen by noting the overlapping of time sectors by all of the units of deposition. The extensiveness of the mixing can be observed by noting the length of the vertical columns. One-fourth of a micron represents approximately 250 years at this site. Thus, a vertical column extending more than 1 micron (1 μm) reveals that the deposition unit includes artifacts ranging over 1000 years apart in age. All of the adequately sampled deposition units at this site reveal ranges of this size or larger. The extent of overlapping between the vertical columns for any two units of deposi-

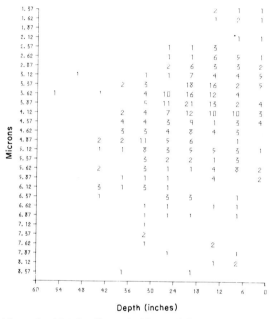

Figure 6. *Total sample of dated artifacts, the Mammoth Junction site. (From Michels 1969: Fig. 1.)*

tion expresses the extensiveness of the mixing. In a case like this one, where all deposition units have large segments of their respective vertical columns overlapping with all of the others, it is reasonable to predict that the net stratigraphic value of this site deposit will be negligible.

We can refine our observation of mixing by the procedure illustrated in Figure 7. The median hydration-rim value for each deposition unit is calculated, thereby expressing the central chronological tendency of each unit. By using the median value to represent the frequency distribution of the artifacts, the scatter diagram becomes two-dimensional, and we can calculate a trend line that will express the long-term chronological patterning of the site deposit (least-squares method). In Figure 7 the trend line has a clear positive slope relative to the two axes of the graph, and this sloping orientation is evidence of the presence of a tendency toward superposition in the site deposit. This means that the deposition units are conforming to the principle of superposition even though they are extensively mixed.

It is often useful to examine the stratigraphic properties of individual excavation units, especially when one wishes to determine where

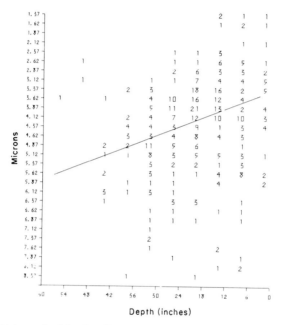

Depth (inches)

Figure 7. *Total sample of dated artifacts, the Mammoth Junction site (with the trend line plotted). (From Michels 1969: Fig. 2.)*

to take carbon samples for radiocarbon dating. Normally, a carbon sample is selected for dating where there is reason to believe that the cultural materials associated with the carbon sample represent valid historical associations and not simply a physical association. In Figure 8 two 5 by 5-foot pits are illustrated, which have been examined using the procedures already described. The size of the samples used in these two cases is not large, and some eccentric bias might be represented in the scatter.

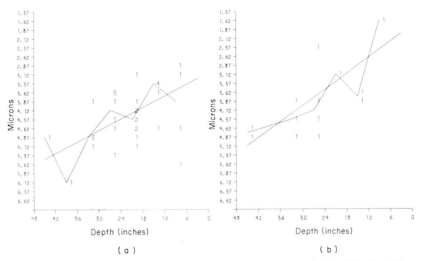

Figure 8. *Mammoth Junction site: (a) Pit 15; (b) Pit 17. (From Michels 1969: Fig. 7.)*

Both pits show a trend slope corresponding to the one prevailing at the site as a whole, yet the median lines of each pit are quite different with respect to their fluctuation patterns. One very important thing to note is the relatively narrow range of hydration-rim values represented in each excavation level.

Figure 9 illustrates two more pits. Notice the very close correlation between the trend lines and the median lines. Such a correlation is a good indication that the net stratigraphic value of such an escavation unit is reasonably high.

The inference to be drawn from these data on pits is that the depositional history of each pit is often significantly unique, and the correlation of arbitrary levels between pits may contribute little reliable chronological or associational information. This does not mean that broad stratigraphic units cannot be commonly relied upon; on the contrary, the fact that a superpositional tendency can be demonstrated for a site indicates that some stratigraphy exists. A completely mixed site would not reveal a tendency towards superposition, since the central chronological tendencies of the depostion units of such a site would not yield a prevailing trend. The stratigraphically meaningful subdivisions of the deposit therefore will vary.

Using an analysis of variance and Scheffe's S method of multiple comparison (Scheffe 1959), it was possible to subdivide the Mammoth

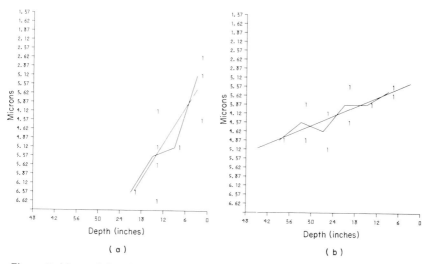

Figure 9. *Mammoth Junction site: (a) Pit 12; (b) Pit 26. (From Michels 1969: Fig. 8.)*

Junction site deposit into four stratigraphically significant units of deposition. The tests indicated that it was necessary to ignore the top 12 inches and the bottom 12 inches of the deposit for the purpose of stratigraphic analysis. The four significant units are (1) 12–24 inches; (2) 24–30 inches; (3) 30–42 inches; (4) 42–48 inches. These units reveal heavy representation of distinctive segments of the micron range. The ranges for each of the four units are considerable, however, and the inventories thereby associated with each represent the refuse of over a millennium of cultural activity.

The Feature Approach to Component Segregation

In archaeological sites, such as the Mammoth Junction site just discussed, where there is no reliable physical stratigraphy, no architecture, and evidence of substantial mixing, the only approach to component segregation is through the isolation of discrete features. *Features*, in archaeological parlance, refer to close contextual relationships among artifacts. Many examples come readily to mind: artifacts included with the corpse at the time of internment, artifacts deliberately placed in storage pits, artifacts in direct association with recognizable segments of a living floor or fire hearths. Controlling for disturbance and intrusive materials is often difficult, but can be managed.

Thus, as a site is excavated, numerous feature assemblages are isolated. We can refer to these as *association lots*. At the completion of excavation these artifact lots can be compared, and grouped into components. Thus, for example, if the formal composition of artifact lots from *Living Floor 1, Burial 13,* and *Hearth 6* is similar, the archaeologist may choose to assign them to the same component.

The feature approach often is used in conjunction with the stratigraphic approach, especially when strata isolate excessively large blocks of time. For example, if we can isolate a 3000-year period stratigraphically in a given rock shelter deposit, we may be able to discriminate between constituent episodes of occupation during that 3000-year period by analyzing the formal composition of specific features located within the stratum.

Methods for Evaluating Intracomponent Artifact Association

There are occasions when objects appear to be associated but really are not. Several items within a single stratum of a stratified deposit, objects in proximity to a feature, substantial numbers of items all found within a constricted segment of an undifferentiated midden deposit—all of these are circumstances in which lot associations seem valid. There are a number of techniques that can be used to test this validity. One such technique, *cross-dating*, has such broad applications in dating that it is discussed separately in Part Two, Chapter 6, of the text. Chronometric techniques that date specific artifacts or features, such as thermoluminescence, dendrochronology, radiocarbon dating, and obsidian dating can also serve this role. Again, however, these techniques have considerably wider and more significant functions that justify fuller treatment in later sections of the book (Part Three, Chapters Seven, Nine, Twelve, and Thirteen, respectively). There are several techniques, however, that are limited in their dating utility, and have value as dating techniques precisely in cases such as described above. They include the chemical dating of bone and the patina dating of stone and glass.

Chemical Dating of Bone

The association of human skeletal remains with an artifact assemblage that includes bone tools can be tested by this set of techniques. Similarly, the association of human skeletal remains with the skeletal remains of extinct fauna can be tested. Finally, the determination as to whether bones presumed to belong to the same individual are, indeed, of comparable antiquity can be accomplished. It was a case of the latter type that brought chemical dating into prominence. This, of course, was the famous discovery of the difference in age between the jawbone and skull bones of Piltdown man.

The Nitrogen Test

Skeletal remains buried in the earth are subject to a wide range of chemical changes. One such change affecting the composition of bone is the progressive loss of organic constituents. The two principal organic constituents of bone are protein (collagen) and fat. The fatty portion of bone is lost very soon after burial. Collagen, on the other hand, disappears much more slowly. When skeletal remains are located within a more or less uniform soil matrix, as occurs when they share an identical history of deposition, there is a high probability that all bone elements among several distinct skeletons will exhibit similar proportions of protein loss. This is due to the fact that the rate of protein loss is determined by the soil chemistry of the matrix in which the bone is found. For this reason the relative age of bones within an archaeological site can be determined by comparing the quantity of their organic constituents—nitrogen, carbon, and chemically bound water. A chemical analysis known as the micro-Kjeldahl method permits convenient determination of the nitrogen content of prehistoric bone. The nitrogen content value then is used as an indicator of the quantity of residual organic matter remaining in the prehistoric bone specimens.

The Fluorine Test

The mineral constituents of skeletal remains also undergo change in composition. Percolating ground water inundates bone remains with a solution of minerals drawn from the local soils. In the process, two kinds of changes in mineral composition can occur. First, the principal constituent of bone, hydroxyapatite, undergoes alteration through the substitution of one element for another. Second, minerals in solution may be added by being trapped in the porous structure of the bone. This second kind of change is what is usually meant by the term *fossilization*. It often involves the addition of lime or iron oxide, thus increasing the density and weight of the bone and giving it a new character. Such changes occur at widely fluctuating rates, and therefore bones buried in the same soils at different times can come to resemble one another in their general fossilized appearance. For this reason, relative dating based on the progressive fossilization of bone is not reliable.

The first kind of change, however, alteration of the hydroxyapatite, has been used as a relative dating technique. These changes are slow and irreversible, involving the permanent substitution of elements. Two such elements that can accumulate in prehistoric bone in this fashion are fluorine and uranium. Fluorine, in the form of soluble fluorides, occurs in trace quantities in almost all ground waters. When fluorine ions come into contact with skeletal remains through water percolation, they tend to displace the hydroxyl ions, transforming hydroxyapatite into fluorapatite. Fluorapatite is less soluble than hydroxyapatite, and the fluorine once fixed as an ultramicroscopic crystalline structure is not readily dissolved out.

Over time, skeletal remains located in soils permeated by ground water accumulate more and more fluorine. The rate of accumulation is determined by the specific conditions of the soil matrix, and therefore varies from one location to another. However, bones that have an identical history of burial will significantly resemble one another in fluorine content. Because the process is essentially irreversible, owing to the dissolubility of the fluorapatite, bone specimens of differing age, although found together through accidental redeposition, can be differentiated, and bones that are contemporary can be identified.

The Uranium Test (Natural Low-Level Radioactivity)

Another way to determine the contemporaneity of bone specimens is by measuring the amount of uranium that has accumulated since burial. Uranium is brought in contact with the bone through groundwater percolation. As groundwater contains trace quantities of uranium, calcium ions in the hydroxyapatite of bone are displaced by the introduction of uranium. The replacement of calcium ions by uranium is a cumulative process so that the longer a bone has lain in the soil, the more uranium it will have absorbed. Since uranium is radioactive, the uranium content of prehistoric bone can be conveniently estimated by measuring the amount of radioactivity present. This is done with aid of a proportional-flow counter. The uranium oxide content of the bone is estimated in parts per million by measuring the frequency of beta radiations per minute.

Generally, however, uranium is not the only source of radioactivity in prehistoric bone. Other so-called *daughter elements* are known to contribute some radioactivity. The error factor that such daughter elements introduce apparently is not regarded as serious. However, because it is not entirely correct to refer to this radioactivity as the product of uranium decay, it is often referred to simply as natural low-level radioactivity. In this context it is not used to estimate uranium content, but to measure variance among bone specimens and the soil matrix environment that contains them. Contemporaneity between the geological stratum and the associated specimens thus presumably can be tested.

Other techniques for determining the uranium oxide content of bone and teeth are available. Haynes *et al.* (1966) refer to a *fluorimetric technique*, and Groff (1966) suggests the analysis of gaseous uranium halides for this purpose. Whatever the technique, a uranium test can serve in the same way as fluorine analysis to distinguish among specimens found in fortuitous association.

The Piltdown Man Controversy

In a shallow gravel pit on Piltdown Common in Sussex, south of London, some two dozen fossil mammalian specimens were found. The gravel, which had originally been the bed of a river, exhibited two easily definable strata—a lower stratum of dark gravels and an upper stratum of light-colored gravels. All the bone specimens appeared to have been water worn, indicating that they had been redeposited and did not lie in their original burial positions. The question of their mutual contemporaneity therefore was raised. The species represented by the bone remains could be grouped in two contrasting faunas: an older fauna, including teeth fragments of an extinct Pleistocene elephant, and a geologically recent fauna that included the remains of beaver and red deer. It appeared that the two faunas had been washed from the two contrasting geological strata and redeposited together.

The importance of this find and of the issue of contemporaneity derived from the fact that among the two dozen bone specimens were the remains of what was purported to be an early fossil of man. The find, popularly known as the Piltdown Man (*Eoanthropus dawsoni*), consisted of the right half of a lower jaw with two molar teeth in place, a canine tooth, and several large fragments of the frontal, parietal, temporal, and occipital bones of the cranial vault. The find produced considerable controversy among human paleontologists, and most were prepared to reject it because the skull was fully modern in its morphology, whereas the jawbone had pronounced apelike characteristics. Acceptance of the association would have seriously undermined the prevailing scientific consensus regarding the evolutionary course of man.

The controversy raged on until 1949 when all the vertebrate specimens from the Piltdown gravels were subjected to fluorine dating. The bones of the earlier fauna contained a substantial quantity of fluorine, 2–3% (3.8% is the theoretical maximum). On the other hand, the amounts of fluorine in the skull and jawbone were determined to be 0.1 and 0.4%, respectively. Although not proving that the skull and jawbone were not contemporaneous, the fluorine test did prove that neither was as old as the Early fauna which, on the basis of the elephant remains, was dated at the Lower Pleistocene. This discovery further strengthened the skepticism of the scientific community regarding the authenticity of the Piltdown Man. Some even went so far as to assert that the jawbone and the canine tooth were deliberately fossilized to match the condition of the human skull bone.

In 1953 samples were taken from the specimens collectively regarded as Piltdown Man and again subjected to chemical analysis. By this time, however, there had been considerable refinement of the procedures for estimating fluorine content of fossil bone. Upon reexamination, the jawbone and canine tooth proved to contain no more fluorine than fresh bones and teeth, whereas the skull bones contained just enough fluorine to indicate that they were not modern. At this same time the nitrogen test, previously described, was also applied, and it was learned that the jawbone and teeth contained nitrogen contents equivalent to freshly dissected specimens. These results clearly demonstrated that Piltdown Man was indeed a hoax, and the controversies that the find had stimulated began to die down. At a still later time, the uranium test was applied to the Piltdown specimens. The findings agreed with those obtained by the fluroine and nitrogen tests. Table 2 provides a summary of the multiple test findings on the Piltdown Man materials.

TABLE 2

Fluorine, Nitrogen, and Uranium Contents of Human and Mammal Remains from the Piltdown Gravels[a]

	Fluorine (%)	Nitrogen (%)	"Uranium" (U_3O_3, ppm)[b]
Fresh bone	0.03	4.0	0
Piltdown jawbone	0.03	3.9	0
Neolithic skull, Kent	0.3	1.9	—
Piltdown skull	0.1	1.4	1
Piltdown "*Elephas* cf. *planifrons*" molar[+]	2.7	Nil	610

[a] After Oakley 1970: 41, Table B.
[b] Equivalent uranium oxide content, estimated in parts per million on basis of beta radiations per minute.

Radiological and Optical Methods of Dating Bone

Dating of prehistoric bones also can be accomplished by radiological and optical methods. The radiological methods make use of x-ray absorption and x-ray diffraction techniques. Optical methods include determination of the index of refraction, birefringence, and variable light absorption or *dichroism*. All these techniques are concerned with measuring the extent to which mineralization has taken place, and with recognizing changes in the micro- and ultramicrostructure of the bony framework itself. A very readable survey of these techniques is provided by Baud (1960). As in the case of chemical analysis of bone, these techniques provide a means of testing the validity of apparent intracomponent associations. Their dating functions are therefore minor in comparison with dating methods used for intercomponent dating.

Patination Dating of Stone Artifacts

The surface of rocks undergoes progressive chemical alteration through time. The term *patina* is used to refer to the visually obvious results of this process. Under certain conditions, the amount of patina can serve as a measure of relative age for stone artifacts. The variables affecting the nature and extent of patina are far too numerous and elusive to allow for its use in chronometric or even relative dating of archaeological components.

It can, however, serve as a possible indicator of stratigraphic mixture of cultural remains. Seemingly well-strafied sites may contain lithic assemblages that exhibit significant variability in the nature and extent of specimen patination. This may serve to call into question the validity of artifact association established by means of stratigraphic analysis. Similarly, a depositional layer at a site may contain a lithic assemblage that exhibits remarkable homogeneity in specimen patination. This may help to clarify at which point to designate the boundary between two cultural strata. Where there are sharp contrasts in the nature and extent of patination between two or more strata at a site, individual intrusive specimens may be reassigned confidently. The use of patination for intersite cross-dating is, on the other hand, a very unreliable activity.

Five types of patination have been recognized (Goodwin 1960). A type of patination observed on flint, chalcedony, and certain types of shales is called *bleaching*. It is caused by the leaching out of silica and its replacement by lime salts. The contrast that can be observed between bleached and unbleached specimens is a reliable one. Gradations in the extent of bleaching, however, are unreliable indicators by which to segregate stone artifact assemblages. Quartzitic sandstones found in well-watered soil deposits exhibit over time *induration of exposed surfaces*. This type of patination is caused by the leaching out of soluble silica and its redeposition at the surface in the form of a chertlike substance called silcrete. As a consequence of this kind of patination, the surfaces of the rock often are transformed into sand. The induration of exposed surfaces is an uncommon type of patination and is of no use for dating. Another type of patination that affects quartzitic sandstone is *limonite penetration and staining*. Limonite clays and salts within a soil matrix can be absorbed by stone artifacts through groundwater action. Such objects may be usefully segregated into groupings of light, moderate, and heavy staining, which may have significant implications for relative age. A fourth type of patination is called *desert varnish*. Under conditions of extreme dryness and intense solar radiation, such as can be found in desertlike settings where artifacts are located at the surface of the ground, the patina assumes the form of a glaze of varying thickness. Artifacts that possess a desert-varnish patina are generally members of a surface collection, where component segregation is normally very difficult to establish. The patination of stone artifacts in such a case can serve, possibly, as a rough indicator of the likelihood that the surface collection represents a single-component site. Considerable uniformity in specimen patinas may indicate that the collection of artifacts represents a single period of occupation, whereas variability among specimens in the thickness of the glaze may suggest that the site surface contains the residue of multiple periods of occupation. A final type of patination involves the *formation of a crust* on stone. The crust is formed by the removal of iron salts through leaching and their redeposition at the surface. This type of patination also is associated with arid environments, and can provide consistent and useful indications of relative age.

READINGS

Ascenzi, A.
   1970   Microscopy and prehistoric bone. In *Science in archaeology*, edited by D. Brothwell and E. Higgs. New York: Praeger.
Baud, C. A.
   1960   Dating of prehistoric bones by radiological and optical methods. In *The application of quantitative methods in archaeology*, edited by R. F. Heizer and S. F. Cook. Viking Fund Publications in Anthropology, No. 28. New York: Wenner-Gren Foundation.
Cook, S. F.
   1960   Dating of prehistoric bone by chemical analysis. In *The application of quantitative methods in archaeology*, edited by R. F. Heizer and S. F. Cook. Viking Fund Publications in Anthropology, No. 28. New York: Wenner-Gren Foundation.
Goodwin, A. J. H.
   1960   Chemical alteration (patination) of stone. In *The application of quantitative methods in archaeology*, edited by R. F. Heizer and S. F. Cook. Viking Fund Publications in Anthropology No. 28. New York: Wenner-Gren Foundation.
Groff, D. W.
   1966   Bone dating: Gas chromatology. *MASCA Newsletter* **2**, No. 1.
Haynes, C. V., Jr., A. R. Doberenz, and J. A. Allen
   1966   Geological and geochemical evidence concerning the antiquity of bone tools from Tule Springs, Site 2, Clark County, Nevada. *American Antiquity* **31**, No. 4: 517–521.
Hurst, V. J., and A. R. Kelly
   1961   Patination of cultural flints. *Science* **134**, No. 3474: 251–256.
Johnson, L., Jr.
   1967   *Toward a statistical overview of the archaic cultures of central and southwestern Texas* Bulletin 12. Texas Memorial Museum.
Lloyd, S.
   1963   *Mounds of the Near East*. Edinburgh University Press: Edinburgh.
Michels, J. W.
   1969   Testing stratigraphy and artifact reuse through obsidian hydration dating. *American Antiquity* **34**, No. 1: 15–22.

Oakley, K. P.
   1970   Analytical methods of dating bones. In *Science in archaeology*, edited by D.
          Brothwell and E. Higgs. New York: Praeger.
Scheffe, H.
   1959   *The analysis of variance.* New York: Wiley.
Wheeler, Sir M.
   1956   *Archaeology from the earth.* Baltimore: Penguin.
Willey, G. R., and P. Phillips
   1958   *Method and theory in American archaeology.* Chicago: University of Chicago Press.

◯

PART TWO

METHODS OF RELATIVE DATING

Earlier, it was stated that relative dating consisted of ascertaining the correct order of events. This, however, is not an entirely adequate definition, for there are two fundamental strategies involved in relative dating that need to be distinguished. First, there is the need to establish a sequence of events. In archaeology this is generally an ordering of recognized phases *within a particular region. The establishment of a sequence of phases can be accomplished by chronologically ordering representative* components *of these phases by means of stratigraphy, seriation, chronometric dating, or some combination of these. Ascertaining the correct order of events therefore is one important objective involved in relative dating. We have also noted earlier that* phases *represent, analytically, categories or classes to which specific archaeological* components *can be assigned. It is precisely this activity of assigning components to one or another phase of a chronological sequence that constitutes the second fundamental strategy of relative dating. This second strategy is often referred to as* correlation dating *or* cross-dating. *It presupposes the existence of a suitable temporally ordered sequence of cultural phases.*

47

Sequence dating *and* cross-dating *therefore constitute the principal topics of discussion in this portion of the book. It has been noted that sequence dating can be accomplished by means of stratigraphy, chronometric dating, seriation, or some combination of these. We have discussed stratigraphy in Part One, in connection with component segregation, and it will be further discussed in Part Two, together with seriation and cross-dating. A discussion of chronometric dating comprises all of Part Three.*

CHAPTER FOUR

Sequence Dating through
Stratigraphic Analysis

Introduction

Stratigraphic analysis of site deposits is one of the most difficult tasks confronting the field archaeologist. Because of the uniqueness of each site with respect to time, depth, geomorphology, sedimentation, climate, and the effects of human occupation, it is difficult to provide useful generalizations of method beyond those given in Chapter Three without reference to a specific set of problems. For this reason, I have chosen to summarize a study of the stratigraphy of Sheep Rock Shelter, Huntingdon County, Pennsylvania. The study, conducted under my supervision by archaeology students at The Pennsylvania State University, illustrates the procedures, problems, and potential results of stratigraphic analysis.

Rock shelters, in contrast to open-air sites, are a principal source of stratified archaeological deposits. First, open-air sites seldom exhibit

49

rigid boundaries to the extent of settlement area available so that successive phases of occupation may not necessarily overlap in space. Second, such sites are subject to erosional forces that can destroy the integrity of depositional layers, should they develop. Rock shelters, however, have finite living platforms forcing successive occupants to reuse the same activity areas year after year. This guarantees superposition of the cultural debris. Furthermore, rock shelters often provide adequate protection against the effects of erosion so that the integrity of the superimposed deposits is maintained. Generally speaking, the volume of cultural midden that accumulates in a rock shelter is related to the amount of protected usable living area; small rock shelters generally contain shallow midden deposits, whereas large rock shelters may contain deep midden deposits. However, even large rock shelters, which contain deep midden deposits, may be poorly stratified. The extent of recognizable cultural stratigraphy present in a shelter is affected by several factors. Those most frequently serving to obscure recognition of the interfaces between cultural strata are:

(1) surface water runoff;
(2) ground water seepage;
(3) postdepositional disturbances such as pitting, dwelling construction, and burrowing by rodents and other small animals.

Sheep Rock Shelter: A Case Study in Methodology

The rock shelters of Pennsylvania usually have only small living platforms and exhibit generally shallow, poorly differentiated archaeological deposits. Sheep Rock Shelter (Plate 1) represents an important exception to this generalization. The site is located in the Appalachian Mountain section of the Ridge and Valley Province. Rocks of this area consist of layers of ancient sediments which have been compacted into beds that have been folded so that the rocks are now tilted. Erosion through the folded layers has created valleys where there were soft rocks and mountains where there were rocks of greater resistance.

The rocks at Sheep Rock Shelter are tilted 25 degrees (25°) from the horizontal toward the southeast. The Raystown Branch of the Juniata River, which flows past the site, has cut a meandering valley

Plate 1. *Sheep Rock Shelter site, Huntingdon County, Pennsylvania.*

into the tilted strata so that the valley walls along the stream rise 250–300 feet. To the northwest, resistant layers have left higher ground, which rises steeply 1100 feet above stream level. The stream cuts through rocks that were laid down as sediments approximately 360 million years ago; some represent deposits of an old delta, and others were laid down on the sea floor offshore from the delta. The delta sediments are red shales and sandstone of the Devonian Catskill formation; the marine rocks are gray and greenish shales and sandstone of the Devonian Chemung formation and contain scattered marine shells.

The shelter itself is located in an undercut notch in the Chemung formation. The notch was cut during past millenia by the Raystown Branch as its waters, flowing then at a higher elevation, were swung in against the outcrop as the stream flowed around a tight bend. Over the years, the stream cut downward and eventually abandoned the notch, leaving a shelf under overhanging rock.

Most of the recently deposited material at the shelter consists of decayed shale derived from the overhang of the shelter and by the creep of similar material from the steep slope at the northwestern end of the site. Occupational debris, naturally derived humus, and rock fall account for the remainder of the site material.

The overhang rises abruptly from the innermost recesses of the shelter toward the drip line (a distance of 15–30 feet) rising from less than 5 to more than 70 feet above the present floor level. This was a very livable shelter. Its high-vaulted overhang permits sunlight to reach the living floor all during the day. Yet the orientation of the rock face protects the shelter from the prevailing winds and keeps large areas of the floor free from moisture throughout the year.

The present usable living area of the shelter measures approximately 3000 square feet (roughly 25 by 120 feet). Artifacts have been found more than 14 feet below the present surface, and shaley gravels continue down another 10 feet to the prehistoric stream level (which is now higher as a result of dam construction). In general, the lower strata are more moist and contain a greater amount of shale relative to soil per unit volume than the upper levels. An exceptionally dry midden comprises the top 2–3 feet of deposit on the western end of the site. The moist condition of the eastern side is largely the result of a small spring at the back of the shelter, which, together with the inclination of the surface, causes rainwater runoff to flow inward from the drip line. This water reaction has tended to obscure strata boundaries sometimes beyond recognition in certain areas. Near the spring, water containing ferromagnesium impurities has combined with the soil to form compact reddish-brown clay, which extends down to bedrock.

On the basis of contrasting sediments the deposit can be divided into five zones (Figure 10). From top to bottom they are as follows:

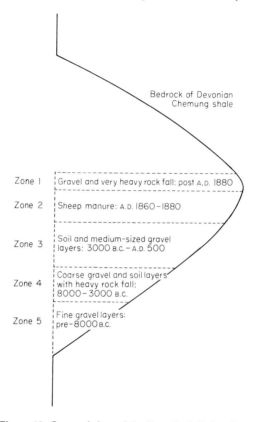

Figure 10. *Geomorphology of the Sheep Rock Shelter deposit.*

Zone 1. This is a surficial layer averaging 4 inches in thickness and consisting mostly of shale chips, very heavy rock fall, and the debris of picnickers, campers, and hunters who have used the site over the past half-century.

Zone 2. This zone comprises a layer of domestic sheep manure 6–18 inches in thickness. The shelter derived its name from its past use as a refuge spot favored by grazing sheep during bad weather.

Zone 3. Soil (including humus, ash, and charcoal) is the predominant component in a deposit also consisting of medium-sized shale chips and rock fall. The zone may be subdivided into dry and wet segments. The dry segment is found in the upper 2 feet of the western end of the site and is flanked on the east and underlaid by a wet segment.

Zone 4. This zone averages about 90 inches in thickness and consists largely of coarse shaley gravels together with soil and humus. A massive rock fall separates two artifact-bearing segments in certain areas of this zone.

Zone 5. This is a thick preoccupational stratum consisting of numerous layers of fine shaley gravels. These form the base of the site deposit and extend down 50–120 inches to bedrock and the prehistoric stream level.

Field Methodology

A grid system was laid out when systematic excavations first began (Figure 11). At that time a datum point and coordinate base lines were established, with grid north perpendicular to the back wall and 44.6 degrees east of magnetic north. The site then was partitioned into squares 5 feet to the side, with the north–south lines running the length of the site (in an east–west direction) and the east–west lines running more or less perpendicular to the back wall of the shelter (in a north–south direction).

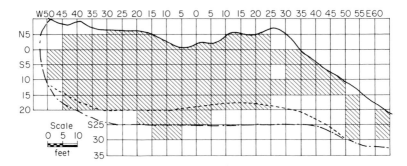

Figure 11. *Sheep Rock Shelter grid system: distribution of excavated squares in relation to the total site area and main habitation area. The hatching indicates squares excavated during the eight seasons of excavations (1958–1967); the long–short dashed line delineates the estimated maximum area of habitation deposit, ~3000 square feet; the dashed line indicates the main habitation area (within the drip line), 2400 square feet. (From Bebrich and Willey 1968: Fig. 2.)*

Each square was excavated as a separate unit by the natural stratigraphy of the deposit, by arbitrary 3- or 6-inch levels, or by a combination of natural and arbitrary levels. Upon the completion of an excavation, unit profiles were drawn for one or more of the surrounding vertical walls, generally by the workers who had excavated the unit.

The intention was that each level be described systematically in terms of color, texture, and composition. Profiles were drawn to scale as accurately as possible, and the scale used was noted on each profile. The Munsell Soil Color Chart aided in standardizing soil color descriptions. A set of soil samples from the site was also taken for reference in describing textural and compositional variations. Both black-and-white and color photography were used as aids in detecting color changes that were sometimes difficult to see with the naked eye. An effort was made to record stratigraphic profiles as soon as possible after exposure so that drying and other weathering processes would not affect level description and drawing accuracy. The drawings were prepared on 8½ by 11-inch sheets of graph paper. All measurements were taken and recorded in the English (inch–foot) system. The vertical measurements were given in inches below the arbitrary zero datum point. Such measurements were accomplished with the aid of retractable metal measuring tapes, a plumb bob and string, line levels, and stadia rods. Upon the completion of the profile drawings, they were attached to the field notes of the appropriate excavation unit.

During the eight seasons of work at Sheep Rock Shelter an estimated 70 individuals, including students, amateurs, and professionals, were involved in the recording of field profiles. With few exceptions, these profiles, numbering some 447, were recorded independently for the 5-foot sections of the grid, generally without regard to the previously drawn profiles of adjacent squares. As would be expected, problems emerged that had to be resolved if the field profiles were to be integrated successfully into composite crosssections of the site. The problems of integration derive from four sources:

1. condition of the deposit.
2. failure to record data.
3. quality of data recorded.
4. data comparability.

Erosion, soil hydration, slumpage, animal burrowing, and poor excavation techniques all affect the condition of the deposit, and can interfere with adequate stratigraphic recording. The profiles of vertical wall sections suffering such disturbance sometimes can be reconstructed with the aid of daily field notes and face-view drawings of completed excavation levels.

Occasionally, a worker neglects to prepare a vertical wall profile for the square he has been excavating. This is the most common failure in data recording, and sometimes can be corrected through reconstruction efforts. Variations in the quality of data recorded has to do with the extent of detail in the observations as well as the degree of accuracy with which the detail was faithfully recorded onto the profile drawings. Problems of comparability of data stemmed principally from the fact that each observer tended to select for emphasis different visual and textural clues to observed stratigraphy. One might depict with considerable detail contrasts in zones of color, and all but ignore variations in soil texture. Another might make fine distinctions between layers of varying-sized gravels, all but ignoring the variation in soil color. Trying to match up such section profiles then becomes difficult, owing to the lack of comparability of the data recorded.

For these reasons it was recommended that the excavator make sure his profile drawings include the following information:

1. Name of recorder; date (including year).
2. Grid square designation.
3. Side wall shown in drawing (using grid coordinates in all cases and cardinal directions of the grid system when applicable).
4. Scale (if possible, all drawings should be prepared to the same scale).
5. Below-datum elevation readings for the termini of all strata boundaries at points of intersection with vertical grid lines.
6. Precise recording of cultural features, including morphology, internal stratification, soil description(s), and the relation of cultural items to feature components.
7. Soil descriptions of all soil components, including color, texture, and composition.
8. Notation of the relation of cultural items to components of the stratigraphy, including unusual concentrations and associations.
9. Precise plotting of rocks and other materials that may indicate slope and location of strata boundaries, particularly at grid junctures, where they may play an important role in the linking of adjacent profiles.
10. Numbering of excavation levels.
11. Cross-checking against previously drawn adjacent and intersecting profiles, noting the nature of the discrepancies, if any, and recommendations for correction.

12. Prepare frequent face-view drawings of square during excavation. These can be used to supplement the profiles and can serve as an independent check on measurements and associations.

Laboratory Analysis

Laboratory study begins with the trial integration of individual field profiles into continuous composite profiles of selected grid lines of the site. First, the original field profiles are removed from their respective field note files. They then are labeled and organized according to grid square. Identification labels include the grid designation of the profile or profiles. For example, "E5/S10–S15; S10/E5–E0" indicates that two intersecting profiles were prepared on the same sheet of graph paper, one of which runs North–South from S10 to S15, and the other East–West from E5 to E0 (see Figure 10, page 53). This form of identification has the advantage of specifying both the location of a profile and the direction from which it was drawn.

All original field profiles were reproduced to actual size using a standard office copying machine. The copies were then spliced together according to the following procedures.

All of the profiles pertaining to a given grid line were arranged in a vertical and horizontal sequence with grid West and North to the left-hand side of the drawing. When necessary, profiles for a given grid line were reversed by carefully tracing the structural element of the copy on the opposite side of the page over a light box.

Adjacent profiles (those lying side by side in the same plane) were aligned first by the vertical below-datum readings indicated on them. They then were checked for continuity of strata, as suggested by the articulation of strata boundaries at grid junctures and by continuity in soil description and soil slope.

About 20% (62) of the profile sections used had to be reconstructed from original field notes because of the problems mentioned earlier involving the condition of the deposit, failure to record data, quality of data recorded, and comparability of data. Reconstruction was accomplished by plotting the below-datum measurements of natural strata for both adjacent squares along the grid line segment to be reconstructed. Next, face-view drawings and daily field record observations regarding the square in question were gleaned for any and all details of deposition that might aid in connecting up the strata that seem to articulate across the interrupted section. Several sections were reconstructed independently by two different persons to insure objectivity.

Finally, integration was achieved by joining the profiles so that the layers could be traced as they extended across the site. If disagreement did not exceed 3 scale inches, the lines forming the boundaries of strata could be altered so as to join in an unbroken fashion. If, however, variance exceeded 3 scale inches but joining of the lines still seemed warranted on the basis of additional data, the lines were then corrected; in this case, however, dashed rather than solid lines were used to warn the user of the possible inaccuracy.

Upon completion, each composite profile was traced in pencil on vellum paper, and the tracing was checked in every detail against the original. Vertical and horizontal scales also were blocked out in pencil and double-checked for accuracy. The pencil tracings were then inked, using the pencil drawn lines as guides. Actual soil descriptions given by each recorder were transcribed onto the composite profiles in place of a small set of standard soil categories so as not to submerge the feature patterns, and because it was felt that they would make the composite profiles better research instruments by providing original descriptive information keyed to the field notes. To further integrate the profiles with the field notes, excavation-level designations were included in parentheses where applicable.

Because of their apparent locational stability with respect to time, cultural features consitute a more or less permanent record of living-floor activities, and combined with evidence drawn from artifact distributions, guide the archaeologist in deciding where on the composite profiles he should locate boundaries between adjacent cultural strata. For this reason all readily available field note data on features were plotted. Thus, rocks, bedrock, ash, charcoal, and burned soil were all shaded in different patterns in order to give the profiles relief and to emphasize the feature areas (see Figure 12).

Altogether, the composite drawings represent about 5530 square feet of profiled deposit, 3060 square feet of which lies along the North–South profiles and 2470 along the East–West profiles (see Table 3).

Cultural Stratum Definition

In the case of Sheep Rock Shelter, the final stage in stratigraphic analysis was to define the cultural strata that corresponded to the major divisions of the Middle Atlantic and Northeastern archaeological

TABLE 3

Name, Location, and Length of Sheep Rock Shelter Composite Stratigraphic Profiles[a]

North–South profiles			East–West profiles		
Name	Location	Length (feet)	Name	Location	Length (feet)
N5	E5–E25	20	W40	S0–S15	15
S0	W40–E30	70	W33	N7–S15	22
S5	W40–E30	70	W30	N8–S25	33
S10	W45–E50	95	W25	N7–S21	28
S15	W40–E27	97	W20	N8–S28	36
S20	W35–E20	55	W15	N5–S30	35
			W10	N4–S30	34
			W5	N1–S20	21
			E0	N3–S20	23
			E5	N3–S25	28
			E10	S0–S20	20
			E15	N5–S20	25
			E20	N5–S20	25
			E25	N5–S15	20

[a]From Bebrich and Willey (1968: Fig. 3).

sequence. The following procedures were used to accomplish this. First, all thirteen radiocarbon dates and all diagnostic (cross-datable) artifacts were plotted on the composite stratigraphic profiles. The composite profiles then were examined for patterning in the distribution of *period-specific* artifacts. For example, the distribution of Early Archaic artifacts were determined and compared with that for Middle Archaic artifacts. Analysis began with the S10 profile because of its central location in the rock shelter. Carrying the above example further, a line was drawn through the deposit on the S10 profile that effectively segregated artifacts cross-datable to the Early Archaic period from artifacts cross-datable to the Middle Archaic period. It was also ascertained that carbon samples dating to the respective periods were located on the appropriate sides of the line. This line thus became the provisional boundary between the Middle and Early Archaic components. To test its reliability, the provisional boundary line then was traced via each of the 14 East–West cross profiles to the adjacent S0, S5, S15, and S20 profiles, where it was determined that the boundary line also served to segregate *period-specific* artifacts

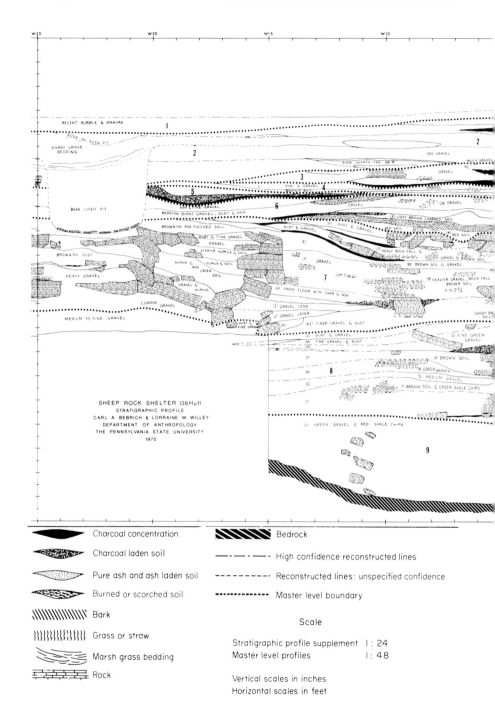

SHEEP ROCK SHELTER (36Hu1)
STRATIGRAPHIC PROFILE
CARL A BEBRICH & LORRAINE M WILLEY
DEPARTMENT OF ANTHROPOLOGY
THE PENNSYLVANIA STATE UNIVERSITY
1970

Charcoal concentration

Charcoal laden soil

Pure ash and ash laden soil

Burned or scorched soil

Bark

Grass or straw

Marsh grass bedding

Rock

Bedrock

—·—·—·— High confidence reconstructed lines

— — — — — Reconstructed lines: unspecified confidence

············· Master level boundary

Scale

Stratigraphic profile supplement   1 : 24
Master level profiles   1 : 48

Vertical scales in inches
Horizontal scales in feet

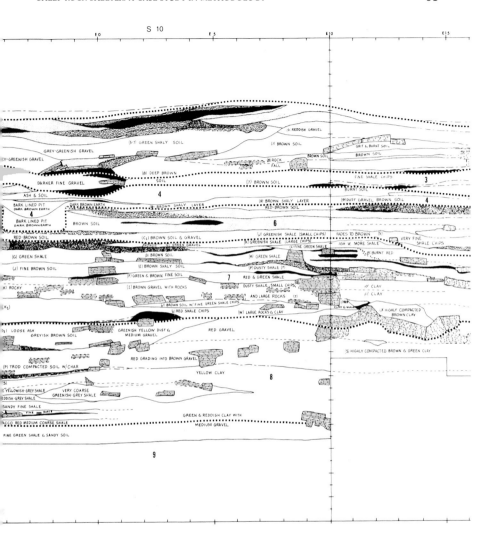

Figure 12. *Sheep Rock Shelter stratigraphic profile (36 Hu1). Scale: stratigraphic profile supplement, 1:24; master level profiles, 1:48. The vertical scales are in inches, the horizontal scales are in feet, and the key to the symbols is given in the legend. (From Bebrich and Willey 1970: Fig. 2)*

and radiocarbon samples for each North–South profile. When a projected boundary line did not adequately partition the components
on some of the North–South profiles, the initial boundary line was
altered to conform with the information on the other profiles. At
Sheep Rock Shelter the natural strata intersect and diverge at numerous points along every profile. Options for altering provisional boundary lines therefore were almost always available.

The above-mentioned procedures were repeated for each successive culture stratum, beginning with the earliest and ending with
the most recent. Eight culture strata and one preoccupational stratum
were defined in this manner (see Figure 11). From top to bottom
they include the following:

Level 1 (post-A.D. 1580).   This constitutes the top layer of the site
and consists of sheep manure and modern refuse. Although it is
associated with the Colonial period, it contains some artifacts uplifted
from the Late Woodland stratum directly underlying it. One radiocarbon date of A.D. 1870 ± 100 was obtained from a hearth apparently
dug into an old Susquehannock bed pit. Such artifacts as French
gun flints, a rifle ball, and a piece of Germantown blue-jean cloth
were found in this level. Level 1 covers the entire site area and
measures about 6–18 inches in thickness.

Level 2 (A.D. 700–1580).   This level consists of Protohistoric and Late
Woodland deposits. The Early and Middle Woodland artifacts found
at this level owe their presence to deep pitting into the earlier deposits.
Current evidence suggests that all such pitting originating from Level
2 is the exclusive by-product of the final aboriginal occupation of
the site—that of the Shenk's Ferry and Susquehannock Indians. Five
radiocarbon dates were obtained from this level: A.D. 1450, A.D. 1460,
A.D. 1490, A.D. 1690, and A.D. 1600 (all with a standard error of ± 100
years). Cultural affinities represented in this stratum include Clem-
son's Island, Owasco, Shenk's Ferry, Monongahela, and Susquehannock. Level 2 covers the entire site area and measures 18–36 inches
in thickness.

Level 3 (500 B.C. to A.D. 700).   This represents the Middle Woodland
deposit. Some Early Woodland ceramics were found in this level
and are accounted for by uplift and disturbances caused by the Middle
Woodland pitting. Middle Woodland pits appear to have served
primarily as hearths, although some might have been intended for
use as food storage pits. Two radiocarbon dates were obtained from

this level. Both were secured from small pits of densely packed charcoal located on the eastern side of the site. The dates are A.D. ± 140 and A.D. 320 ± 140. Diagnostic projectile points indicate use of the shelter by groups in contact with or representing cultures to both the west and north: Raccoon side-notched, Snyders, Fox Creek stemmed, and Jack's Reef corner-notched. Only one ceramic type was identified for this period, Sheep Rock cord-marked: a locally evolved ware possibly of Point Peninsula affiliation. Level 3 appears to have covered the entire site area, but was considerably disturbed by deep pitting during Protohistoric times. Before disturbance, the stratum had an estimated thickness of 6–18 inches.

Level 4 (1000–500 B.C.). This level constitutes the Early Woodland deposit. Some terminal Archaic and Transitional period artifacts were found in this level, generally in the lower portions, and owe their presence to uplifting and to excavation of at least two medium-sized pits by Early Woodland inhabitants. No radiocarbon dates definitely assignable to this period were obtained from Level 4. Three related varieties of pottery resembling Vinette I were recovered, however, together with two projectile-point types (Meadowood and Juniata stemmed) that have Vinette I associations elsewhere. Level 4 covers most of the site area but appears to lens out on the far western end of the site. The level measures 0–30 inches in thickness.

Level 5 (1500–1000 B.C.). This is a relatively thin stratum constituting the Transitional period deposit. Although soil accumulation may have proceeded at normal rates, diagnostic artifacts show a highly restricted distribution which is confined to the central and western portions of the site. Several varieties of transitional points were recovered from Level 5: Susquehanna, Perkiomen, Fish Tail, and Frost Island. One radiocarbon date of 1270 B.C. ± 160 was obtained from a small hearth believed to be associated with the Frost Island component of this period. Level 5 measures 0–8 inches in thickness.

Level 6 (3000–1500 B.C.). This level constitutes the Late Archaic deposit. The level appears to be relatively undisturbed and little difficulty was encountered in defining its boundaries. Several varieties of points were associated with this stratum: Brewerton side-notched, Brewerton corner-notched, Helgramite, Bare Island-Wading Water, Genesee, Rossville, and Savannah River. Two radiocarbon dates were obtained from Level 6: a date of 2350 B.C. ± 180 secured from a hearth forming part of a Brewerton living floor, and a date of 1850 B.C. ± 180, which appears to represent charcoal sweepings from the same floor contaminated by carbonaceous material derived from a later context. Level 6 is continuous throughout the site and measures 12–36 inches in thickness.

Level 7 (5000–3000 B.C.).   This constitutes the stratum of Middle Archaic deposition. The base of the level was dated at 5100 B.C. ± 250. At least two distinct components are represented in this stratum, the earliest, termed the Raystown River phase, dating 5000–4000 B.C., and the latest, an early Laurentian phase, dating 4000–3000 B.C. Diagnostic point types from this stratum include Raystown stemmed, an early Laurentian corner-notched form, and a type much resembling the Halifax type. Level 7 is continuous throughout the site and measures 18–48 inches in thickness.

Level 8 (8000–5000 B.C.).   This constitutes the Early Archaic deposit. The top of the stratum is marked by a radiocarbon date of 5100 B.C. ± 250; a second radiocarbon date of 6920 B.C. ± 320 was obtained from the middle of the level. Only three diagnostic artifacts were found in Level 8, two Kirk serrated points and one LeCroy point. The deepest artifacts were found at the base of this stratum at 204 inches below datum. Level 8 is continuous throughout the site and measures 12–48 inches in thickness.

Level 9 (pre-8000 B.C.).   This constitutes the pre-occupation deposit. This level is composed mostly of the fine angular, bedded shale, and occasional rock fall. Level 9 is continuous over the site and measures 50–120 inches in thickness.

Sheep Rock Shelter illustrates both the information to be gained and the difficulties to be met within analyzing the stratigraphy of a deep site. Throughout the world such sites serve as cornerstones in the construction of regional chronologies.

READINGS

Bebrich, C. A., and L. M. Willey
   1968   The stratigraphy of the Sheep Rock Shelter. In *Archaeological investigation of Sheep Rock Shelter, Huntingdon County, Pennsylvania*, edited by Joseph W. Michels and James S. Dutt. Occasional Papers in Anthropology, Number 5, Department of Anthropology, Pennsylvania State University; pp. 33–92.
Biek, L.
   1970   Soil silhouettes. In *Science in archaeology*, edited by D. Brothwell and E. Higgs. New York: Praeger.
Butzer, K. W.
   1971   *Environment and archaeology*. Chicago: Aldine-Atherton.

Cornwall, I. W.
  1958 *Soils for the archaeologist*. London: Phoenix House.
  1970 Soil, stratification and environment. In *Science in archaeology*, edited by D. Brothwell and E. Higgs. New York: Praeger.
Heizer, R. F.
  1959 *The archaeologist at work*. New York: Harper & Row.
Hole, F., and R. F. Heizer
  1969 *An introduction to prehistoric archaeology*. New York: Holt.
Lloyd, S.
  1963 *Mounds of the Near East*. Edinburgh: Edinburgh University Press.
Schmid, E.
  1970 Cave sediments and prehistory. In *Science in archaeology*, edited by D. Brothwell and E. Higgs. New York: Praeger.
Wheeler, Sir M.
  1956 *Archaeology from the earth*. Baltimore: Penguin.

CHAPTER   FIVE

Sequence Dating through Seriation

Introduction

The archaeologist investigating the remains of past cultures usually encounters them in the form of components such as pit or trench levels, caches, house floors, and graves. These collections, in turn, are composed of types of artifacts. In other words, a component would be considered a group of artifacts that were probably manufactured at approximately the same time and place. Many of the components recovered from a single region would differ in their artifact contents because, among other reasons, types of artifacts originate at different times and increase and decrease in popularity at different times.

One implication that can be drawn from this is that if a series of components derive from a culture that changes through time, their relative placement on an axis of time is a function of their similarity. That is, components representing cultural phases that are temporally close will have relative artifact type frequencies that are very similar; conversely, components that are not temporally close will have dissimilar relative artifact type frequencies. If this is the case, a seriation (ordering) of the components can be made in which, if time were the causative agent (and not such factors as irregularities in culture change, spatial variation, social and functional variation, mixture, or change), the results would represent the temporal placing of the components. The determination of the direction (early to late), however, would require independent data, such as that available through cross-dating with previously established sequences, or chronometric dating of any two points within the series.

In general, the term *seriation* means the placing of items in a series so that the position of each best reflects the degree of similarity between that item and all other items in the data set. Thus, seriation is one form of scale analysis. It arranges items by position alone, and does not use variation in metric distance between item positions as an expression of degree of similarity. As such it is simpler than the scaling procedures that use the distance between the item points to show the magnitude of the similarity between the items.

The Brainerd-Robinson Technique

In 1951, Robinson (1951), a sociologist, and Brainerd (1951), an archaeologist, sought to obtain a mathematical measure of similarity among collections which would depend upon the comparative frequencies of a number of artifact types common to the collections. They wanted to quantify the comparison of collections by devising a measure of how similar or dissimilar the relative artifact type frequencies are for various pairs of components. These measures of similarity are called *indexes of agreement* or *agreement coefficients*.

With the determination of the agreement coefficient one can tell whether, for example, Component 3 is closer in time to Components 2 or 5. If the agreement between the percentage of distributions of Components 2 and 3 is greater than the agreement between Components 3 and 5, then Components 2 and 3 are closer temporally than Components 3 and 5.

Suppose there are a number of components for which the agreement coefficients between the percentage distributions in *all possible* combinations of the two has been determined. These coefficients show how close together temporally all possible pairs of these components are. If the components are arranged in chronological order, the agreement coefficients should show some kind of a pattern.

To determine patterning, the coefficients of agreement between pairs of components are plotted in asymmetric table or matrix in which the collections are listed along the top and left margins, beginning from left to right and from top to bottom, respectively. The agreement coefficients are placed at the intersections. If the collections are arranged chronologically along the margins, the resulting table of agreement coefficients will show high values clustering about the diagonal. If the chronological order of the components is not known, they are rearranged along the margins until the above-mentioned pattern of agreement coefficients is approximated.

The Brainerd–Robinson technique for seriation is based on the calculation of the agreement coefficient. The basic data needed are those in a table listing the percentage of different types of artifacts within each of a number of archaeological components (it is assumed that the artifact types already have been established and that the components are properly segregated). The first step in calculating the agreement coefficient is the tabulation of the percentage of each artifact type in each component. Next, each component is compared to all other components with regard to the percentages of each type and the smaller percentage, regardless of which component it belongs to, is always subtracted from the larger.

The resulting percentage differences from the comparison of the types in one component to another are then added together to give the total difference between any two components (Figure 13). This total is then subtracted from the figure 200; the remainder is the *agreement coefficient*. The reason for the figure 200 is that if two collec-

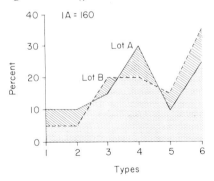

Figure 13. *Areas of agreement and disagreement for a Robinson index of agreement (IA-160) between two hypothetical assemblages, Lots A and B. Stippling indicates agreement; hatching indicates disagreement. (From Johnson 1968: Fig. 3.)*

tions are compared that have all types in common, then their maximum similarity would be 200%. The agreement coefficients then are
entered in the matrix (Figure 14).

The Brainerd–Robinson technique soon proved itself to be widely

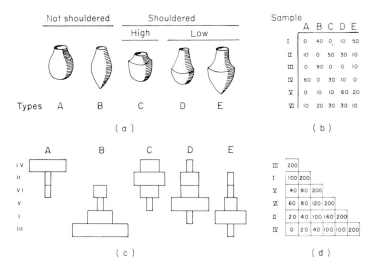

Figure 14. *Seriation: (a) a likely typological classification of a collection of ceramics; (b)
frequency (percent) of each type in six samples; (c) bar-graph seriation of the samples; (d)
Brainerd–Robinson seriation of the samples. (From Jelinek 1962: Fig. 1. Reproduced by permission
of the Society for American Archaeology from* American Antiquity, *Vol. 28.)*

applicable to the relative dating tasks of archaeology, but was
employed only rarely because of the enormous investment of time
and effort required when more than a very few components are to
be seriated. Although the calculation of agreement coefficients takes
up considerable time when large numbers of artifact types and components are involved, the major deterrent to ready application of this
technique has been the time and effort involved in manipulating the
items within the matrix toward achieving the best approximation to
an ideal pattern. Every time the position of a row is changed, the
position of the corresponding column has to be changed.

The process was made somewhat easier with the aid of an ordering
board designed by Brainerd. The ordering board is a block of wood
cut up into 1-inch cubes with ¼-inch diameter holes drilled through
all four sides. Metal rods pass through all block cubes constituting

a column and/or row within the matrix. Each block cube represents a similarity score between two items or components. Thus, a column or row of such blocks represents the total set of similarity scores between a single item or component and all other items or components. To change the position of an item, the operator has to lift up all the blocks in the column and row affected by the positioning of the item. The metal rods are used for this purpose. There is always the danger that the blocks will slip off the rod by accident during one of the item manipulations, and chaos would ensue.

However, even with this mechanical aid, seriation remained a time-consuming process for larger numbers of artifact types or components. Table 4 lists the number of essentially different permutations for sets of items or components consisting of from 2 to 20 members. It is obvious that manual rearrangement of the order of components within the matrix would be extraordinarily burdensome for sets consisting of more than five items.

TABLE 4
Number of Essentially Different Item Permutations for Values of n *below 21[a]*

n	$\dfrac{n!}{2}$
2	1
3	3
4	12
5	60
6	360
7	2,520
8	20,160
9	181,440
10	1.82×10^6
11	2.00×10^7
12	2.40×10^8
13	3.12×10^9
14	4.36×10^{10}
15	0.66×10^{12}
16	1.04×10^{13}
17	1.78×10^{14}
18	3.20×10^{15}
19	0.61×10^{17}
20	1.22×10^{18}

[a]From Johnson 1968: Table 1.

Computer-Assisted Seriation

Ascher and Ascher (1963) presented the first published computer program for the Brainerd–Robinson technique. The Aschers' basic procedure in ordering the Robinson matrix of agreement coefficients is to have the computer insert one row and column at a time, gradually increasing the matrix from two row–columns until the full matrix size is reached. Each placement decision is based on the assumption that those already ordered are correct. As each new row–column is introduced, it is successively tried in each position until its proper position is found. Once a position is found that satisfies certain criteria, the row–column is inserted in that position and remains there without further testing.

Because anthropological data are rarely ideal, some row–columns cannot be ordered in the sense that they do not *behave* properly in relation to other row–columns (that is, they do no fully satisfy the criteria for placement). In the Aschers' program, these are held aside until all those that can be ordered are in a proper relationship. Those held aside are then tested against the row–columns already ordered until their *best* position is found—*best* is described as the position most closely approximating the ideal matrix model in terms of the least number of negative signs. The placement of these withheld row–columns, however, is not allowed to influence the relative positions of those already placed.

As the Aschers' state (1963), their technique is not based on extensive comparisons of all possible placements. Instead, each row–column is placed as soon as it satisfies the criteria or, in the case of a withheld row–column that is subsequently inserted, when it approximates the criteria to some degree. They point out that this can lead to different *final* orderings if the order of the input is changed.

The reason the Ascher technique did not involve extensive comparisons of all possible placements has to do with the incredible number of essentially different item permutations involved in orderings consisting of more than six-item sets or artifact collections. One programmer has estimated that 20 artifact collections would demand a minimum of 600 hundred billion years of computer time to try all one quintillion, two-hundred twenty quadrillion essentially different permutations! So, although the use of an electronic computer does solve the problem of unwieldiness originally associated with the use of the Brainerd ordering board, it still does not solve the time problem.

The Aschers' procedure was a short cut, but one that gave heavy influence to the original ordering of collections in the matrix. Kuzara *et al.* (1966) tried out a different strategy of computer-assisted seriation that would significantly reduce the influence of the original ordering, but retain the desired economy on computer time. Their technique involved three stages:

Stage I. This consists of moving row–column 1 into position 2, so that the original row–column 2 then occupies position 1; next, the original row–column 1, which is now in position 2, is moved down to position 3. The procedure is continued until row–column 1 is tried in all positions of the item array. A matrix coefficient is used to compare the different permutations, and the permutation producing the best ordering coefficient is held in storage. This permutation is then used as a new starting matrix, and row–column 2 is tried in the same fashion as row–column 1 in all positions. If a particular shift in the position of row–column 2 yields a better ordering coefficient, the corresponding item permutation is held in memory. Using this permutation as a starting matrix, row–column 3 is shifted through all positions, continuing the process through all items.

Stage II. This starts with the item permutation having the best ordering coefficient that was found in Stage I, and the whole process is repeated again. This is continued until the best ordering obtained by trying every row–column in every successive position is identical to the previous best ordering.

Stage III. In this stage Stage I and II procedures are repeated, but the input array at the beginning of each Stage I action is randomized (Figure 15).

Two subsequent computer programs have been written that constitute refinements and improvements on the basic design worked out by Kuzara, Mead, and Dixon. One is called the Phoenix-II program, written by Hole and Shaw (1967), and another, called Program Seriate, written by Craytor and Johnson (1968). One of the characteristics common to several of the computer programs is the fact that they are written with sufficient generality that they can accept data in a variety of forms and can use a wide range of similarity scores in the item seriation. This range of options augments the versatility and convenience associated with this technique of relative dating, making it more attractive to archaeologists.

Although there are a number of different kinds of agreement coefficients or similarity scores that can be used in seriation dating, the

73

CASE CSCLB/BR/02/64-1008-01 - ARTIFACT FREQUENCIES IN UNORDERED LOTS

LOTS	TYPES										
	1	2	3	4	5	6	7	8	9	10	11
1	3	2	0	1	0	0	0	0	25	9	0
2	23	2	0	0	0	0	0	0	24	36	1
3	34	4	0	0	21	5	0	0	19	55	1
4	68	2	0	0	23	9	0	0	11	44	2
5	94	6	1	0	45	1	0	0	17	25	0
6	79	6	5	0	36	6	0	0	6	46	0
7	58	5	0	1	14	6	0	2	1	43	0
8	51	15	1	2	22	9	0	0	0	13	0
9	51	16	3	0	16	6	0	0	1	13	0
10	105	3	3	0	30	13	0	0	0	9	0
11	57	6	0	1	29	0	0	0	5	0	0
12	57	6	0	1	29	0	0	0	5	0	0

(a)

CASE CSCLB/BR/02/64-1008-01 - UNORDERED COEFFICIENT MATRIX - COEF A = 0.659722

LOTS	1	2	3	4	5	6	7	8	9	10	11	12
1	200	128	99	87	65	83	78	57	48	50	36	35
2	128	200	169	110	96	100	93	69	57	59	45	44
3	99	169	200	118	115	109	102	77	67	69	55	52
4	87	110	118	200	156	170	162	143	141	127	126	114
5	65	96	115	156	200	171	168	158	147	142	136	129
6	83	100	109	170	171	200	186	155	155	153	137	143
7	78	93	102	162	168	186	200	160	163	156	146	141
8	57	69	77	143	158	155	160	200	164	175	174	153
9	48	57	67	141	147	155	163	164	200	165	171	146
10	50	59	69	127	142	153	156	175	165	200	177	165
11	36	45	55	126	136	137	146	174	171	177	200	163
12	35	44	52	114	129	143	141	153	146	165	163	200

(b)

CASE CSCLB/BR/02/64-1008-01 - COEF A AND SEQUENCE PER ORDERING - RANDOM NUMBER = 54420698

	1	2	3	4	5	6	7	8	9	10	11	12
0.659722	1	2	3	4	5	6	7	8	9	10	11	12
2.479167	5	6	7	9	11	12	10	8	4	3	2	1
0.659722	1	2	3	4	5	6	7	8	9	10	11	12
0.659722	12	11	10	9	8	7	6	5	4	3	2	1
0.659722	1	2	3	4	5	6	7	8	9	10	11	12
0.659722	12	11	10	9	8	7	6	5	4	3	2	1

(c)

CASE CSCLB/BR/02/64-1008-01 - ORDERED COEFFICIENT MATRIX - COEF A = 0.659722

LOTS	1	2	3	4	5	6	7	8	9	10	11	12
1	200	128	99	87	65	83	78	57	48	50	36	35
2	128	200	169	110	96	100	93	69	57	59	45	44
3	99	169	200	118	115	109	102	77	67	69	55	52
4	87	110	118	200	156	170	162	143	141	127	126	114
5	65	96	115	156	200	171	168	158	147	142	136	129
6	83	100	109	170	171	200	186	155	155	153	137	143
7	78	93	102	162	168	186	200	160	163	156	146	141
8	57	69	77	143	158	155	160	200	164	175	174	153
9	48	57	67	141	147	155	163	164	200	165	171	146
10	50	59	69	127	142	153	156	175	165	200	177	165
11	36	45	55	126	136	137	146	174	171	177	200	163
12	35	44	52	114	129	143	141	153	146	165	163	200

(d)

Figure 15. Example of seriation program results: (a) a listing of the input data (in this case, figures representing actual specimen frequencies, though percentages or previously computed matrices also may be input); (b) the matrix of agreement coefficients in the same order as the input data, with the ordering criterion and value of the matrix coefficient expressed so that later comparison of the ordered matrix to the input unordered matrix will be facilitated; (c) a listing of the results of each ordering, including the matrix coefficient value and the resulting order of the collections each time; (d) the best-ordered matrix, with the matrix coefficient value. (From Kuzara et al. 1966: Fig. 1. Reproduced by permission of the American Anthropological Association from American Anthropologist Vol. 68, No. 6, 1966.)

most suitable appears to be standardized scores that state similarity in terms of an equal-unit scale. That is, a given difference in score size between two high-value scores must mean the same thing as the same size difference between two low-value scores. The Robinson index of agreement continues to remain popular with seriation analysts on both of the above counts. In addition, it is noted for reducing the effect of moderate interassemblage mixture on the resultant similarity scores and for giving strong weight to dominant characters of the assemblages being compared.

Alternative Techniques for Seriation Dating

The Ford Method

The Brainerd–Robinson technique of similarity matrix analysis for which there are now six published computer programs is not the only approach to seriation dating. One of the earliest techniques involved the experimental ordering of artifact components in such a way that the relative frequencies of various artifact types yielded a best fit to lenticular curves. The method recently has been restated and illustrated by the archaeologist Ford (1962), who was one of the main proponents of the method for the purposes of seriational dating (see Figure 14a, b, and c for an illustration of bar graphing in conformity with such curves).

The Contextual Analysis Method

Dempsey and Baumhoff (1963) have proposed a method of seriation based on a system of measurements called contextual analysis. The method depends on knowing which artifact types are present and which are absent at each site rather than on their relative frequency of occurrence.

A matrix of agreement scores analogous to those used in the Brainerd–Robinson method is first constructed. Here, however, the index of agreement between each pair of sites is simply a count of what Dempsey and Baumhoff call common *responses*. If an artifact is present at both sites being compared, or absent from both sites, a count is made. For artifacts present at one site but absent from the other, no count is included. Thus, with 26 characteristics, the maximum agreement score possible is 26, and the minimum zero.

The technique is intended to be used to isolate major differences between sites. To illustrate, let the horizontal line in Figure 16 stand for the time dimension, and let the points A to J indicate the correct position of ten burial sites. According to the basic hypothesis, the pattern of artifact types present at Site A will be most similar to that of Site B, and progressively less similar to each of the later sites. Site J will show the same sort of progression in the opposite direction. Site E, on the other hand, will show maximum agreement with Site F, and progressively less agreement with both earlier and later sites. Also, because of their position near the middle of the time scale, Sites E and F may be expected to show higher average agreement with all of the sites than do Sites A and J. The value of the average

Figure 16. *A hypothetical sequence of ten sites. (From Dempsey and Baumhoff 1963: Fig. 3. Reproduced by permission of the Society for American Archaeology from* American Antiquity, *Vol. 28.)*

agreement scores attained by the separate sites should be a direct function of their closeness to the mean point of the time scale. Furthermore, to establish relative chronological positions, the direction from the mean as well as the distance from the mean must be established.

According to the authors, contextual analysis provides a simple way of accomplishing this. First the sample is dichotomized into two equal groups. In Figure 16, Sites A to E have been assigned to Group II. Next, the average agreement of every site within each of the two groups is determined, and the difference between the two averages is recorded. Site A, for example, will show a much higher average agreement with Group I than with Group II. This disparity is expressed as a single difference score by subtracting the mean of Site A with Group II from its mean with Group I. For Site J the situation is reversed, and the same process of subtraction will result in a large difference score, which is opposite in sign to that obtained by Site A. Sites E and F, on the other hand, will show approximately the same means with both groups: their difference scores will be close to zero. The proper chronological order of those two sites becomes clear in their *difference* scores, for Site E will have a slightly higher mean with Group I and a slightly lower one with Group II. Similarly, the correct chronological ordering of all ten sites will be expressed in the *difference* scores. Site A will obtain the highest difference score, and the younger sites progressively lower ones, with Site J, the youngest site, obtaining the lowest difference score.

Lipe (1964) has suggested that because of its dependence on presence-and-absence counts, the Dempsey–Baumhoff ordering technique may not be as useful as the Brainerd–Robinson technique in two kinds of situations:

(1) when artifact mixture has occurred;
(2) when the types used in the seriation are defined on the basis of continuously varying attributes and overlap one another to some extent because of normal variation in the attributes.

The Three-Pole Graph Method

Another technique of seriation dating has been developed by Meighan (1959) and is called the *three-pole graph method*. This technique uses only three types of artifacts from the components to be seriated. In beginning a seriation of this type, the first step is selection of the trait to be seriated. This trait must have the following characteristics:

(1) abundance;
(2) measurable diversity (more than one type);
(3) long time span in terms of the sample to be seriated (the feature should occur throughout the time span studied).

If pottery is present this is likely to be the best feature or trait for seriation.

Assuming that pottery is used for the seriation, the next step is to reduce the number of pottery types to three for purposes of the analysis. The reduction to three types may be done in several ways.

1. Selecting the three most abundant types will usually work. In this case all other types are omitted from the seriation, although they sometimes may be used as a check on the results as described below.
2. In cases where a large part of the pottery sample consists of a common type (such as plain ware), occurring in about the same proportion throughout the time span of the sample, the common type may be skipped and the seriation done with the next three most common types.
3. Closely related types may be lumped together to reduce the

categories to three. This is useful in cases where the sample is small and the types numerous, but lumping of types can lead to erroneous results and should be avoided. In practice, according to Meighan, it takes such a short time to do the seriation that it is often feasible to plot all the possible ways in which the collection can be reduced to three types. This provides an internal check for consistent results and rapidly eliminates those combinations which cannot yield a seriation (for example, types that do not overlap in time).

After selecting the three categories, the percentages of each are calculated. For purposes of the seriation it is assumed that these categories are the only three types present (that is, total 100%), and the relationships between these three types are used to determine the sequence. With the percentages in hand, the figures may be plotted on triangular coordinate paper, yielding a three-pole graph. Examine Lot 23 on Figure 17. The point on the graph where the three lines intersect represents the proportions: A, 23%; B, 5%; C, 72%. Lot 23 was plotted as follows: on the line a–A the line at 23 was located.

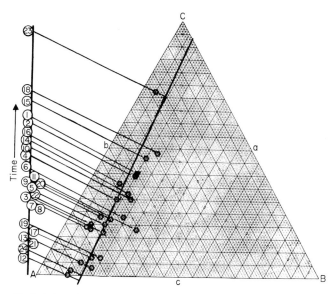

Figure 17. *Seriation of 24 structures at Paragonah, Utah: (a) Snake Valley gray; (b) Snake Valley B/gray; (c) Snake Valley corrugated. (From Meighan 1959: Fig. 1. Reproduced by permission of the Society for American Archaeology from* American Antiquity, Vol. 25.)

Along this line (23) was found the junction with the line numbered five as counted along the line b–B. This is automatically at the point 72 units along the line c–C; hence, this point represents the relationship between the three percentages.

When all the lots are entered on the graph, the resulting points usually will be seen to cluster along an axis. A line is drawn through the scattered points using a least-squares best fit (Ascher 1959). This line provides the seriation, and the points should be arranged along the line in their proper time sequence.

Cowgill, in a review of the comparative studies on seriation dating of Hole and Shaw (Cowgill 1968: 519), comes to the conclusion that when all one wants to do is just get the right chronological sequence, there is no method that works any better than the very easy three-pole graph technique.

Archaeologists are thus in possession of several different techniques of seriation dating that have been proven effective in relatively dating a number of sites within a somewhat delimited region. Each has advantages and drawbacks peculiar to it, and students interested in utilizing one or another of these techniques should consult the appropriate references listed at the end of the chapter.

Problems Connected with Seriation Dating

Artifact-Type Distribution Patterns

The occurrence of artifact types in a collection of sites usually follows a predictable pattern: They originate, achieve popularity, and then decline in popularity—eventually to disappear. Thus, the frequency of occurrence of any artifact type in any area will have a curvilinear relationship to chronological time. Dempsey and Baumhoff (1963) have theorized that in any actual sample of sites, four different patterns of artifact-type distributions may be expected to occur. Figure 18 presents these four patterns in generalized form. Pattern I applies to those types, already in use at the time of the earliest site, that have fallen into disuse by the time of the latest. Pattern II will occur for artifact types whose span of use covers the entire chronological period of the sites. Pattern III will be shown by artifact types that wlll appear after the time of the first site and disappear before the last. Finally, Pattern IV includes those which first appear sometime after the earliest sites and are still in use at the time of the latest.

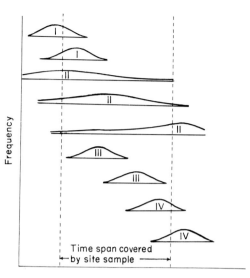

Figure 18. *Varieties of artifact-type distribution patterns. (From Dempsey and Baumhoff 1963: Fig. 1. Reproduced by permission of the Society for American Archaeology from* American Antiquity, *Vol. 28.)*

Dempsey and Baumhoff (1963) point out that according to the basic hypothesis of Brainerd and Robinson, sites that lie close together on the time dimension are expected to show similar relative distributions of artifact types, whereas sites far apart in time will show dissimilar distributions. They argue that whereas artifact types whose distributions are described by Patterns I, II, and IV in Figure 18 tend to support this hypothesis, Pattern III distributions present complications. In Pattern III the time of maximum frequency always falls within the range of time covered by the sites. Furthermore, the minimum frequency, zero, may occur in sites widely separated in time. Dempsey and Baumhoff thus conclude that artifact types showing Pattern III distributions will always introduce error. If types of this pattern occur with high frequency, they caution, there is a strong possibility that the earliest and latest sites will be considered contemporaneous! Thus, any factors which tend to increase the relative frequency of Pattern III distributions will complicate the problem of establishing chronology by purely statistical means. Such factors as a long time span between earliest and latest sites will do this, as will rapid rate of change of artifact types.

The Spatial Aspects of Seriation

Seriation dating involves the assumption that artifact types used in seriation originated at a single locus and subsequently spread outward from that point. Thus, an artifact type used in seriation, in order to have utility, must occur at two or more sites. A second assumption that must be made in seriation dating is that sites further removed from the locus of origin of any type will show the occurrence of that type, at a given frequency, later in time. This means that a type might continue to be present at some distant site even after it had disappeared from its point of inception.

These two assumptions have been analyzed and made more explicit through the work of Deetz and Dethlefsen (1965). They have developed a model in which rate of change and dimensions of spatial and temporal units are held constant. The model shown in Figure 19 illustrates the spread of a single type outward in two directions from a center, indicated as locus M on the horizontal axis. Loci N–P and N'–P' are progressively more distant from locus M, and distances between all adjacent loci on the space axis are equal. The vertical axis of the model represents time, with each number unit, 1 through 10, representing a time segment of equal duration. The frequency of the type is indicated by percentage bars at each locus, with a uniform rate of change of 25% for each time unit. Thus, although an identical pattern of increase and decrease of the type occurs, its appearance at a given frequency occurs at a later point in time at each locus further removed from M. This phenomenon, referred to as the *Doppler effect* by Deetz and Dethlefsen, must always be taken into consideration when conducting seriation analysis.

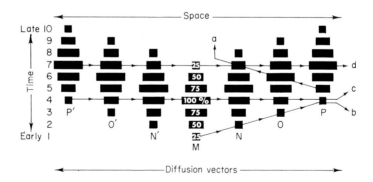

Figure 19. *Model illustrating the spread of a single type from a point (M) outward in two directions. (From Deetz and Dethlefsen 1965: Fig. 1.)*

Sample Size

The primary data in most kinds of seriation dating is the set of percentages of artifact types within each component. These values are normally the building blocks for the coefficients of similarity that are to be analyzed and seriated. If the number of objects in a component is small, there is the possibility that the relative percentages of types computed with such a sample will be unrepresentative of the relative proportions of types characteristic of that site, or more accurately, of that point in time. Sampling error caused by the smallness of the sample is often the most serious form of error, but also one of the easiest to detect and to control. Many of the early seriation exercises were conducted without due attention placed upon sample size. In selecting site collections for seriation, a rough working guideline is to include only assemblages which consist of at least 100 objects.

Conclusion

As Dunnell has pointed out, "a seriation is not a chronology; chronologies are inferred from seriations" (Dunnell 1970: 317). It is important for an analyst to ascertain whether the ordering resulting from seriation analysis has been affected by sample size, lack of comparability of seriated units, the Doppler effect, or by anomalous artifact-type distributions.

READINGS

Ascher, M.
  1959 A mathematical rationale for graphical seriation. *American Antiquity* **25**, No. 2: 212–214.
Ascher, M., and R. Ascher
  1963 Chronological ordering by computer. *American Anthropologist* **65**, No. 5: 1045–1052.
Brainerd, G. W.
  1951 The place of chronological ordering in archaeological analysis. *American Antiquity* **16**, No. 4: 301–313.
Cowgill, G. L.
  1968 A review of "Computer Analysis of Chronological Seriation" by Frank Hole and Mary Shaw. *American Antiquity* **53**, No. 4: 517–519.
Craytor, W. B., and L. Johnson, Jr.
  1968 Refinements in computerized item seriation, *Museum of Natural History, Bulletin* No. 10. University of Oregon.
Deetz, J., and E. Dethlefsen
  1965 The Doppler effect and archaeology: A consideration of the spatial aspects of seriation. *Southwestern Journal of Anthropology* **21**, No. 3: 196–206.

Dempsey, P., and M. Baumhoff
 1963 The statistical use of artifact distributions to establish chronological sequence. *American Antiquity* **28**, No. 4: 496–509.

Dunnell, R. C.
 1970 Seriation method and its evaluation. *American Antiquity* **35**: 305–319.

Ford, J. A.
 1962 A quantitative method for deriving cultural chronology. *Technical Manual, 1.* Washington, D.C.: Pan American Union, General Secretariat, Organization of American States.

Gelfand, A. E.
 1971 Seriation methods for archaeological materials. *American Antiquity* **36**: 263–274.

Hole, F. and M. Shaw
 1967 Computer analysis of chronological seriation. *Rice University Studies, Monographs in Archaeology* **53**, No. 3.

Johnson, L., Jr.
 1968 Item seriation as an aid for elementary scale and cluster analysis. *Museum of Natural History, Bulletin* No. 15, University of Oregon.

Jelinek, A. J.
 1962 Use of the cumulative graph in temporal ordering. *American Antiquity* **28**: 241–243.

Kendall, D. G.
 1963 A statistical approach to Flinders Petrie's sequence dating. *Bulletin of the International Statistical Institute* **40**: 657–680.

Kuzura, R. S., G. R. Mead, and K. A. Dixon
 1966 Seriation of anthropological data: A computer program for matrix ordering. *American Anthropologist* **68**, No. 6: 1442–1455.

Lipe, W. D.
 1964 Comment on Dempsey and Baumhoff's "The Statistical Use of Artifact Distributions to Establish Chronological Sequence." *American Antiquity* **30**, No. 1: 103–104.

Meighan, C. W.
 1959 A new method for the seriation of archaeological collections. *American Antiquity* **25**, No. 2: 203–211.

Renfrew, C., and G. Sterud
 1969 Close-proximity analysis: A rapid method for the ordering of archaeological materials. *American Antiquity* **34**: 265–277.

Robinson, W. S.
 1951 A method for chronologically ordering archaeological deposits. *American Antiquity* **16**, No. 4: 293–301.

Rouse, I. B.
 1967 Seriation in archaeology. In *American historical anthropology*, edited by C. L. Riley and W. W. Taylor. Carbondale: Southern Illinois University Press.

Rowe, J. H.
 1961 Stratigraphy and seriation. *American Antiquity* **25**: 324–330.

Troike, R. C.
 1957 Time and types in archaeological analysis: The Brainerd-Robinson technique. *Bulletin of the Texas Archaeological Society* **28**: 269–284.

CHAPTER SIX

Cross-Dating

Introduction

Cross-dating becomes a strategy of relative dating once a culture phase sequence has been established for a local area. Cross-dating is the assignment of a site component to a local culture phase sequence. Cross-dating therefore is closely dependent upon sequence dating. Since archaeological manifestations of culture occur within a geological framework, many of the geochronological techniques of cross-dating can be applied. In addition, time-sensitive variation in the makeup of artifact assemblages offers an opportunity for cross-dating by means of culture trait comparisons.

Cross-dating, as mentioned earlier, involves a special idea of *contemporaneity*. Seldom is it reasonable to assume that a site component coexisted with another site component with which it may cross-date. Rather, the resemblances established during culture trait comparison only authorize the archaeologist to assume that the component occurred sometime during the same *period* as the site component with which it has been cross-dated.

Cross-dating does not always involve the correlation of cultural units. In some cases cross-dating is attempted in order to establish contemporaneity between a culture phase and a particular climatic setting, a particular fauna, or local topographic features. Thus, cross-dating is valuable in connection with ecological analysis. What makes this possible is the fact that cross-dating can be performed with data from geomorphology, paleontology, and palynology. These scientific disciplines provide knowledge about the ecology of the past—and ecological analysis, both for the purpose of explaining culture change and for the purpose of more fully understanding cultural behavior, has become an important subject in American archaeology.

In this chapter, we will review the geochronological methods of cross-dating as well as those involving culture trait comparisons. It is in the latter category that the use of historical records is discussed.

Geomorphology

Although it may safely be said that all archaeological sites are to be found in a geological context, only in the case of some sites is that context geologically significant. The great bulk of late Prehistoric and Historic sites are located at the surface or under a very shallow mantle of recent soils and vegetation. For such sites the geomorphologist can be of little service. For a site to be geologically significant, it must be *stratified*. Geologists mean something quite different by this term than do archaeologists. For the geologist, a stratified site is one for which the cultural assemblage can be associated with different geomorphic events. Examples of such events might include the raising or lowering of the sea level, down-cutting by streams, alluviation, wind erosion, the retreat or advance of glaciers, solifluction, and volcanic eruptions. In practice, the archaeological deposit has to be either within the sediments resulting from one or another of the above-mentioned events (or similar ones), or beneath such sediments.

When the archaeological sites of a given area are geologically stratified, cross-dating is possible. Yet, without benefit of paleontological or palynological time markers the geologist is often limited in the geographical range of his correlations. The allowable range, however, can be large enough to accommodate the cross-dating needs of an archaeologist confronted with the task of analyzing a localized interaction sphere.

Sedimentation Cross-Dating of Upper Pleistocene Sites

A good example of this is provided by Klein (1969) in his study of the Kostenki–Borshevo sector of the Don River basin in the Soviet Union. Here, Soviet archaeologists have been successful in uncovering cultural remains dating to the Upper Paleolithic period. Archaeological research in the area dates back to the late 19th century, and is still continuing at the present. The Kostenki–Borshevo region is an area of approximately 35 square kilometers (35 km²). More than two dozen sites have been discovered within the area. Many are multicomponent sites, and a major task confronting interested archaeologists is to cross-date the components of the various sites within the area.

The sites under study all occur on the western side of the Don River Valley. In the Kostenki–Borshevo sector, the slopes of the western side are quite steep. The oldest deposits, forming the substratum of the western slopes, are Upper Devonian clays. In almost all areas of this sector the Upper Devonian clays are overlaid by deposits of Lower Cretaceous age. These, in turn, are overlaid by a series of Upper Cretaceous sediments consisting first of sand, then soft limestone, and ultimately compact limestone. Above the Upper Cretaceous sediments can be found deposits formed during the Pleistocene, consisting of either till (sediments laid down by a glacier) or colluvial loam (sediments accumulated on or at base of a hillside as a result of water runoff erosion and other processes of soil flow).

The till deposits are located in the upper segment of the western slope and represent a remnant of an originally far more widespread deposit left behind by a glacier which covered this region during the Riss Glacial period. Overlying the till in various locations is a soil, now partially eroded, formed during the Eem Interglacial period. This soil, in turn, is covered by gray-brown loams that were formed during the Wurm glacial period. The gray-brown loams cover much of the slope. The upper zone of the loams has weathered during recent times, producing a chernozem soil (very black and rich in humus and carbonates). A thin layer of volcanic ash, resulting from a Late Pleistocene volcanic eruption in the Caucasus Mountains, can sometimes be found imbedded within the loams. In addition, interspersed within the loams are beds of buried humus that had eroded from older soils and been redeposited as colluvium.

Three river terraces, all concealed beneath nonalluvial deposits, have been recognized on the western slope of the Don River in the Kostenki–Bershevo sector (Figure 20). Each terrace is designated by the height its colluvial overburden reaches above the *low-water* level of the river. The first river terrace averages 8–10 meters (8–10 m), the second 15–20 m, and the third 35–40 m. The terraces are narrow, with a maximum width of 60–70 m, 30–40 m, and 40–50 m, respectively for the first, second, and third terraces. Furthermore, the western slope has been exposed to severe water runoff erosion that has formed a pronounced network of ravines and gullies. Many of the larger ravines have as many as three terraces. Since the ravine terraces articulate with the river terraces of the Don proper, and since the ravine terraces are structurally similar to those of the Valley, the two sets of terraces are treated as equivalent.

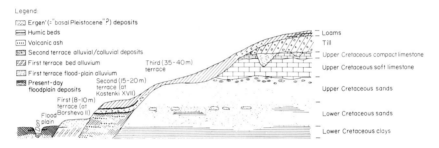

Figure 20. *Geomorphology of the western slope of the Don Valley in the Kostenki–Borshevo region. The key to the symbols is given in the legend. (From Klein, R. G. "Man and Culture in the Late Pleistocene," Fig. 7. San Francisco: Chandler Publ., 1969. Reproduced by permission.)*

Archaeological sites are rare on the third (highest) terrace. Two sites that have been found there are Kostenki XIII, located in the colluvial loam covering the terrace, and Kostenki XVIII, intruding into the Late Cretaceous sands that form its base. The second terrace is the locus of the majority of the sites in the region (Figure 21). They are found in the colluvial deposits that rest upon the terrace. Although poorly preserved in the Don River Valley proper, these colluvial deposits are well preserved in the ravines. Intensive agricultural activity has facilitated the discovery of many of these sites.

Throughout the area, the second terrace exhibits a characteristic soil morphology. Late Cretaceous sands serve as the base of the terrace profile. First to overlie these are the bedded and sandy loams interspersed with lenses of rolled limestone pebbles. Two layers of humic

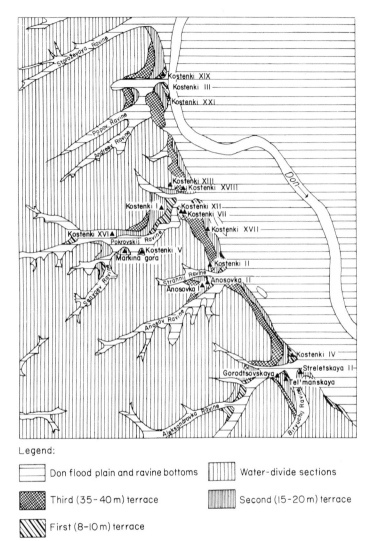

Legend:

| | Don flood plain and ravine bottoms | | Water-divide sections |

| | Third (35-40 m) terrace | | Second (15-20 m) terrace |

| | First (8-10 m) terrace |

Figure 21. *Geomorphological map of the Kostenki area. The key to the symbols is given in the legend. (From Klein, R. G. "Man and Culture in the Late Pleistocene," Map 3. San Francisco: Chandler Publ., 1969. Reproduced by permission.)*

loam separated by a bed of nonhumic loam are found above. In some areas the nonhumic loam separating the humic layers contains lenses (soil deposits that in cross-section appear biconvex in outline) of the previously mentioned volcanic ash. Finally, above the upper humic layer are nonbedded gray-brown loams.

Although there are differences in detail from place to place, the above description is sufficiently characteristic that the stratigraphic sequence can serve as an instrument for associating components of various sites. Figure 22 illustrates the kinds of results that were obtained in the geomorphological cross-dating of sites within the colluvial deposits of the second terrace.

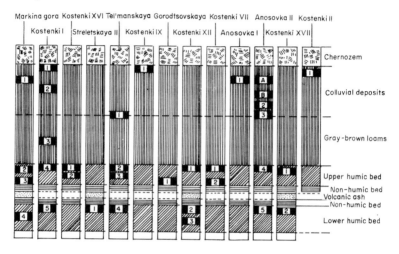

Figure 22. *Comparative stratigraphy of the Kostenki–Borshevo sites: second supra-flood-plain terrace (15–20m). (From Klein, R. G. "Man and Culture in the Late Pleistocene," Fig. 8. San Francisco: Chandler Publ., 1969. Reproduced by permission.)*

Beach Strand Cross-Dating

People who regularly exploit the food resources of a seacoast can be expected to locate their settlements at water's edge. The resulting settlement pattern is a string of dwellings or camp spots that hug the beach crest, just above the high tide mark. If, as has often happened, a new beach develops forward through processes of erosion and redeposition, subsequent groups will string out their dwellings along the newly formed beach crest, abandoning the former. The interval of time between when the beach is formed and when it is stranded marks a period to which many of the archaeological remains located in or on that beach can be assigned. Opportunities for cross-dating become more important the more extensive the stranded beach system.

Cross-dating is based on the opportunity for *intrastrand* correlations of archaeological remains. *Interstrand* comparisons of sites can add another dating dimension to the study of ancient beaches. A series of parallel beach strands, for example, constitutes an ordered sequence of occupation that lends itself to sequence dating. Archaeological sites located on the fifth strand back from the present beach are probably younger than sites located on the twenty-fifth strand back. Some persons refer to this as *horizontal stratigraphy*.

Alaska is one area where the study of beach strands has been of considerable interest to the archaeologist. From the modern-day Eskimo back to at least 3000 B.C., arctic hunter gatherers have camped at the edge of the sea. Among the many sections of the Alaskan coast that exhibit multiple stranded beaches, one especially good area has come in for an extensive archaeological investigation—Cape Krusenstern, at the northeastern margin of Kotzebue Sound (Giddings 1966). Some of the beach strands at Cape Krusenstern extend more than 12 kilometers (12 km); linking in time settlements that are out of sight of one another. Over the past 5,000 years, 114 successive beaches have been formed at Cape Krusenstern (Figure 23). Their

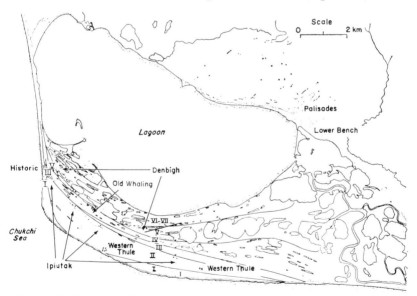

Figure 23. *Sketch map of Cape Krusenstern beaches. The most recent beaches are in the foreground; the oldest beaches are back toward the lagoon. Segments 1–VII correspond to Beaches 1–104. The Lower Beach and Palisades sites are at the upper right. (From Giddings, J. L. Cross dating the archaeology of Northwestern Alaska.* Science, *153: 127–135, Fig. 4. Copyright 1966 by the American Association for the Advancement of Science.)*

crests were of coarse sand and gravel covered with a thin mantle of sod that failed to conceal the archaeological traces of prehistoric settlement.

House pits of Eskimos who lived there during the past century were found on the first set of beaches (Figure 24). Multiroom semisubterranean houses of the Western Thule culture were found on the ninth and successive strands. Further back, the archaeological remains of the Birnick culture lay partially exposed. In the vicinity of the thirty-fifth strand, the large, square pit houses and clusters of shallow summer lodges representing Ipiutak culture were found. The *Choris-Norton-Near Ipiutak* cultural tradition extends over approximately 15

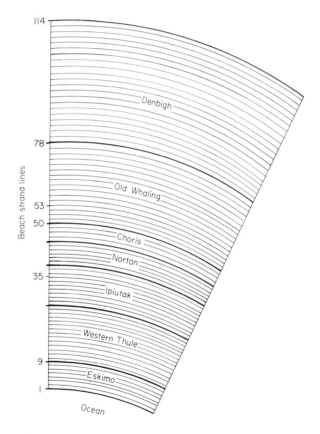

Figure 24. *Cape Krusenstern, Alaska: Beach strand line chronology. (From Giddings, J. L. Cross dating the archaeology of Northwestern Alaska.* Science, 153: 127–135, Fig. 11. Copyright 1966 by the American Association for the Advancement of Science.)

consecutive strand lines. Here, hearths, tent sites, and quantities of artifacts were discovered. Bones of the right whale were frequently encountered upon the crest of Beach 53, and in association with an *Old Whaling* culture settlement having both winter and summer dwellings. Finally Beach 78 back to Beach 104 represented a sector that contained many hearths and tent encampments assignable to the Denbigh flint complex.

Unconformities can interrupt a beach strand system where the sea has eaten back into part of the beach series. Another complication can arise, when, through a shift in the direction of the prevailing winds, the trend of beach formation is altered. Through careful study of aerial photographs, it is often possible to trace individual beach strands despite unconformities and shifts in the axis of beach formation.

Paleontology

Paleontology, the study of ancient life, adds an important dimension to geomorphology in the context of dating. Alone, geomorphological evidence can be used to cross-date sites providing that they are located in reasonable proximity to one another. This is because the geological events that serve as time markers may only have had local occurrence. A good example might be volcanic activity such as the deposition of lava or ash. Archaeological sites in the vicinity of such events may have a stratigraphic relationship to these deposits. Other sites of the same age outside of the zone of volcanic activity would not exhibit these important stratigraphic clues. However, if time-marker fossils were associated with both the volcanic and nonvolcanic deposits it would be possible to establish the geological contemporaneity of all the sites in question.

Paleontology has recognized subdisciplines, such as invertebrate paleontology, vertebrate paleontology, micropaleontology, and paleobotany. They reflect useful fossil categories from the standpoint of analysis. Paleontologists, regardless of their specialization, work with the fossil remains of organisms. Most commonly these remains consist of the hard parts of animals, such as shell, bone, and teeth, or of pollen—in the case of paleobotany. In addition, however, some sedimentary deposits allow for the preservation of remarkably detailed impressions of the whole animal or of the entire leaf structure of a plant. Finally, in very rare instances, the entire animal or plant is preserved under conditions of glacial freeze, peat bedding, oil pools, or extreme aridity.

Cross-dating by fossils is possible because of the nature and consequences of biological evolution. Evolution is an ongoing process involving all forms of plant and animal life. Evolutionary changes in most species can become cumulatively so significant that it is advantageous to discriminate between early and late populations by means of a classification or *taxonomic* scheme. The consequence of this is, of course, the proliferation of *varieties* of life forms, each of which has at some point in time come into taxonomic being and at some other point in time passed into taxonomic or True extinction. If it can be established that the fauna or flora at widely separated archaeological sites consists of a uniform mix of biological types, then it is possible to infer a kind of contemporaneity between these sites.

The most useful fossils for cross-dating are ones that are (1) easily identifiable, (2) abundant, (3) of wide geographical range, and (4) of short temporal duration. Such fossils are termed *index* or *guide* fossils. Other indicators, however, also can be used. Fossil combinations involving fossils of long temporal duration, for example, can be useful when they consist of individual fossil types with overlapping but not concurrent temporal ranges. In such cases, the overlapping segment may be sufficiently brief in duration that it can serve cross-dating purposes. Finally, some fossil types, although of long duration, may fluctuate significantly in their abundance. A specific period may have occurred during which such a fossil is characteristically abundant or rare.

An understanding of the environmental conditions under which fossil animals lived is also very important in the context of cross-dating. Differences between the faunal assemblages of two areas might suggest different time periods whereas in reality the two areas are contemporaneous but differ in environment.

Micromammalian Cross-Dating in Europe

During the Pleistocene epoch, Europe was marked by repeated fluctuations in temperature. A sequence of geomorphic events was initiated at the onset of each cold or warm episode. Some of these events previously have been referred to in the discussion of sedimentation cross-dating. The principal factor was, of course, glaciation. The onset of cold would cause the growth of ice fields and usher in associated geomorphic consequences. With a warming episode, ice fields would melt, causing heavy water runoff with widespread erosional effects. Geochronologists thus divide the Pleistocene into a series of glacial and interglacial periods representing the most significant fluctuations, and subdivide glacial periods into *stadial* and *interstadial* episodes to mark minor climatic fluctuations.

In Pleistocene archaeology, then, the first task of the geochronologist is to determine by inspection of the geomorphological evidence at a site whether the geomorphic events to be inferred represent a *warm* period or a *cold* period. The question then to be asked is "which warm or cold period? " since there are many of both during the two million years of the Pleistocene epoch. It is with this question that paleontology makes its initial contribution. Through many years of study, paleontologists have identified the distinctive fauna of each of the major Pleistocene periods. Fossil mammals, because of their abundance in the fossil record and because of the rapid rate at which some have speciated, supply the principal index fossils. Traditionally, the elephant, rhinoceros, bear, hyena, pig, bovid, deer, and antelope have provided the index fossils. Thus, for example, one can subdivide the Pleistocene into three periods simply using the elephant: the Upper Pleistocene is the period of *Elephas primigenius*; the Middle Pleistocene is the period of *Elephas antiquus*; and the Lower Pleistocene is the period of *Elephas meridionalis*. Although there is an overlap in the time ranges of these species, the time of first appearance of each serves to mark the beginning of a period.

From the standpoint of archaeological research, considerable difficulty is often met with in attempting to rely on the identification of large mammals, such as those mentioned above. For one thing, the remains of large mammals are often badly broken up, burned, or incomplete as a result of butchering and cooking activities. Second, the inhabitants may have specialized in the game they hunted, so that an insufficient variety of species is at hand with which to classify the *fauna*. Finally, fine divisions in the geochronological time scale are often indicated not only by differences in the taxonomic composition of a faunal assemblage, but also by the relative frequencies of constituent species. Seldom do archaeological sites yield large mammals in sufficient numbers that percentage counts are at all meaningful. For these reasons, paleontologists are concentrating more and more on micromammals—small mammals such as rodents and shrews. They are often found in large numbers, their presence is independent of hunting strategy or luck, and they yield a number of good index fossils.

A recent example is provided by archaeological research at the Vértesszöllös site, near Budapest, in Hungary (Kretzoi and Vértes 1965). The site is located on the alluvial plain of the Atalér River. The plain joins Terrace IV of the Danube River system [the site is 15 kilometers (15 km) south of the Danube River]. Stratigraphically, the site was formed on a calcareous-mud surface overlying travertine sediments. The cultural layer, some 5 centimeters (5 cm) thick and 14 m long, is situated in a travertine–calcareous mud matrix but extends up into an overlying loess deposit. Based on geomorphology, Vértesszöllös appears to have been occupied at the end of a warm period just before it shifted to a subsequent cold period.

Fossil remains of large mammals were absent from most of the seven stratigraphic layers, and when present, were in a poor state of preservation. They were thus of little value in trying to pin down *which* warm period–cold period transition was represented at the site. Fortunately, the lower five strata, including the culture-bearing horizon, contained the remains of micromammals. A Hungarian faunal sequence involving micromammal index fossils (among others) had previously been established and tentatively correlated with the Pleis-

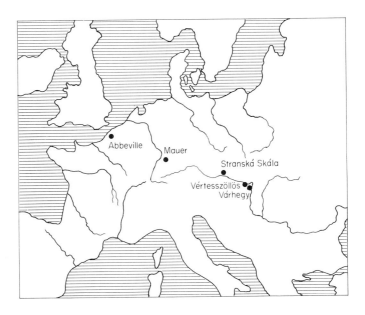

Figure 25. *Important Lower Paleolithic sites in Europe.*

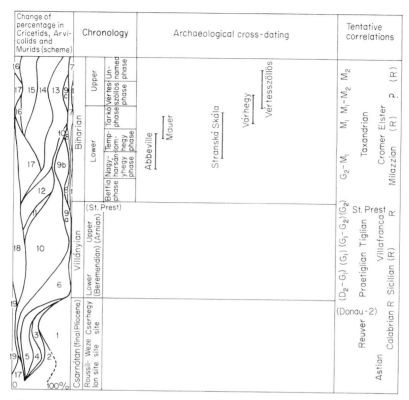

Figure 26. *Correlation table of five archaeological sites of lower Pleistocene Age. The numbers of the graph to the left indicate: (1) Murids; (2) Trilophymus; (3) Baranomys; (4) Cseria; (5) Propliomys; (6) Dolomys; (7) Myodes (Clethrionomys); (8) Pliomys; (9a) Lagurodon; (9b) Prolagurus; (9c) Lagurus; (10) Mimomys; (11) Kislángia; (12) Allophaiomys; (13) Pitymus; (14) Microtus; (15) Arvicola; (16) Lemmus (and Dicrostonyx; (17) Cricetus; (18) Allocricetus; (19) Cricetinus. (From Kretzoi, M. and L. Vértes, Upper Biharian (Inter-mindel) pebble-industry site in Western Hungary.* Current Anthropology **6**, *No. 1: Fig 5. Reproduced by permission.)*

tocene stratigraphic sequence (see Figure 26). Using this for reference, the micromammals of Vértesszöllös revealed that the site had been occupied at the end of the Mindel I–Mindel II interstadial period.

Reexamination of the micromammalian assemblages at other important European archaeological sites (Figure 25) allowed the researcher to go further and to attempt a cross-dating that spanned a good portion of Europe (Kretzoi and Vértes 1965). The results are given in Figure 26 and represent one of the most rigorous cross-dating attempts so far for European Lower Pleistocene data.

Cross-Dating by Fossil Pollen Analysis

Fossil pollen analysis or *palynology* serves principally as a technique for paleoecology and only nominally as a technique for archaeological cross-dating. Still, reference to a pollen sequence or *chronology* sometimes can reveal the relative temporal placement of an archaeological site.

Pollen analysis involves documenting changes in vegetation through time by means of pollen counts. Wind-pollinated trees, shrubs, and grasses release large quantities of pollen grains no more than 0.01–0.1 millimeters (0.01–0.1 mm) in diameter and less than 10^{-9} grams (10^{-9} gm) in weight. The pollen grains are easily held in air suspension and propelled by winds over distances up to 100–250 km. Over the year, but principally in the flowering season, pollens representing the composite vegetation of a region accumulate on the ground (pollen *rain*) up to several thousand grains per square centimeter. The *exine,* or outer shell, of the pollen grain protects it from rapid deterioration. For this reason, a good number of pollen grains may be preserved indefinitely. Preservation is enhanced by low oxidizing and acidic soil environments. Stratified sediments of annual pollen rain build up over a time and serve as recoverable fossils of past plant life.

For regions with a history of significant climatic change, a pollen sequence will exhibit qualitative and quantitive differences in the floral composition of succeeding periods. A pollen *chronology* defines each period in terms of the percentage composition of key floral genera. And an archaeological site can be "dated" by matching up its pollen spectrum with a segment of the regional pollen diagram.

In most cases, a soil sample of approximately 20 cubic centimeters centimeters (20 cm³) will yield enough pollen to make a satisfactory count. The sample usually is collected in a test tube or jar that can be tightly sealed. The archaeologist drives a section of soil into the container, taking care to avoid contamination by surrounding strata.

Selection of the sediment to be sampled is critical in two ways. First, it is important that the archaeologist fully understand the relationship between the sediment to be sampled and the cultural component he wishes dated. Sedimentary disconformities, erosional surfaces, traces of fire, and other human and natural disturbances have to be watched for. Second, not all sediments of even a small site equally preserve fossil pollen. Careful inspection of the chemistry and morphology of the soil can aid in selecting the most promising sediments.

Laboratory preparation and microscope analysis of the pollen sample must be conducted by trained specialists. There are many variations in the pollen extraction technique. Some merely reflect preferences of individual palynologists, others are intended to accommodate the fragility of certain pollens or the intractability of certain soil matrices. A technique used on samples removed from midden pit features in the upper levels of Sheep Rock Shelter (see Chapter Four) by the palynologist Kovar is given below (Kovar 1967).[1]

1. A certain amount of the material from each jar was passed through a 1-millimeter (1-mm) sieve. The coarse fraction retained in the sieve was washed repeatedly with a stream of distilled water to remove any minute particles which might have adhered to the coarser fragments. The remains were then examined to determine whether they contained any significant materials, such as fruits, seeds, charcoal fragments, etc.

2. The fine fraction, which had passed through the sieve, was collected in a 50-milliliter (50-ml) plastic centrifuge tube, and after adding distilled water and stirring, was centrifuged at about 3000 revolutions per minute (3000 rpm) for approximately 20 min.

3. After pouring off the supernatant water, a 10% potassium hydroxide (KOH) solution was mixed with the sample.

4. The centrifuge tube was placed into a water bath, and its contents were brought to the boiling point.

5. The sample was allowed to cool, centrifuged, and repeatedly rinsed with distilled water until all KOH had been washed out.

6. After the last washing, the contents of the tube were thoroughly mixed with a saturated solution of zinc chloride ($ZnCl_2$).

7. The mixture was let stand for about 10 min in order to allow the heavier, nonpolliniferous materials to settle.

8. The remaining supernatant liquid was poured into a folded piece of Tygon tubing which was placed, with both ends up, into a 50-milliliter (50-ml) plastic tube so that both ends protruded about ½ inch above the rim of the tube.

[1]Kovar, A. J. (May, 1967) Report on the Pollen Analysis of the Samples from the Sheep Rock Shelter in *Archeological Investigations of Sheep Rock Shelter* Vol. I, pp. 96–97.

9. The mixture was then centrifuged at about 1000 revolutions per minute (1000 rpm) for approximately 10 min. During this procedure the heavier inorganic material settled at the bottom (near the bend) of the Tygon tubing while the lighter organic particle, including pollen, remained suspended near the upper end.
10. The top layer, containing the organic material, was collected in another 50-ml plastic centrifuge tube.
11. To make sure that all organic material was extracted from the sample, the somewhat compacted material which had settled at the bottom of the Tygon tubing was stirred and re-centrifuged and again the top layer was collected.
12. The collected top liquid was diluted in distilled water and a few drops of hydrochloric acid (HCl) were added in order to eliminate a white precipitate that might have formed at this point.
13. The diluted material was centifuged and rinsed at least twice in order to make sure that all $ZnCl_2$ had been eliminated.
14. To the very fine material which remained at the bottom of the centrifuge tube, a small amount of Methyl Cellosolve was added, and the whole was centrifuged again to eliminate the remaining water.
15. After this, more Methyl Cellosolve was added to the material, which was then stored in a properly labeled small vial.

After all samples had been thus processed, the permanent slides for each sample were prepared in the following manner:

1. A small drop of semiliquid diaphane was placed on a cover glass and evenly spread over it.
2. A small amount of the material preserved in the vial was placed on the diaphane, and a drop of Bismark Brown stain was added.
3. The diaphane, the sample, and the stain were mixed thoroughly by means of a dissecting needle.
4. The cover glass then was inverted, placed on a microscope slide, and gently pressed against it until the mixture was completely distributed under the cover glass.
5. The properly labeled slide was allowed to dry for 4–5 days and was then ready for pollen identification and pollen count.

The identification and counting of pollen is carried out under magnifications ranging from 200 to 1000× with the aid of a binocular microscope. A sample of either 100 or 200 pollen grains is identified, and the percentage composition of differing floral genera is computed. The result, called the *spectrum* is combined with other spectra to form a stratigraphic pollen *diagram* (Figure 27).

A *regional* pollen *chronology* is derived from the correlation of a number of pollen diagrams collected at archaeological sites from throughout the region. The correlation usually is based on evidence provided by an independent chronological scale, such as radiocarbon dating, geomorphology and paleontology, or culture trait comparisons.

A good example is provided by Paul S. Martin's (1963) Southern Arizona post-pluvial pollen chronology. Using numerous radiocarbon dates, as well as paleontological and geomorphological controls, he was able to correlate the spectra of nine separate pollen diagrams and construct a chronology that spans the whole archaeologically significant time range for southern Arizona (Figure 28). With such a chronology, pollen cross-dating becomes a real possibility for that region.

Cross-Dating by Correlation of Culture Traits

Although the geochronological methods reviewed above are important, by far the most common approach to site component cross-dating is that of culture trait comparison and correlation. There is a universal tendency of people who have frequent interpersonal contact to share many cultural traits. The village or band would, of course, be a basic unit of shared culture due to the daily interaction that takes place among young and old alike in a single settlement. Villages or bands linked together in trade, in protective alliances, in marriage, or in simple proximity, would represent, perhaps, a second order of shared cultural traits. Some have referred to these as *interaction spheres*. Although a considerable degree of cultural resemblance can be expected, it is generally less than what obtains within a single community.

Whole regions may share a number of culture traits. Some of these traits are shared simply as a result of extended, long-term proximity or common cultural ancestry. Linguistic dialect, world view, etiquette, subsistence pattern, and basic technology usually are included in this category. Other traits, however, may be shared as a result of

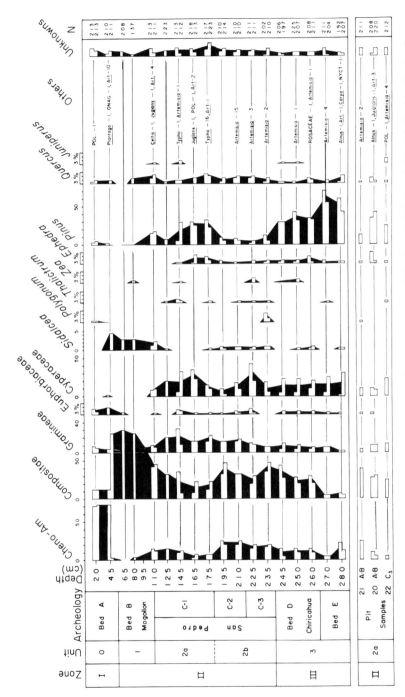

Figure 27. Pollen diagram of Cienega Creek site, Point of Pines. (By permission from "The Last 10,000 Years," Fig. 29. Paul S. Martin, Tucson: Univ. of Arizona Press, copyright 1963.)

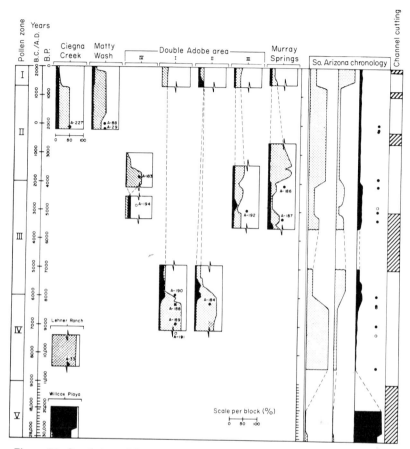

Figure 28. *Correlations of desert grassland pollen diagrams, southern Arizona postpluvial pollen chronology: hatching, Compositae; shading,* Pinus; *stippling, Cheno-Am; (●) ^{14}C dates; (○) ^{14}C dates discarded. (By permission from "The Last 10,000 Years," Fig. 36. Paul S. Martin. Tucson: Univ. of Arizona Press, copyright 1963.)*

regional integrating forces, such as regional markets, military conscription, public works, labor conscription, and regional ceremonial centers. Such activities, which are usually sponsored by political leaders who are attempting to integrate the region, bring individuals from widely separated communities into face-to-face association. The exchange of items in the material culture of differing communities is facilitated, along with the acquisition of a common body of knowledge and experience. One consequence may be community specialization in craft and food production, thus leading to widespread uniformity in some aspects of material culture.

CARL A. RUDISILL LIBRARY
LENOIR RHYNE COLLEGE

Finally, interregional cultural resemblances can emerge under the stimulus of long-term population proximity, migration, long-distance trade, warfare, and a high-mobility settlement pattern. Usually such traits are so general in nature that they are of little or no chronological value. There are exceptions, some quite spectacular, especially in the case of those cultures that can be classified on the basis of their complexity as *civilizations*.

Multiple community participation in a common cultural tradition, although fundamental, is not the only prerequisite for cross-dating. A second requirement is that some of the shared traits must undergo change through time (see Chapter Five). And finally, the traits must be archaeologically recoverable. This latter requirement effectively confines cross-dating efforts to the realm of material culture. In summary, then, one must seek out material culture traits that are susceptible to change through time and that characterize communities throughout the geographical area within which cross-dating is to be attempted.

Material Culture

Archaeologists have drawn traits useful for cross-dating from all of the craft industries of Prehistoric man—stone, ceramics, wood, bone, and shell, as well as metal. He looks for traits that are ephemeral, inconsequential—that are governed by the canons of style rather than utility. Thus, for example, he focuses not on the presence or absence of a stone knife in the tool kit, but on the shape of the knife, on the retouch or refinishing, or on the type of stone selected. Similarly, stone projectile tips are ubiquitous, but the geometry of shape, the size and weight, and the quality of workmanship are often time-related variables. Architecture, from modest family dwellings to monuments of religious or secular splendor, vary enormously—in shape, size, building materials, techniques of construction, ornamentation, and function. Within a single culture area a good many of these differences are time related. For a thorough survey of archaeological chronologies of the Old World see Ehrich (1965).

Ceramic Artifacts

The problem of the degree to which variation in form, material, technique, and embellishment is possible without affecting function places limits on the potential for cross-dating of some crafts. Crafts that permit considerable plasticity, therefore, are most popular among archaeologists. For this reason, ceramic artifacts dominate the field of culture cross-dating. A pottery vessel can take a bewildering number of forms, is subject to a wide range of decorative techniques, and can be embellished by an unlimited number of discrete motifs and designs.

As an example, Table 5 provides a coded attribute system for Mesoamerican pottery vessels used (in a somewhat modified form) by the Pennsylvania State University Kaminaljuyú Project. It illustrates the vast range of discrete trait variation in a single technology. Computers now are being used to aid in summarizing and comparing assemblages when attribute complexity reaches this level.

TABLE 5
A Mesoamerican Pottery Attribute System[a]

General Vessel Form

Bowl
  spherical
  hemispherical
  basal angle
  basal shoulder or flange
  flattened base,
  simple silhouette

Dish

Basin

Vase
  cylindrical

florero

Cup–goblet

Jar
  tecomate
  straight neck
  angular neck
  flaring neck

Comal–saucer
  comal, simple

Vessel Wall Forms

Spherical

Convex

[a] After Wetherington and Kolb: 1968.

TABLE 5 (*continued*)

Vessel Wall Forms (continued)

Beveled

Shouldered

Straight

Concave

Vessel Lip Forms

Rounded

Flat

Bilateral taper

External taper

Internal taper

External bolster

Internal bolster

Thickened externally

Thickened bilaterally

Thickened internally

Wedge, bilateral

Wedge, internal

Wedge, external

Straight lip, rim flange

Beveled lip, rim flange

Labial flange, horizontal

Labial flange, beveled

Vessel Base Form

Flat

Concave

Convex

Basal shoulder

Basal flange

Basal angle

TABLE 5 (*continued*)

Surface treatment

Unsmoothed	Low burnished
Intentionally roughened	Streak burnished
Plain matte or unburnished	High burnished
Slipped matte	Pattern burnished (matte
Finger smoothed or patted	and burnished areas)

Surface decoration technique

Deep narrow incised	Modeled
Deep wide incised	Round punctated
Narrow shallow incised	Wedge punctated
Broad shallow incised	Lunate punctated
Incised zone separation	Notched fillet rim
Simple grooved	Appliqued segment
Complex grooved	Pierced wall
Vertical fluted	Rocker stamped
Horizontal fluted	Channelled
Gadrooned	Frescoed
Excised	Negative painted
Gouged–incised	Painting
Plano–relief	

Design motifs

Simple linear	Complex geometric
Simple geometric	Complex curvilinear
Simple curvilinear	Zonal painting
Complex linear	Representational

Correlation of Trait Complexes

Normally, cross-dating is not successful if only a single trait is being compared. For one thing, the trait may be absent at some sites. For another, the trait may not be sufficiently distinctive to secure high confidence that its presence at several sites is truly a result of contact by contemporaneous groups and not merely fortuitous.

In order to insure scientific confidence and to make the comparisons widely applicable, archaeologists tend to compare *complexes* of traits rather than single traits. Thus, a culture phase will be defined in terms of what is distinctive about (a) its lithic assemblage, (b) its architecture and settlement pattern, (c) its pottery, (d) its subsistence pattern, and (e) its burial practices. When a sufficient number of these distinctive traits occur at a site, cross-dating to that phase can take place with considerable confidence.

Sometimes there is sufficient complexity in a single, highly ubiquitous industry to provide for rigorous cross-dating without recourse to other domains of material culture. Pottery is perhaps the best example of such an industry. Pottery fragments are virtually indestructible and are found in abundance throughout pottery-using culture areas. Vicissitudes in style affect pottery heavily, and provide for extensive time-related variability. As a result, many archaeological regions have ceramic chronologies established for the purposes of sequence and cross-dating.

Continuing with the Mesoamerica example, Table 6 summarizes the ceramic chronology of the important Highland Guatemala site of Kaminaljuyú. For each of the principal occupational periods at the site a *complex* of diagnostic ceramic traits has been isolated for cross-dating purposes. Figure 29 illustrates the points made in Table 6, and also reveals the continuities and discontinuities in style that make up the ceramic tradition of this area. Cross-dating is an important task at a site like Kaminaljuyú, with its 200 earthen mounds, its 6 square kilometers (6 km²) of settlement area, its 1,800 years of occupation, and its constituent rural population spread over the whole of the Valley of Guatemala at hundreds of discrete farming hamlets and district centers.

Exotics and Cross-Dating by Historic Artifacts

Up to now, the discussion of cross-dating by correlation of cultural traits has focused largely on *shared* traits—traits that imply a common cultural tradition. There are, however, special occasions when *alien artifacts* intrude upon the material culture of a region. When such artifacts are discovered at a site, the archaeologist will often refer to them as *exotics* or *trade pieces*. They are important for cross-dating precisely because they are alien.

Their presence signifies contemporaneity between all *receiving* settlements and the *donor* culture. A clear example of this was the introduction of European artifacts into the material culture of Protohistoric Indian society of eastern North America. Glass beads, metal axes, buttons, knives, guns, and crockery all found their way into the artifact assemblages of Indian settlements, and demonstrate contemporaneity with the European colonists and traders. Fashion also prevailed in the manufacture of European goods, and items ranging from smoking

TABLE 6
Summary Characterization of Diagnostic Ceramic Complexes at Kaminaljuyú[a]

1. *"Las Charcas": The Middle Formative Period*

   Orange Ware: Color ranges from dull orange through beige; surface from dull to glossy. Streaky or mottled in appearance. Forms: flat-based simple silhouette bowl: subspherical, hemispherical, and incurved rim bowls. Decoration is done by grooving, fluting, and modeling. Designs tend to be curvilinear and linear.

   Streaky Gray-Brown Ware: Gray-white to buff and brown. Forms: S–Z angle bowls, hemispherical bowls with incurved rim, shallow inturned rim bowls with medial flange.

   Pallid Red Ware: Pale red-orange to brown. Forms: large, deep hemispherical bowl with flattened lip and parallel horizontal incising on the rim; deep bowl with restricted mouth and decorated at the shoulder break with horizontal incising, vertical ticking, or fingernail punctation; large vertical-necked jar with heavy bolstered lip, lip articulating strap handles, and decorated with curvilinear incisions around the upper body.

2. *"Providencia–Sacatepequez": The Late Formative Period*

   Fine Red Ware: Begins during this period but persists beyond it. Although the ware itself is not diagnostic, the specific vessel forms are. Forms: standing-wall bowls, small-mouthed and subspherical bowls, composite silhouette bowls with faceted shoulder or medial flange. Decoration: the red surface slip is painted with a purple or magenta pigment. The painting is used to outline vessel zones (such as the lip, rim, or flange) or the fill in design elements executed by grooving or modeling.

   Zinc Orange Ware: Hard-slipped with a medium-fine paste that has a mottled surface color of orange to buff-orange. Surface texture is an even polish. Decoration: groove incising of motifs such as a horizontal scallop, or zigzag with framing lines above and below. Forms: flaring-wall bowls with flat base, small-shouldered bowls with flaring, slightly bolstered lips.

   Polished Black Ware: Occurs in the form of incurved rim bowls, decorated with simple grooving or modeling.

   Utatlan Bichrome Ware: Uncommon but diagnostic. It occurs in the form of simple flat-based bowls decorated in red and black zones that are separated by broad incising.

3. *"Verbena–Arenal": The Terminal Formative Period*

   Fine Red Ware: Composite silhouette bowls, ranging from S–Z to basal angles to basal shoulder to faceted flange. Walls are everted, either flaring or straight. Lips are beveled internally (to the horizontal) and flared externally. Lip and body decoration involves scalloping, faceting, grooving, and the modeling of low-relief effigies. Vessel supports: solid, conical tripod or tetrapod nubbins. A special diagnostic form is the "toad bowl": a shallow vessel with stylized head and limbs appliqued during the drying process.

   Verbena White Ware: A medium-to-coarse red-paste ware with a soft white slip. Decoration involves incising through the slip to reveal the ulterior red paste in patterns such as hatching, crosshatching, and triangular hatching. Forms: subspherical, hemispherical, and flat-based simple bowls.

TABLE 6 (*continued*)

Black-Brown Ware: Subspherical bowls, composite silhouette bowls, cylindrical and "flower-pot" vases. Nubbin supports are common. Decoration: fine and coarse incising a linear and curvilinear design.

Polished Black Ware: Occurs in the form of a hemispherical bowl with hollow tripod conical supports and rim effigies. Surface treatment: coarse incising and excising gouging.

Red-on-Buff Ware: Globular jars with loop handles curving above the lip. Decoration: the unslipped buff surface takes a red-brown pigment in a bold execution of design elements.

4. *"Aurora": The Early Classic Period*

Esperanza Flesh Color Ware: Surface ranges from an unslipped but polished orange-cinnamon with lustrous streaks to an irregular creamy buff wash with little or no polish. Forms: simple hemispherical, basal angle, and basal shoulder bowls. Distinctive feature: ring-stand supports.

Brown and Red-Orange Ware: Form: shallow bowl or dish. Distinctive feature: large, hollow, mammiform or globular supports.

Coarse Incised Black-Brown Ware: Occurs with conspicuously more low-relief carving than during the previous period.

Painted Cream Ware: Occurs as a large, shouldered, flaring-neck jar with designs in purple paint. An important diagnostic is the large, flat-based basins with tripodal, solid conical supports and hollow rim-head effigy figures.

5. *"Amatle I–Esperanza": The Middle Classic Period*

Diagnostic "Trade Wares" occur during this period. They include *Thin Orange, Peten Polychrome*, imported cylindrical vases on slab tripodal supports, and imported basal-flange bowls with hollow mammiform supports. Surface treatment, combining both Peten and Mexican influences, include carved, plano–relief, painted, and stucco designs. Several locally produced wares are also diagnostic.

Amatle Bichrome Ware: Simple hemispherical basal angle, and basal shouldered bowls. Decoration: geometric and effigy motifs painted onto the vessel interior is a reddish-purple pigment, over a previously applied cream or orange slip.

Brown-Gray Wares: Globular jars with pinched fillet crescents on the shoulder; also utility vessels in a "frying pan" form with handles.

Mud Ware: crudely executed shallow hemispherical bowls.

Polished Brown-Black Ware: Occurs in cup and goblet forms.

Red-Brown Ware: A coarse ware with appliqued spikes that occurs in a barrel-shaped, deep-bowl form, as well as in other shapes.

6. *"Amatle II": The Late Classic Period*

Amatle Hard Ware: A well-fired ceramic, generally gray but often buff-orange. Well smoothed but not polished. Forms: vases; squat, wide-mouthed jars; large jar with a high, straight neck and everted lip.

Amatle Polychrome Ware: It is an evolved Amatle bichrome distinguished from its antecedent by the addition of white elements or lines, new decorative motifs, and the occasional expansion of the ring base into a taller annular base.

[a]After Wetherington (1970).

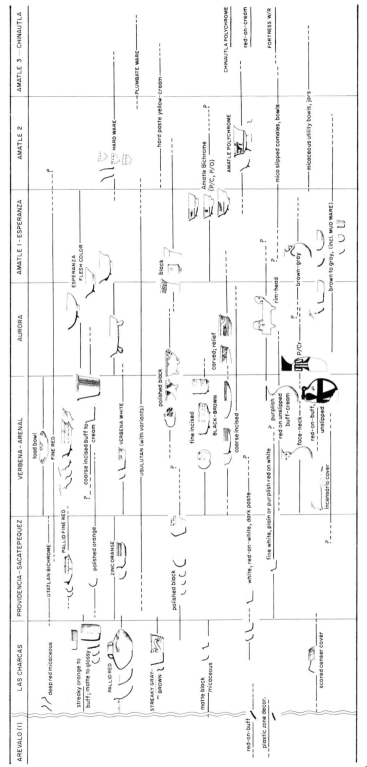

Figure 29. *The ceramic sequence of Kaminaljuyú: a provisional interpretation.* (*From Wetherington 1969.*)

pipes to the buttons of men's trousers underwent stylistic modifications that are time related. Going through the records of old manufacturing firms, historians have been able to reconstruct a chronometric sequence of trait variation for specific classes of European goods. Thus, for example, the discovery of a specific type of brass-and-hook fastener can be identified as having been manufactured sometime after 1650 A.D.

Exotic traits generally can be found in cultures that have achieved high levels of economic and political complexity, or in those in contact with such cultures. There are many reasons for this—all having principally to do with the need for incentives to carry out long-distance trade. Only complex societies can raise armies and seek to conquer and exact tribute from distant lands. The exchange of legations, diplomacy, and reciprocal gifts of fine and rare objects are matters of concern to chiefdoms, monarchies, states, and empires. And it is the elaborate religious institution that is a characteristically heavy consumer of exotic goods and valuables. Finally, only large and powerful political entities can provide the security that the long-distance flow of goods requires. Troubled times in the relations of neighboring societies often can be detected by evidence of an interruption in the flow of exotic goods. When empires do prevail, the striking uniformity in some traits that occurs among constituent archaeological regions makes possible the recognition of *horizon markers*—traits that are short-lived but widely disseminated. They may range from a particular type of metal coin to a distinctive architectural tradition.

READINGS

Bishop, W. W., and J. D. Clark (Editors)
    1967 *Background to evolution in Africa.* Chicago: University of Chicago Press.
Butzer, K. W.
    1971 *Environment and archaeology.* Chicago: Aldine.
Ehrich, R. W. (Editor)
    1965 *Chronologies in Old World archaeology.* Chicago: University of Chicago Press.
Epstein, D.
    1968 *Buttons.* New York: Walker.
Giddings, J. L.
    1966 Cross-dating the archaeology of northwestern Alaska. *Science* **153**, No. 3732: 127–135.
Godden, G. A.
    1964 *Encyclopedia of British Pottery and Porcelain Marks.* New York: Crown Publ.

Klein, R. G.
1969 *Man and culture in the Late Pleistocene.* San Francisco: Chandler Publ.
Kovar, A. J.
1967 Report on the pollen analysis of the samples from the Sheep Rock Shelter. In *Archaeological Investigations of Sheep Rock Shelter,* edited by J. W. Michels and I. F. Smith, Vol. I, pp. 85–112. Department of Anthropology, Pennsylvania State University, University Park, Pennsylvania.
Kretzoi, M., and L. Vértes
1965 Upper Biharian (Intermindel) pebble-industry occupation site in Western Hungary. *Current Anthropology* **6**, No. 1: 74–87.
Martin, P. S.
1963 *The last 10,000 years.* Tucson: University of Arizona Press.
Noel Hume, I.
1970 *A guide to artifacts of Colonial America.* New York: Knopf.
Oakley, K. P.
1964 *Frameworks for dating fossil man.* Chicago: Aldine.
Patterson, T. C.
1963 Contemporaneity and cross-dating in archaeological interpretation. *American Antiquity* **28**, No. 3: 389–392.
Rowe, J. H.
1962 Worsaee's law and the use of grave lots for archaeological dating. *American Antiquity* **28**, No. 2: 129–137.
Smiley, T. L. (Editor)
1955 *Geochronology.* University of Arizona Physical Science Bulletin No. 2.
Wetherington, R. K.
1969 *Illustration of ceramic sequence at Kaminaljuyú, Guatemala: A provisional interpretation.* Unpublished drawing, The Kaminaljuyú Project, Pennsylvania State University.
1970 *The Ceramic Sequence at Kaminaljuyú* (A Preliminary Version). Unpublished manuscript, The Kaminaljuyú Project, Pennsylvania State University.
Wetherington, R. K. and C. Kolb
1968 A Mesoamerican pottery attribute system: Preliminary version. Unpublished manuscript, Kaminaljuyú Project, The Pennsylvania State University.

PART THREE

METHODS OF
CHRONOMETRIC DATING

The following seven chapters describe the principal methods of archaeological dating that can produce chronometric results. A number of radioactive isotope systems of dating have been omitted since they are applied exclusively to geochronological objectives which benefit archaeology only indirectly, if at all.

The emphasis of this section of the book is on the promise for the future. With the exception of radiocarbon dating, the methods described are not widely in use. Many of them are relatively new, and have been slow to be adopted. All, however, are well enough established that their promise for the future looks very bright indeed!

The methods are evolving in an interdependent manner. For example, radiocarbon dating is calibrated by reference to dendrochronological scales; archaeomagnetic dating depends on both dendrochronology and radiocarbon dating; and fission-track dating and potassium argon dating serve to scale each other. As one method becomes more precise and more reliable, its utility as a scale for critically evaluating another method increases. With better scales, error can be detected more accurately and corrected more effectively, in turn making the latter method more reliable.

It is not uncommon, nowadays, for an archaeologist to deliberately seek out deposits that permit him to recover samples for several different dating methods. At Kaminaljuyú, Guatemala, for example, the author and his colleagues were able to recover obsidian, fired clay, charcoal, and diagnostic pottery, all in association, at a number of different locations. Such data give the archaeologist new flexibility and a new perspective in the interpretation of chronology, and at the same time aid those researchers working to improve the dating techniques represented.

The dating techniques described in this section are based on principles and procedures that span a broad segment of the biological and physical sciences. Perhaps no other context so vividly illustrates the modern role of science in archaeology.

CHAPTER SEVEN

Dendrochronology

Introduction

Dendrochronology is a method that uses tree-ring analysis to establish chronology. A major application of dendrochronology is in archaeology, as a tool for establishing tree-ring dates. This method makes it possible to date individual ruins to within a year, or even a season, of the day they were built. Often, the tree-ring analysis from a site can give strong clues about the length of occupation, certain periods of building or repair activities at the site, as well as demonstrate practices of reuse or stock piling by early inhabitants.

Another application of tree-ring analysis is the inference of past environmental conditions (Fritts 1963, 1965, 1966). Although this type of data could be extremely valuable to archaeologists, these studies will not be discussed here.

Because of the accuracy of the chronometric scale established by tree-ring analysis, there now is an effort to use these scales for calibrating dates established with other dating methods, in particular, carbon-14 (Suess 1970, Ralph 1971).

Discovery of the Technique

The annual cycle of tree-ring formation has been known for a long time, and for many years tree rings were counted to establish the ages of growing or dead trees. However, the modern science of dendrochronology was pioneered by A. E. Douglass, an astronomer who had set out to investigate sunspot cycles by tracing climatic factors reflected in the growth of trees. From his earliest studies, which were purely climatic in their objectives, he went on to establish, in a systematic manner, an absolute chronology for the southwestern United States.

Douglass started his investigation in 1904, studying the yearly rings of the yellow pines in the Flagstaff and Prescott areas. He succeeded in counting back 500 years, starting with the outermost rings. In the process, he discovered that the rings were always of a definite relative width in relation to the adjacent rings on different tree sections. Thus, tree rings of particular species of trees appeared to occur in a specific pattern, which, when recognized, could be correlated to older tree sections in order to extend the chronology farther and farther into the past. Indeed, the tree-ring sequences correlated even with specimens of wooden sections collected from prehistoric ruins. During subsequent years, Douglass (1919, 1928, 1936), obtained specimens from various sites in the southwest to extend the chronological record of the yellow pine to A.D. 700. He and other workers in the field continued in their efforts to extend the chronology further into the past. The tree-ring sequence for the southwestern United States now goes back to 59 B.C.

Thus, a study that started as an aid in the study of climate, and used archaeological data to extend the chronology, has provided an important tool for archaeologists in their efforts to solve archaeological problems. Since the discovery of the technique, hundreds of prehistoric ruins have been dated. Current research in dendrochronology is concerned with establishing chronologies for other species of trees and in different parts of the world where it can be applied. Efforts are being made to simplify the method of recording and to standardize ring sequences with the aid of computers.

The Underlying Process in Dendrochronology

Tree-ring analysis is based on the phenomenon of formation of annual growth rings in many trees, such as conifers. These rings can be recognized most clearly in trees that grow in areas with regular seasonal fluctuations in climate, with dry and wet seasons or mild and cold seasons alternating regularly. Usually, trees produce one ring every year from the cambium—the layer of soft, cellular tissue that lies between the bark and the old wood. In the spring, or generally at the start of the growing season, groups of large, thin-walled, light-colored cells are added to the existing wood. As the season progresses, these cells merge gradually with new cells, which become increasingly smaller, darker, and more thickly walled, until the production of cells stops abruptly at the end of the summer or the wet season. The process is repeated the following year, and a clear line thus is formed between the summer growth of one year, with its small, dark cells, and the new spring growth of the following year with its large, light-colored cells. The growth rings of trees vary throughout. This variation is caused by two major factors: First, the thickness varies with the age of the tree, the rings becoming narrower as the tree gets older. The inner rings of a tree are therefore wider than its outer rings. This factor is independent of climate and location, and must be considered and taken into account when the rings are analyzed. The second factor that affects the thickness of growth rings is the change in climate from one year to another. In years with unfavorable weather, such as drought, the growth rings will be unusually narrow. On the other hand, during years with exceptionally large amounts of rain, the tree will form much wider growth rings. Most of the trees in a given area will show the same variability in the width of their growth rings because of the climatic fluctuations they all endured. Such trees are said to be *sensitive*; those that do not exhibit variability are said to be *complacent* (Figure 30). In the semiarid southwestern United States, with its frequent drought conditions, the rings often will be very narrow, even microscopic. The pattern of narrow and wide rings that *sensitive* trees in an area display is the basis for cross-dating among specimens. This pattern is unique, since the year-to-year variations in climate are never exactly the same, and the resulting wide and narrow ring sequences will not be exactly the same through a long period of time.

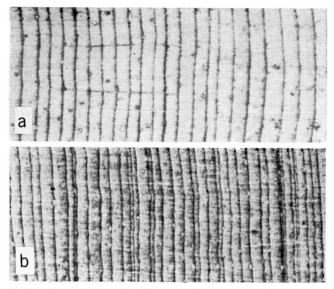

Figure 30. *Sanded cross sections of bristlecone pine showing (a) complacent and (b) moderately sensitive growth-ring response. (From Ferguson, C. W. Bristlecone pine: Science and esthetics. Science, **159**: 839–846, Fig. 7. Copyright 1968 by the American Association for the Advancement of Science.)*

In regions having modern trees that can serve as cross-dating controls, the assignment of calendar years to each of the individual tree rings within a specimen is possible. Even where the modern tree-ring controls are not available, relative dating can be undertaken.

Field Work Applications

It should not be assumed that tree-ring dating can be applied universally, since only certain trees in an area cross-date with each other and only certain areas in the world contain cross-datable trees. Cross-dating between separated areas is seldom successful. In the southwestern United States, tree flora have the following characteristics with respect to tree-ring dating. The most commonly dated tree is the Douglas Fir, since it is well represented at archaeological sites, and because the rings are consistent in form and easy to read. Yellow pine is equally valuable for similar reasons. Piñon, with much fainter rings, has been found to be compatible with tree-ring series constructed of other woods. Juniper, although widely distributed in the southwestern United States, is not of dendrochronological importance, since it is characterized by an eccentric center and almost microscopic rings. Cottonwood, oak, and walnut have *complacent* growth-ring response, and are therefore of little value for dating purposes. Sagebrush is datable, and since it is usually recoverable in the form of charcoal from fireplaces, it is of special archaeological interest.

Not every piece of wood or charcoal will have datable rings. Trees that grow on steep slopes, narrow hilltops, or in very rocky soil, where runoff is rapid and soil moisture light, are inclined to show supersensitive records, with many rings absent in years when no growth took place in the stem of the tree. Others, growing near the bottoms of valleys or on the banks of streams or in springs or similar spots, have such an abundant permanent supply of water that their rings are all of equal size and thus are classifiable as *complacent*. Trees that lend themselves best to dating are those which grow in well-drained, gently sloped soils. The rings of such trees will have sufficient character or variation in width to make them easily datable.

The number of rings included in the specimen is also important in determining its value for dating. Unless unusually strong and easily recognizable ring groupings are present, sequences of less than 25 or 30 years are undatable. An ideal section will cover 60–200 years, with an average ring size that is easily discernible under a 6× lens. Branches of trees are often difficult to date, as rings tend to be absent or double. Charcoal fragments, which were probably largely branches of small bushes and trees, and were used as firewood, too often lack the outside rings, thereby preventing the determination of the actual date of the activity with which they are associated.

Various methods for the field collection of tree-ring samples have been developed. A full section is usually sawed off from one end of a preserved wood beam no longer in place. In the case of a very large log, a V-shaped cut, extending from the side to a point just beyond the center is sometimes made. For beams that still support roofs in standing dwellings, a tube with a set of teeth on one end and a bit head fastened to the other has been designed. This implement, operated in a power or hand brace, will remove a core from the beam. Furthermore, use of a core driller has made it possible to take large numbers of cores rapidly and conveniently.

Most charcoal and timbers found buried in damp earth will crack when they are exposed to the air and allowed to dry too rapidly. Such materials therefore are kept in the shade and allowed to dry slowly. They are then saturated with a solution of gasoline and paraffin. When the gasoline evaporates, the specimens are left impregnated with paraffin, which acts as a binding material. Coating with a thick shellac is another method of preservation, and is considered effective on thin, delicate wooden or charcoal pieces.

The Technique of Analysis

Before actual study can begin, a specimen must be surfaced so that its cellular structure is visible and its ring series can be examined with clarity. Proper surfaces are absolutely essential in the process of achieving precise dates. Charcoal and soft or rotten wood are prepared with a razor blade, a technique that is rapid but fairly difficult to master. Good results can also be obtained on small sections with a sliding microtome. For large cross sections, sanding is undertaken. There now exist specially designed sanding devices that can produce full transect surfaces which satisfy the most rigorous requirements, although hand-held sanders with graded papers can also be used.

In the analysis of tree-ring specimens, the first objective is the establishment of cross-dating between samples. When chronometric dating is desired, the process is carried one more step, and cross-dated specimens are matched against a master chronology, which itself is a product of previously cross-dated pieces. Essentially, what is involved is the recording of individual ring series and their comparison with other series. Consequently, the initial requirement is the positive identification of each of the visible growth increments within the sample.

Different systems of tree-ring dating, and there are several currently being used throughout the world, are mainly alternate ways of representing growth patterns and establishing cross-dating. Such variation reflects differences in local conditions of tree growth and certain types of ring chronologies.

One method called the Douglass method, has been applied successfully in the southwestern United States. It is applicable when highly sensitive trees constitute the main source of datable specimens, and the degree of correlation between ring readings is very high. The technique emphasizes both those rings that deviate from the normal (for example, narrow or broad rings) and the internal relationship of these rings within the overall series. Comparison of the rings of one log specimen with another is accomplished in three ways:

(1) the memory method;
(2) skeletal plots;
(3) precisely measured ring widths.

The memory method, that is, memorizing all of the ring patterns encountered, is a very rapid and convenient way of comparing specimens but it does require a thorough knowledge of the local chronology.

When working with large quantities of materials or with samples that are either temporally or geographically unfamiliar, skeleton plotting has proved to be a valuable technique (Figure 31). The skeleton plot is a graph that exhibits the relative widths of diagnostic rings. It is free of any age trend within the specimens since the size of each ring is judged in relation to neighboring rings. Thus, skeleton plots of a uniform scale can be compared with each other conveniently, and if cross-dating does obtain, the plots may be integrated.

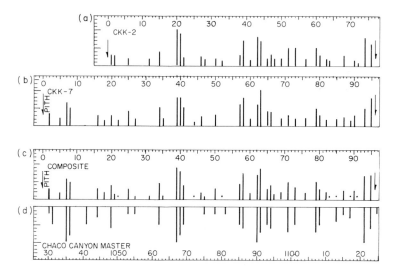

Figure 31. *Comparison of skeleton plots: (a, b) skeleton plots of the ring series in two beams from the prehistoric ruin Kin Kletsok, Chaco Canyon, New Mexico; (c) composite of (a) and (b); (d) regional master chronology for Chaco Canyon. The matching of (c) with (d) establishes the tentative dating of specimens. The length of each vertical bar on the graph in inversely proportional to the relative width of the ring; average ring widths are not recorded, and extralarge rings are indicated by the letter B. (From Bannister, B. Dendrochronology. In "Science in Archaeology," edited by D. Brothwell and E. Higgs. New York: Praeger, 1970.)*

Several different instruments designed to accurately record widths along a radius have been developed. These include the Craighead–Douglass measuring instrument, the De Rouen Dendro-Chronograph, and the Addo-X. After the measured values are translated into plotted graphs, both visual and statistical comparisons can be made (Figure 32).

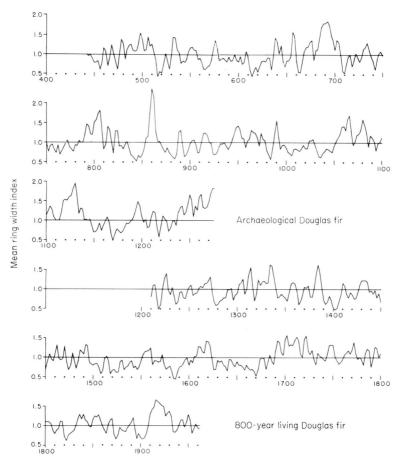

Figure 32. *Five year running means of corrected tree-ring indices from Mesa Verde (plotted on every even year from A.D. 442 to 1962). (From Fritts, Smith, and Stokes 1965: Fig. 10. Reproduced by permission of the Society for American Archaeology from* American Antiquity, *Vol. 31.)*

All that relative dating requires is that tree-ring samples be available and that specimens cross-date with each other. The establishment of chronometric dates, however, is another matter. Even though contemporaneous relative-dated specimens may be merged into a composite whole, forming a floating chronology, it is still necessary to build a known tree-ring chronology that goes back far enough to overlap and cross-date with the unknown segment. Starting with modern samples of known date, successively older and older specimens are cross-dated and incorporated into the matrix until a long-range tree-ring chronology is established (Figure 33). This procedure may take years to accomplish, but, once done, the ring patterns contained in samples of unknown age can be cross-dated with the master chronology and assigned chronometric dates.

The Douglass system has been applied successfully outside of the United States (Mexico, Turkey, and Egypt, among others). However, in Europe and elsewhere, where precipitation is heavy, the trees are not as sensitive and do not lend themselves to cross-dating. In such areas various methods of statistical analysis involving coefficients of parallel and opposite variation, logarithmic plotting, special mechanical devices for automatically comparing series, and other innovations have been devised.

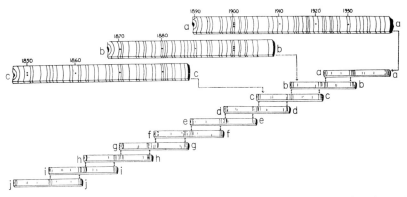

Figure 33. *Chronology building. (a) radial sample from a living tree cut after the 1939 growing season; (b–j) specimens taken from old houses and successively older ruins. The ring patterns match and overlap back into prehistoric times. (From Bannister, B. Dendrochronology. In "Science in Archaeology," edited by D. Brothwell and E. Higgs. New York: Praeger, 1970.)*

The validity of tree-ring dating ultimately depends upon the precision with which cross-dating can be accomplished. High-confidence ring correlations can be secured by means of the *forecast-and-verification* method, involving the search and comparison of additional ring characteristics once trial correlations have been made. When a sufficient number of positive verifications are found, the probability of chance correlations becomes acceptably low.

Interpretation of the Tree-Ring Dates

As with so many other dating techniques, there is the basic problem of the time relationship that exists between the date of a specimen and the archaeological manifestation being dated. Bannister (1962) has set forth the four classes of time relationships as they are represented in tree-ring dating:

1. According to Bannister, the most common type of error encountered in the interpretation of tree-ring dates is caused by the presence of reused beams. The labor involved in felling a tree with stone tools and in transporting it motivated aboriginal builders to recover logs from nearby abandoned ruins whenever possible. The reuse of timbers in later structures can result in error since the tree-ring date, although correct, is being applied to the wrong structure.

2. Error may occur when artifacts in a room are dated by the application of tree-ring dates derived from logs that were used in the construction of the room. The problem is not serious in short occupation sites, such as pit houses and small masonary structures. However, in sites of long occupation the problem can become critical.

3. Error may result from the practice of reoccupying or remodeling older rooms or dwellings. In such cases it is common for the occupants to remove weakened structural timbers and replace them with new timbers. Tree-ring dates derived from such samples will introduce error into the analysis.

4. Error can result from dates obtained from nonconstruction specimens found within or associated with structures—thinking that the date refers to the structure itself. Thus, charcoal and wood found in room fill or in trash mounds sometimes give more recent dates than the architectural features with which they are loosely associated.

Bannister offers two solutions to these four types of error: the clustering of tree-ring dates and clustering or archaeological traits. Errors of Type 1 and 3 usually can be corrected, provided enough wood samples are available for deriving multiple dates from the same feature. If there are a number of dates that cluster about a single point in time, then dates that deviate from the cluster represent reused or repair timbers (depending upon whether they are earlier or later than the majority). The evaluation of the contemporaneity of artifacts within a room fill can contribute to the solution of error Types 2 and 4. In both cases the problem involves the temporal relationship between the dated structure, or object, and the associated artifacts. Artifact inventories that appear to represent multiple episodes of occupation within a long period of time indicate that physically associated tree-ring dates cannot be utilized for dating the cultural materials. On the other hand, if the artifact inventory appears to consist of archaeologically contemporaneous specimens, it is likely that the tree-ring dates will be chronologically associated as well as physically associated.

The Problem of Outside Rings

A tree-ring date is the year in which the last ring present on a specimen was formed. To distinguish between dates based on *true* last-rings and *remnant* last rings, we refer to cutting dates (sometimes called bark dates) and noncutting dates. The term *cutting date* is applied to specimens possessing the last exterior ring that grew on the tree before it died, regardless of whether the tree was killed by human activity or died of natural causes. When a specimen is thought to have lost exterior rings, or there is no evidence to indicate otherwise, the tree-ring date is referred to as a *noncutting date*.

The confirmation of cutting dates is based on the following:

(1) finding bark or bark cells on the outside of the specimen;
(2) determining if the outside ring seen in the cross-section of a specimen extends without a break;
(3) locating the presence of beetle galleries on the exterior surface;
(4) ascertaining the presence or absence of a distinctive patina on the surface of the log.

In the absence of evidence indicating cutting dates, the dendrochronologist may either estimate the number of rings lost or state only that the date is a noncutting date.

Application of Dendrochronology in Archaeology

There are several prerequisites to the successful application of dendrochronology in an archaeological region. First, there must be sufficient wood or charcoal specimens at archaeological sites in the region. Second, the wood must have been well-enough preserved that both the cellular and ring structures are accessible. A third requirement is that the specimens cross-date. As indicated previously, in order for cross-dating to be feasible, the samples must contain clearly defined rings that show fluctuations of thickness throughout the series. The rings must be the result of factors that induce uniform responses in trees within the region. Finally, the cross-dated floating chronology of archaeologically recovered specimens must be anchored to an established master chronology tied by cross-dating to our calendar.

The southwestern United States has many sites with preserved construction timber. One result has been that this region has now one of the most sensitive and accurate archaeological chronologies to be found anywhere in the world. Thousands of individual tree-ring dates from hundreds of archaeological sites have been determined by the Laboratory of Tree-Ring Research at the University of Arizona in Tucson (Figure 34).

Other areas in which this dating method has been used extensively are Alaska, northern Mexico, Germany, Norway, Great Britain, and Switzerland. However, many of the chronologies established have yet to be tied to a master chronology, and are therefore not chronometric (Clark and Renfrew 1972). Preliminary applications of this technique are also reported for the midwestern and northwestern United States, Turkey, Egypt, Japan, and Russia.

Probably the most spectacular master chronology available for tree-ring dating is to be found in east central California, where a 7,100-year tree-ring chronology has been developed for bristlecone pine (*Pinus aristata* Engelm) (Ferguson 1969). Living trees contributed over 4,000 years of this record, owing to the incredible longevity of this species. Dead trees that could be accurately cross-dated to these living specimens extended the chronology back to 5110 B.C. Recent studies have shown that the master chronology produced with bristlecone pine can be used to cross-date with local chronologies derived from trees as far away as 1,600 km to the east and south and about 480 km to the north. The bristlecone pine chronology undoubtedly will be pushed even farther back in time, and its applications to archaeological dating will continue to be explored.

READINGS

Bannister, B.
    1962   The interpretation of tree-ring dates. *American Antiquity* **27**, No. 4: 508–514.

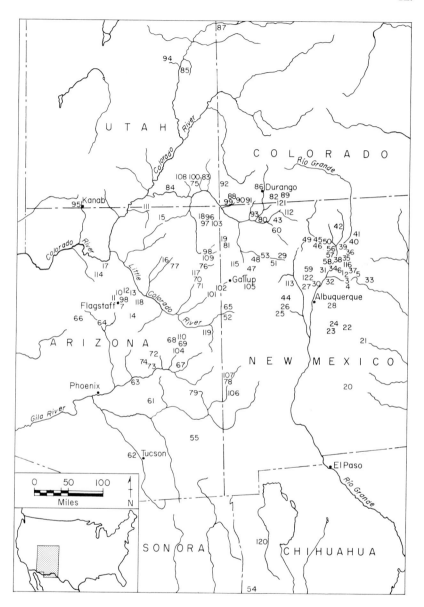

Figure 34. *Map of the southwestern United States showing the location of archaeological sites and site areas with dated tree-ring specimens. (By permission from "An Appraisal of Tree-Ring Dated Pottery in the Southwest," p. viii. David A. Bretternitz, University of Arizona Anthropological Paper No. 10. Tucson: Univ. of Arizona Press, copyright 1966.)*

1970   Dendrochronology. In *Science in archaeology*, edited by D. Brothwell and E. Higgs. New York: Praeger.

Bannister, B., and T. L. Smiley
  1955   Dendrochronology. In *Geochronology, with special reference to southwestern United States*, edited by T. L. Smiley, pp. 177–195. University of Arizona Bulletin, Vol. 26, No. 2, Physical Science Bulletin No. 2, Tucson.

Bell, R. E.
  1952   Dendrochronology in the Mississippi Valley. In *Archaeology of eastern United States*, edited by J. B. Griffin, pp. 345–351. Chicago: University of Chicago Press.

Breternitz, D. A.
  1966   An appraisal of tree-ring dated pottery in the Southwest. *Anthropological Papers of the University of Arizona*, No. 10.

Clark, R. M., and C. Renfrew
  1972   A statistical approach to the calibration of floating tree-ring chronologies using radiocarbon dates. *Archaeometry* **14**: pp. 5–19.

Damon, P. E., A. Long, and D. C. Grey
  1970   Arizona radiocarbon dates for dendrochronologically dated samples. In *Radiocarbon variations and absolute chronology*, edited by I. V. Olsson. New York: Wiley.

Douglass, A. E.
  1919   *Climatic cycles and tree-growth, Vol. I.* Washington, D.C.: Carnegie Institution of Washington.
  1928   *Climatic cycles and tree-growth, Vol. II.* Washington, D.C.: Carnegie Institution of Washington.
  1936   *Climatic cycles and tree-growth, Vol. III.* Washington, D.C.: Carnegie Institution of Washington.

Ferguson, C. W.
  1968   Bristlecone pine: Science and esthetics, *Science* **159**: 839–846.
  1969   A 7104-year annual tree-ring chronology for bristlecone pine, *Pinos aristata*, from the White Mountains, California. *Tree-Ring Bulletin* **29**: 3–29.

Fritts, H. C.
  1963   Recent advances in dendrochronology in America with reference to the significance of climatic change. *Arid Zone Research (UNESCO)* **20**: 255–263.
  1965   Dendrochronology. In *The quaternary of the United States*, edited by H. E. Wright and R. V. Frey. Princeton, New Jersey: Princeton University Press.
  1966   Growth-rings of trees: Their correlation with climate. *Science* **154**: 973–979.

Fritts, H. C., D. G. Smith, and M. A. Stokes
  1965   The biological model for paleoclimatic interpretation of Mesa Verde Tree-Ring Series. *American Antiquity* **31**: 101–121.

Giddings, J. L., Jr.
  1940   The application of tree-ring dates to arctic sites. *Tree-Ring Bulletin* **7**, No. 2: 10–14.

Glock, W. S.
  1937   *Principles and methods of tree-ring analysis.* Washington, D.C.: Carnegie Institution of Washington. (Publication No. 486.)

Haury, E. W.
  1935   Tree-rings—The archaeologist's time piece. *American Antiquity* **1**, No. 2: 98–108.

Lister, R. H.
1968 Archaeology for layman and scientist at Mesa Verde. *Science* **160**: 489–496.
McGregor, J. C.
1965 *Southwestern Archaeology*. Urbana, Illinois: University of Illinois Press.
Michael, H. N.
1971 Climates, tree-rings, and archaeology. In *Dating techniques for the archaeologist*, edited by H. N. Michael and E. K. Ralph. Cambridge, Massachusetts: M.I.T. Press.
Oswalt, W. H.
1958 Tree-ring chronologies in south central Alaska. *Tree-Ring Bulletin* **22**: 16–22.
Ralph, E. K.
1971 Carbon-14 dating. In *Dating techniques for the archaeologist*, edited by H. N. Michael and E. K. Ralph. Cambridge, Massachusetts: M.I.T. Press.
Ralph, E. K., and H. N. Michael
1970 MASCA radiocarbon dates for sequoia and bristlecone-pine samples. In *Radiocarbon variations and absolute chronology*, edited by I. V. Olsson. New York: Wiley.
Scott, S. D.
1966 Dendrochronology in Mexico. *Papers of the Laboratory of Tree-Ring Research* No. 2, The University of Arizona.
Smiley, T. L.
1951 A summary of tree-ring dates from some Southwestern archaeological sites. *University of Arizona Bulletin* **22**, No. 4.
Smiley, T. L., S. A. Stubbs, and B. Bannister
1953 A foundation for the dating of some late archaeological sites in the Rio Grande area, New Mexico: Based on studies in tree-ring methods and pottery analyses. *University of Arizona Bulletin* **24**, No. 3: Laboratory of Tree-Ring Research Bulletin. No. 6.
Stallings, W. S., Jr.
1949 *Dating Prehistoric Ruins by Tree-Rings*, rev. ed. Tucson: Laboratory of Tree-Ring Research, University of Arizona.
Suess, H. E.
1970 Bristlecone pine calibration of the radiocarbon time scale 5400 B.C. to the present. In *Radiocarbon variations and absolute chronology*, edited by I. V. Olsson. New York: Wiley.
Zeuner, F. E.
1958 *Dating the past*. London: Methuen.

CHAPTER EIGHT

Archaeomagnetic Dating:
Paleoorientation and Paleointensity

Introduction

Archaeomagnetic dating is based on the known fact that the direction and intensity of the earth's magnetic field vary over the years. Clay and clay soils contain magnetic minerals, and when the clay is heated to a certain temperature, these minerals will assume the direction and a proportional intensity of the magnetic field which surrounds them. They will retain this direction and intensity after they are cooled. By measuring these quantities, the age of the sample can be determined if the changes in the earth's magnetic field at that location are known.

Clay or clay soils, when heated to a dull red heat and allowed to cool down in the earth's magnetic field, will acquire a weak permanent magnetism. Such thermoremanent magnetism is the result of

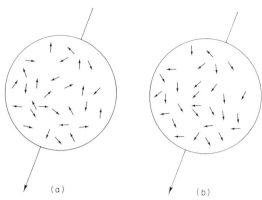

Figure 35. *Thermoremanent magnetism: (a) unbaked clay–particles are in random directions and the net magnetic effect is very small; (b) baked clay–thermal agitation has freed the magnetic particles from the original direction constraints, causing them to assume preferential alignment in conformity with the earth's magnetic field; this alignment is stabilized upon return to normal temperature. The arrows indicate the direction of the earth's magnetic field at the time of firing. (After Aitken, M. J. "Physics and Archaeology." Fig. 2.4. New York: Wiley, 1961. Reproduced by permission.)*

the ferromagnetism of magnetite and hematite. The average iron oxide content of the earth's crust if 6.8%, and most soil and clay, and some rocks, can be expected to contain significant quantities of magnetite and/or hematite. As the temperature is raised, the magnetic particles of these substances are aligned by the earth's magnetic field; on cooling again, the particle directions remain fixed. Figure 35a illustrates the situation in a lump of unbaked clay by representing the particles as little bar magnets. The net magnetic effect is zero since on the average every little magnet is balanced out by another pointing in the reverse direction. Figure 35b shows the situation after baking; the lump of clay now can be regarded as a very weak permanent magnet. A wide range of magnetization can be obtained, depending on the proportions of hematite (the latter has stronger magnetism), the temperature of baking, and the magnetic field in which cooling takes place.

The Magnetic Moment

The magnetic field of the earth at any given point is defined by three measurements: the angle of declination, the angle of dip and the magnetic intensity (Figure 36). When a needle is suspended at its center of gravity so that it can swing freely in all directions, and

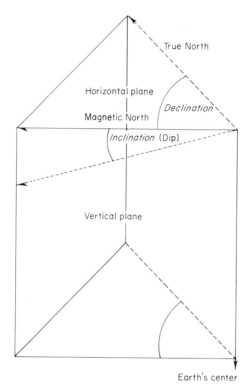

Figure 36. *The magnetic moment.*

is then magnetized, it will assume an inclination to the horizontal direction. The angle that the needle makes with the horizontal is called the *magnetic dip*. Magnetic dip is strongly latitude dependent, varying from 0 degrees (0°) at the magnetic equator to 90° at the magnetic poles. In addition to inclination, the needle will exhibit definite directions in a figurative horizontal plane. The directions defined by the needle are called *magnetic north* and *magnetic south*. The angle between magnetic north and geographic north is called the angle of declination.

If the same needle is fixed onto a horizontal axle at its center of gravity with the axle pointing to magnetic east–west so that the needle can swing freely, it will assume the angle of magnetic dip. If one were now to turn the needle 90° on its axle, the torque required to restrain it from returning to its dip position would be a measure of the *magnetic intensity*. Magnetic intensity is also strongly latitude dependent. The intensity on the magnetic equator is less than half that at the magnetic poles.

Description of Physical Process

Some magnetic oxides (hematite, for example) occur as very small grains $[10^{-5}$ to 10^{-6} centimeters $(10^{-5}$ to 10^{-6} cm$)]$ dispersed in clay. Others, such as magnetite, are dispersed in the form of larger grains $(10^{-1}$ to 10^{-2} cm$)$. For the small-grained oxides, each grain can be considered as a single magnetic particle, spontaneously magnetized along a direction determined by the shape of the grain. Larger grained oxides consist of a number of discrete particles, each of which possesses a distinctive magnetic orientation. If the temperature is high enough, the original magnetic orientation of the particles can be obliterated. This is possible when the thermal agitation energy of the grain is comparable to the energy available for retaining orientation along the preferred axis of the grain. The probability of this occurring is a function of temperature. The temperature above which magnetic orientation is possible is called the *blocking temperature*, and it bears a very close relation to the Curie point of each different magnetic oxide. The *Curie point* is the temperature above which a substance ceases to exhibit ferromagnetic properties. Blocking temperatures vary, anywhere from room temperature to 675 degrees centigrade (675°C). Since thermal agitation does not favor any particular direction, and tends to destroy any preferential alignment, the earth's magnetic field constitutes the only effective force during such periods. The orientation of the earth's magnetic field is manifested in the alignment of magnetic particles in the substance being burnt. However, since the intensity of the earth's magnetic field is relatively small, the alignment achieved by the field is far from complete, and only a portion of the magnetic particles exhibit an alignment pattern conforming to it. The remaining particles exhibit random orientation. When the temperature falls below the blocking temperature of the magnetic oxide in question, reorientation is no longer possible and the particles possessing alignment with the earth's magnetic field are frozen. This fixed alignment of magnetic particles is what is referred to as *thermoremanent magnetism*.

Factors Contributing to Error

Archaeomagnetic dating is based on the assumption that the remanent magnetization of the sample refers to the earth's field that existed when the archaeological feature cooled down for the last time. There is, however, the possibility that subsequent heating may have produced a secondary magnetization, as in the case of accidental fire. Usually visual inspection of the archaeological context of the burnt feature will suggest this if it is at all a possibility. In addition there are three causes from which remanent magnetization can be acquired without reheating: time, chemical change, and strong magnetic fields.

Time: For those magnetic particles possessing a blocking temperature just above ordinary room temperature, a remanent magnetism builds up as time elapses since initial thermal agitation. This type of remanent magnetism is referred to as *viscous magnetization*. Viscous magnetization can be removed by heating to 60 degrees centigrade (60°C), and cooling in a zero magnetic field; this leaves the major part of the thermoremanent magnetism intact.

Chemical Magnetization: Certain chemical changes in a sample can cause a magnetic mineral to be formed. Such a mineral will have a remanent magnetization in conformity with the earth's magnetic direction at the time of its formation. This chemical remanence has the stability of thermoremanent magnetism and cannot be separated, but can be mistaken for thermoremanent magnetism. The external field direction observed, therefore, may not correspond to the time of the last cooling but to this later period. Such chemical changes seldom occur in well-fired clays.

Strong External Fields: Baked clays containing magnetite are subject to particle reorientation caused by lightning flashes even at normal temperatures. A flash of lightning has a magnetic intensity sufficient to overcome the remanent stability of the magnetic particles, thus causing what is termed *isothermal remanent magnetism*. Such magnetism, however, can be separated from thermoremanent magnetism by techniques of demagnetization known as *washing* techniques. Demagnetization involves cooling the specimen down to standard room temperature from a temperature short of the thermoremanent magnetism blocking temperature in a zero magnetic field.

Field Collecting Procedures and Measurement Preparation

The primary consideration in selecting suitable burnt features for magnetic dating is whether any movement has occurred in the sample since baking. Disturbed features will introduce unknown amounts of error in the results. Second, there is the practical question of whether the samples can be extracted without breaking. Third, they should be well baked and free from impregnation of organic matter. Finally, since local magnetic fields can introduce error, it is desirable to obtain at least 5 samples from any single locality, and preferably as many as 20.

The Archaeological Research Laboratory in England, one of the principal institutions conducting research and development in this technique, has published a rating of the quality of various kinds of features with respect to archaeomagnetic dating:

Category I (good):   Structures containing a substantial floor of well-baked clay.

Category II (average):   Kilns and ovens having an intact circumference of solid wall, not less than a foot in height; well-built clay hearths.

Category III (poor):   Unsubstantial hearths, kilns with incomplete walls, patches of burning, iron-smelting sites.

Category IV (very poor):   Stone structures, poorly-fired tile, and brick ovens.

Once the best sampling area of the feature to be dated has been selected, the next step is to isolate a series of close-spaced, tiny pillars of burnt clay which can fit into the 2 by 2-inch brass frame of the extraction jig. This is a time-consuming process, since such pillars have to be excavated out from the surrounding material. The task must proceed cautiously so as not to dislodge or break off the stump-like projections that are being isolated. Dental picks, awls, knives, chisels, and other small hand tools are employed for this purpose. The burnt clay matrix is often very hard and makes the job especially difficult.

The extraction jig then is mounted, in turn, over each isolated sample. The brass frame is slipped carefully over the pillar, and with the aid of modeling clay it is carefully leveled (by reference to built-in bubbles for leveling, and oriented to present-day magnetic north. The orientation is carried out with a Brunton compass that fits over the top of the jig. Dental plaster then is poured into the frame, surrounding and covering the pillar of clay. The plaster is smoothed flush with the top of the brass frame while still wet. After the plaster has dried (a matter of a few minutes), a cutting instrument is carefully insinuated beneath the frame, and the base of the tiny pillar is cut off flush with the frame. The sample now can be moved. It is turned upside down and additional plaster is poured over the bottom and smoothed flush with the frame. Once dry, the frame is removed and a perfect 2 by 2 by 2-inch cube of white plaster is revealed. Notations are inscribed on the surfaces of the cube indicating orientation and provenience. When the cubes are received at the dating laboratory, they are routinely *washed* clean of any viscous remanent, chemical, or isothermal magnetization by means of thermal demagnetization from a temperature of 60°C to standard room temperature.

Measurement Procedure

Robert DuBois, a specialist in archaeomagnetic dating, uses what is referred to as a *parastatic magnetometer* in his specially constructed dating laboratory at the University of Oklahoma. This magnetometer embodies the principle of the compass needle. It consists of three

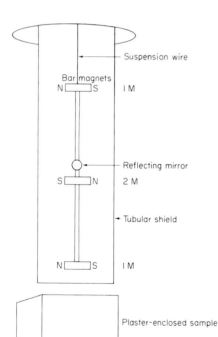

Figure 37. *The parastatic magnetometer (the middle magnet is twice as strong as the two end magnets). (From National Geographic Society painting, Weaver 1967. Adapted, with permission, from illustrations appearing in the National Geographic Magazine.)*

tiny bar magnets, spaced on a slender rod suspended from a very fine wire of phosphor bronze or quartz. The entire assembly is enclosed within a plastic tube that protects it from air currents (Figure 37). A thin beam of light shines on a mirror glued to the rod, then reflects, like a pointer, to a numbered scale (see Figure 38). The horizontal component of the earth's magnetic field is annulled by passing an electric current through large coils of wire that surround the magnetometer by means of a wooden scaffolding. Locally produced magnetic fields with a vertical gradient are annulled by the use of the three bar magnets. The upper and lower magnets are equal in strength and antiparallel to the middle magnet, which has double strength. With this arrangement there is zero torque from any vertical gradient magentic field. The entire apparatus is housed in a building

Figure 38. *Recording apparatus for parastatic magnetometer. (From National Geographic Society photo, Weaver 1967. Adapted, with permission, from illustrations appearing in the National Geographic Magazine.)*

located far from electric transformers and heavy traffic, and the building itself is built entirely of concrete and wood.

The three magnets act like a double set of diametrically opposing magnets of equal strength. Since the pull on the two parts of each magnet system is equal and opposite, the effect of the earth's field is cancelled and the beam of light points to zero. When a sample is placed on a platform directly beneath the suspended magnets, the entire assembly above it rotates slightly. This rotation is caused by the lower magnet, which is affected more strongly than the other magnets, and swings toward the direction of the sample, rotating the entire assembly as it moves. The reflected beam of light moves across the scale, exactly like a compass needle, indicating just how far the clay sample has caused the magnets to turn.

By setting the sample on its top and bottom, its angle of declination is measured directly; the angle of dip is calculated from readings taken when the sample is set on each of its four sides. These values then are used to calculate where the geomagnetic pole was located when the clay was fired. Measurements on a number of samples enable the investigator to compute a *mean vector*. This is the common and recommended practice, since samples taken from any sizable archaeomagnetic feature usually show always appreciable differences in the direction and intensity of their remanent magnetism. The differences in the angles of declination of ten samples taken from a well-preserved kiln will rarely be less than 5° (Table 7). These differences, which do not seem to follow any logical pattern, are too great to result from any faults in collection or measurement; they usually are not caused by accidental shifting of position, nor does it appear that they can be explained by any of the disturbing factors already mentioned.

Another type of magnetometer in use applies the principle of electromagnetic induction. Thus, if a magnet (in this case, an archaeomagnetic sample) is brought close to a coil or wire and there moved, an electrical voltage is set up between the ends of the coil. The voltage is greatest when the direction of the magnet's field is in alignment with the plane of the coil. The voltage can be measured by attaching the coil to a galvanometer. Disturbing magnetic fields are annulled by surrounding the apparatus with a system of Helmholz coils. Samples are measured in three positions at right angles to each other, and their magnetic direction is ascertained from the three readings. One variant of this type of magnetometer is called a ballistic

TABLE 7

Measurements Made in Paris, Oxford and Cambridge of Samples from a Kiln at Grimstone End, Suffolk[a]

Sample No.	Declination (degrees)			Inclination (degrees)			Viscosity[b]
	Paris	Oxford	Cambridge	Paris	Oxford	Cambridge	Paris
1	5.5W	1.2W	1.7W	66.4	65.6	63.5	0.9
2	6.0W	4.2W	4.0W	65.7	66.2	66.0	1.3
3	5.7W	3.2E	4.0W	67.9	67.5	67.0	0.7
4	4.25W	3.8W	3.0W	61.3	61.6	63.0	1.4
5	4.0W	2.8W	1.0W	62.7	60.7	65.0	0.4
6	2.6W	2.1W	2.5W	66.2	63.9	65.5	1.2
7	5.0W	1.9W	9.0W	66.4	65.4	68.0	0.4
8	1.8E	1.0W	0.0	67.9	68.4	67.0	0.6
9	9.5E	8.6E	10.5E	67.2	67.5	67.5	2.5
10	7.9W	5.5W	3.0W	63.9	63.6	65.5	1.1
Average	3.0W	1.1W	1.8W	65.6	65.0	65.8	

[a]From Cook (1970: Table A).

[b]The value for viscosity is the percentage decrease in the vertical component after inversion.

magnetometer, and it works by turning the sample quickly through half a circle, so producing a direct current. In the spinning magnetometer (a second variant), the sample is rotated continuously to produce an alternating current.

Chronometric Dating Applications

A chronometric date can only be obtained for a sample if the secular variation curve has been established for the region in question. The principal *field* determining magnetization is the earth. This field has several components, each of which varies more or less irregularly. The *secular* or *long-term variation* is thought to be compounded of (1) the main field of the earth, which has its North Pole to the north of Hudson Bay and is static over long periods, and (2) of several regional disturbances, which are distributed erratically and have ranges of up to 1000 miles. These regional disturbances have a limited period of growth and decay and move from east to west at a rate of about 1° in 5 years. For this reason the direction and intensity

of the earth's magnetic field at one place does not necessarily have
a completely systematic relation to its direction and intensity at another
place some hundreds of miles away.

Secular variation curves have been established for varying time
segments at only a handful of regions of the world. Thus far England,
France, Germany, Japan, and the southwestern United States have
received the most attention. Calculation of the secular variation curve
of a given region requires the presence of an independent chronometric scale with which to measure a chronologically staggered series
of archaeomagnetic determinations. In London, for example, declination and dip have been recorded for the past 400 years. These measurements provide the basis of a very sensitive secular variation curve
for the period 1600–1968 A.D. In the southwestern United States,
samples were selected for dating that were associated with timbers
dated by dendrochronology or with charcoal dated by radiocarbon
dating. In the absence of more rigorous chronometric dating
techniques, archaeomagnetic samples are assigned *estimated dates*
based on the current archaeological knowledge of the region.

DuBois (Weaver 1967) recently has established a secular variation
curve for the southwestern United States based on clay samples collected from fire pits in 16 pre-Columbian Indian villages (Figure 39).

Figure 39. *Locations of archaeomagnetic samples in the southwestern United States. The
arrows denote the site sampled and approximate paleomagnetic direction at the time of
occupation. (From National Geographic Society painting, Weaver 1967. Adapted, with permission, from illustrations appearing in the National Geographic Magazine.)*

By determining the magnetic alignment of his samples, whose ages were already known from carbon-14 dating or tree-ring analysis of timbers found in the same ruins, DuBois worked out a polar *calendar* extending back almost 2000 years. The geomagnetic pole seen from the vantage point of the southwestern United States, has meandered 8,800 miles during that period of time (Figure 40). He reports that he can achieve accuracy to within 50 years, much greater accuracy than possible with the radiocarbon samples of the same hearths (Weaver 1967).

As of this writing, only one archaeomagnetic dating laboratory is operational in the United States, and this is the one at the University of Oklahoma under the supervision of Robert DuBois. He is currently involved in the collection of datable samples from all over the North and South American continents for the purpose of establishing a

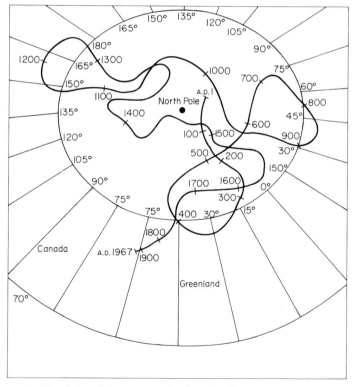

Figure 40. *Meandering of the geomagnetic pole with reference to the southwestern United States. (From National Geographic Society painting, Weaver 1967. Adapted, with permission, from illustrations appearing in the National Geographic Magazine.)*

series of secular variation curves that will provide the basis for wide-spread application of this dating technique by archaeologists throughout the New World.

M. J. Aitken and others in Britain continue to extend and refine existing secular variation curves for European regions, and to assist in the establishment of new ones. Scientists in Eastern Europe and Asia also are working at similar tasks in their own regions. Until these curves are more numerous and in operational status, archaeomagnetic dating will continue to remain a technique of limited applicability. There is every reason to predict, however, that in a relatively short time this technique will be almost as ubiquitous as radiocarbon dating.

Dating by Archaeomagnetic Intensity Measurements

A related, but different method of chronometric dating also based on the principles of archaeomagnetism is *paleointensity* dating. This method, still in its experimental stage, can be applied to disturbed burnt clay features as well as a whole range of portable ceramic artifacts, including pottery, figurines, and bricks. This is possible because, unlike *directional* archaeomagnetic dating, which requires knowledge of *in situ* declination and dip, archaeomagnetic intensity dating only requires knowledge of the intensity of the magnetic field at the time of firing.

Although this technique can make use of the same samples as *directional* archaeomagnetic dating, and although it requires the same measuring apparatus, it is fundamentally a different kind of dating technique. It has different capabilities and limitations, different sources of error, and lags significantly behind *directional* archaeomagnetic dating in research and development.

The principle underlying the technique is that the thermoremanent magnetization of burnt clay is proportional to the intensity of the magnetic field acting on the clay as it cools down from heating. By comparing the strength of the thermoremanent magnetization found in an archaeological burnt clay sample with the value acquired after reheating in the present-day earth's magnetic field, the *ratio* of the prehistoric and present-day fields can be obtained.

With the aid of an independent chronometric scale, such as dendrochronology, these ratios can be used to construct a secular variation curve of the earth's magnetic field intensity for a given archaeological region. Individual ratio determinations of diagnostic clay artifacts from sites within that region then can be dated by locating the points along the curve with which they correspond.

Selection of Samples

V. Bucha, a geophysicist in Czechoslovakia, has played a prominent role in the refinement of the technique, originally developed by Thellier in France. Bucha (1967) reports that he has had good results with burnt clay, kilns, and fireplaces, and less satisfactory results with brick, pottery, and furnace slag.

Samples are selected on the basis of color. Burnt-clay artifacts or features having *brown-red* or *red* colors tend to give reliable results (these colors result from baking at a temperature of between 500 and 900°C). Fired bricks tend to be exposed to temperatures above 1000°C, and this has been thought to be a source of error in measurement due to the possibility that magnetite may have been formed spontaneously at such high temperatures. Gray- or black-colored furnace slags and pottery with *brown-red* exteriors but gray or black interiors also present inconsistencies in dating results. A further consideration is whether the original heating of the sample was uniform. For this reason, it is better to date specimens of smaller size that were baked uniformly throughout than to use a large sample, which may have been heated unevenly.

Laboratory Procedures

The specimens to be measured are cut to a cubic form, generally no larger than 2 cm. Measurements of the thermoremanent magnetization intensity are made on any of the magnetometers described earlier. In the rotating type of magnetometer, readings of intensity are taken directly from the galvanometer. With the parastatic type, it is possible to restrict the swing of the magnet system by suspending it on a torsion fiber, and permitting the intensity of the specimen to be calculated from the degree to which it can deflect the magnet system when at a given distance from the specimen.

In order to control for error, a step-by-step technique of heating to successively higher temperatures and taking intensity measurements at each step must be used. Using a thermostatically controlled oven with a magnetic shield, the samples are heated successively, first in one position and then in a reversed position, to temperatures of 100, 150, 250, 300, 350, 400, and 500°C. A curve then is generated from the *sum* of the measurements obtained for the initial and reversed positions for each temperature, and a second curve is derived from the *differences* between these measurements. Figure 41 gives the first and second curves (demagnetization curve and magnetization curve, respectively) for baked clay from the archaeological site, Zelénky, in Czechoslovakia. In addition, the figure gives a plot (c) of the demagnetization value corresponding to a given temperature (*y* axis) versus the remagnetization value for the same temperature (*x* axis). Ideally, these points lie on a straight line, the slope of which gives the value of the coefficient *k* (the ratio of the original field intensity to the present one).

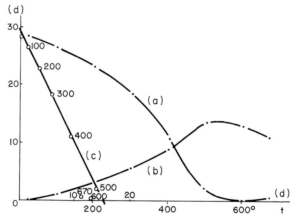

Figure 41. (a) Demagnetization curve and (b) remagnetization curve for a sample from Zelénky, Czechoslovakia. The straight line (c) shows the relationship between demagnetization and remagnetization for various maximum temperatures (horizontal scale d is applicable for this); k = 202. (From Bucha, V. Intensity of the earth's magnetic field during archaeological times in Czechoslovakia. Archaeometry, **10**: 1967, Fig. 3. By permission of Cambridge University Press.)

This graphical method permits the analyst to judge more reliably which points should be taken into consideration and which must be excluded. If it is possible to draw a straight line through at least four successive points, and if this line is defined for at least two-thirds of its course between the *y* and *x* axis, the results should be valid.

Archaeological Applications

The results of recent studies of archaeomagnetic intensity in France, the Soviet Union, Japan, Czechoslovakia, and England have yielded new knowledge about the variation of intensity of the earth's magnetic field for the geologically Recent period. A program for establishing secular variation curves for various parts of the world seems to be under way. Such curves will enable archaeologists to date disturbed features as well as portable artifacts of clay.

Probably the best example of an intensity variation curve that is now operational is the one produced by Bucha (1967) for Czechoslovakia, and extended several thousand years with additional data from Turkey (Figure 42). The graph indicates that the earth's magnetic

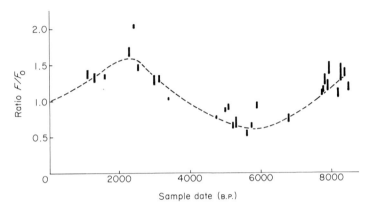

Figure 42. *Secular intensity–variation curve, Czechoslovakia (B.P., before present). (From Bucha, V. Intensity of the earth's magnetic field during archaeological times in Czechoslovakia. Archaeometry,* **10:** *1967, Fig. 10. By permission of Cambridge University Press.)*

field intensity has its maximum around 400 B.C. when the value of the field reaches 1.6 times its present intensity. The minimum occurs between 4000 and 3500 B.C. when the field drops to around 0.6 times its present intensity. For still older periods, the intensity of the magnetic field once again is higher.

READINGS

Aitken, M. J.
    1961   *Physics and archaeology.* New York and London: Wiley (Interscience).
    1966   Magnetic field work. *Archaeometry* **9:** 200.
Aitken, M. J., and H. N. Hawley
    1966   Magnetic Dating—III, Further archaeomagnetic measurements in Britain. *Archaeometry* **9:** 187–197.

Aitken, M. J., and H. N. Hawley
  1967   Archaeomagnetic measurements in Britain—IV. *Archaeometry* **10**: 129–135.
  1971   Archaeomagnetism: Evidence for magnetic refraction in kiln structure. *Archaeometry* **13**: 83–86.
Aitken, M. J., and G. H. Weaver
  1962   Magnetic dating: Some archaeomagnetic measurements in Britain. *Archaeometry* **5**: 4–22.
Aitken, M. J., H. N. Hawley, and G. H. Weaver
  1963   Magnetic dating: Further archaeomagnetic measurements in Britain. *Archaeometry* **6**: 76–80.
Athauale, R. N.
  1966   Intensity of the geomagnetic field in India over the past 4000 years. *Nature* **210**: 1310–1312.
Bucha, V.
  1965   Results of archaeomagnetic research in Czechoslovakia for the epoch 4400 B.C. to the present. *Journal of Geomagnetism and Geoelectricity* **17**: 407–412.
  1967   Intensity of the earth's magnetic field during archaeological times in Czechoslovakia. *Archaeometry* **10**: 12–22.
  1971   Archaeomagnetic dating. In *Dating techniques for the archaeologist* edited by H. N. Michael and E. K. Ralph. Cambridge, Massachusetts: M.I.T. Press.
Bucha, V., and J. Mellaart
  1967   Archaeomagnetic intensity measurements on some Neolithic samples from Catal Hüyük (Anatolia). *Archaeometry* **10**: 23–25.
Bucha, V., R. E. Taylor, R. Berger, and E. W. Haury
  1970   Geomagnetic intensity: Changes during the past 3000 years in the western hemisphere. *Science* **168**: 111–114.
Burlatskaya, S. P., I. E. Nachasova, T. B. Nechaeva, O. M. Rusakov, G. F. Zagniy, E. N. Tarhov, and Z. A. Tchelioze
  1970   Archaeomagnetic research in the USSR: Recent results and spectral analysis. *Archaeometry* **12**: 73–86.
Cook, R. M.
  1958   Intensity of remanent magnetization of archaeological remains. *Nature* **181**: 1421–1422.
  1970   Archaeomagnetism. In *Science in archaeology,* edited by D. Brothwell and E. Higgs. New York: Praeger.
Cook, R. M., and J. C. Belshe
  1958   Archaeomagnetism: A preliminary report on Britain. *Antiquity* **32**: 167–178.
DuBois, R. L.
  1968   Personal communication. Guatemala City.
Haigh, G.
  1958   The process of magnetization by chemical change. *Philosophical Magazine* **3** (8th series): 267–286.
Harold, M. R.
  1960   Magnetic dating III—The spinning magnetometer. *Archaeometry* **3**: 15–21.
Kitazawa, K., and K. Kobayashi
  1968   Intensity variation of the geomagnetic field during the past 4000 years in South America. *Journal of Geomagnetism and Geoelectricity.* **20**: 1–7.
Malin, S. R. C.
  1969   Geomagnetic secular variation and its changes, 1942.5 to 1962.5. *The Geophysical Journal* **17**: 415–441.

Nagata, T., K. Kobayashi, and E. J. Schwarz
   1965   Archaeomagentic intensity studies of Southern and Central America. *Journal of Geomagnetism and Geoelectricity* **17**: 399–406.
Sasajima, S.
   1965   Geomagnetic secular variation revealed in baked earths from western Japan. *Journal of Geomagnetism and Geoelectricity* **17**: 413.
Schwarz, E. J., and K. W. Christie
   1967   Original remanent magnetization of Ontario potsherds. *Journal of Geophysical Research* **72**: 3263–3269.
Tanguy, J. C.
   1970   An archaeomagnetic study of Mount Etna: The magnetic direction recorded in lava flows subsequent to the twelfth century. *Archaeometry* **12**: 115–128.
Thellier, E.
   1938   Sur L'aimantation des terres cuites et ses applications géophysiques. *Ann. Inst. Phys. Globe* **16**: 157–302.
   1966   Le champ magnétique terrestre fossile. *Nucleus* **7**: 1–35.
Thellier, E., and O. Thellier
   1959   Sur L'intensité du champ magnétique terrestre dans le passé historique et géologique. *Annals of Geophysics* **15**: 285–376.
Watanabe, N.
   1958   Secular variation in the direction of geomagnetism as the standard scale for geomagnetochronology in Japan. *Nature* **182**: 383–384.
   1959   The direction of remanent magnetism of baked earth and its application to chronology in Japan. *Journal of the Faculty of Science, Tokyo University* **2**, Section 5: 1–188.
Weaver, G. H.
   1966   Measurement of the past intensity of the earth's magnetic field. *Archaeometry* **9**: 174–186.
   1970   Some temperature related errors in palaeomagnetic intensity measurements. *Archaeometry* **12**: 87–96.
Weaver, F.
   1967   Magnetic clues help date the past. *National Geographic* **131**: 696–701.

CHAPTER NINE

Radiocarbon Dating

Introduction

Radiocarbon dating is by far the most widely used method of chronometric dating available. It gained acceptance among archaeologists during the late 1950s, and is now undertaken in such volume that commercial dating laboratories have sprung up to compete for the business. Research and development laboratories at universities across the country and elsewhere have refined the technique and have extended the range of materials to which the method can usefully be applied.

Underlying Principles of the Technique

Radiocarbon dating had its origin in a study of the possible effects that cosmic rays might have on the earth and on the earth's atmosphere. Willard F. Libby, Nobel Laureate in chemistry for his pioneering work in developing this technique, has provided us with a thorough account of the early research in this method (Libby 1961). He credits Serge Korff with having discovered that neutrons are produced when cosmic rays enter the earth's atmosphere. These particles, being uncharged, are very effective in causing transmutations in the nucleus of any atom with which they collide. Neutrons were found to have an intensity that corresponded to the generation of about two neutrons per second for each square centimeter of the earth's surface. Libby theorized that, upon entering the earth's atmosphere, they would react with nitrogen-14. The reaction produces a heavy isotope of carbon, carbon-14, which is radioactive. Knowing that there are about two neutrons formed per square centimeter per second, each of which forms a carbon-14 atom, and assuming that the cosmic rays have been bombarding the atmosphere for a very long time in terms of the lifetime of carbon-14 (carbon-14 has a half-life of 5730 years), Libby observed that a steady-state condition should have been established in which the rate of formation of carbon-14 would be equal to the rate at which it disappears to re-form nitrogen-14.

The two carbon-14 atoms per second per square centimeter go into a mixing reservoir that consists not only of living matter, but also of the dissolved carbonaceous material in the oceans, which can exchange carbon with the atmospheric carbon dioxide. For each square centimeter of the earth's surface, there are about 7.25 grams (7.25 gm) of carbon dissolved in the ocean in the form of carbonate, bicarbonate, and carbonic acid, and the biosphere itself contains about 0.33 gm per square centimeter of surface. Adding all the elements of the reservoir, Libby observed that one arrived at a total of 8.5 gm of diluting carbon per square centimeter, and that the two carbon-14 atoms disintegrating every second should be contained in 8.5 gm of carbon. Libby found this to be the actual value observed, to within 10%.

Libby argued that, by accepting the above assumptions, one can assert that organic matter, while it is alive, is in equilibrium with the cosmic radiation, and all radiocarbon atoms that disintegrate in living things are replaced by the carbon-14 entering the food chain by photosynthesis. At the time of death, however, the assimilation process stops abruptly. There is no longer any process by which carbon-14 from the atmosphere can enter the body. At that time, the radioactive disintegration process takes over in an uncompensated manner and, according to the law of radioactive decay, after 5730 years the carbon that was in the body while it was alive will show half the specific carbon-14 radioactivity that it showed previously. In the disintegration process, the carbon-14 returns to nitrogen-14, emitting a beta particle in the process. The half-life is measured by counting the number of beta radiations emitted per minute per gram of material. Modern carbon-14 emits about 15 counts per minute per gram, whereas carbon-14, which is 5700 years old, should emit about 7.5 counts per minute per gram.

The Half-Life of Carbon-14

The present "official" half-life of carbon-14 is 5568 ± 30 years, and was derived from the weighted average of three determinations: 5580 ± 45 years, 5589 ± 75 years, 5513 ± 165 years. During both the Fifth (1962) and Sixth (1965) International Radiocarbon Dating Conferences, serious consideration was given to changing this established half-life in light of very solid evidence that it was incorrect. Three new and independent determinations of the half-life of carbon-14 were reported at the 1962 meeting. Using these reports as a basis, the participants of the conference agreed that the average of the three new values, 5730 ± 40 years, was the best value available. The same decision was reached at the 1965 conference. The primary reason for the decision to continue using Libby's original half-life of 5568 years was to avoid the confusion that would result from such a change. Individual users of carbon-14 dates are encouraged to use the new half-life value to achieve closer correlation with dates derived by other means. Conversion from the old to the new value can be done simply by multiplying the old date by a factor of 1.029.

Error in the Radiocarbon Calendar

When Libby initiated the method, it was necessary for him to assume that the worldwide inventory of natural carbon-14 had been constant for several mean lifetimes of carbon-14 (a mean lifetime is approximately 8000 years). Since the production of carbon-14 in the upper atmosphere is by the reaction

$$^{14}N + n = {}^{14}C + {}^{1}H$$

and since there is an abundant supply of nitrogen, this constancy is dependent upon the cosmic ray intensity and, therefore, upon the intensity of the magnetic field of the earth. When the magnetic field is greater, fewer cosmic rays reach the upper atmosphere.

Measuring the intensity of the magnetic field of the earth in past times has become possible through developments in archaeomagnetic dating. The results of such dating suggest that fluctuation in intensity can account for at least half of the magnitude of radiocarbon deviations (Ralph 1971, Bucha 1971).

In order to assess the magnitude of the discrepancies between radiocarbon years and calendar years that may have been produced through such magnetic intensity fluctuations, or through other causes, the staff of the Radiocarbon Dating Laboratories of the University of Pennsylvania and the University of California and the staff of the Laboratory of Tree-Ring Research at the University of Arizona collaborated on the radiocarbon dating of wood samples for which a true age had been established through dendrochronology. The series of wood samples were correlated with points on a master tree-ring log that extends from the present back to 5145 B.C.

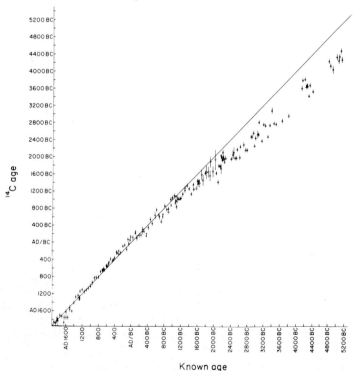

Figure 43. *Carbon-14 dates on Sequoia and bristlecone pine tree-ring samples. (From Ralph 1971: Fig. 1.1.)*

In Figure 43 one can see that the most pronounced fluctuation between radiocarbon chronology and absolute time is a long-term one that starts in the first millennium B.C. and continues back in time to the present limit of dated samples. In addition to this long-term deviation from steady-state carbon-14 inventories, there appear to be some shorter-term fluctuations. These can be of sufficient magnitude as to cause ambiguity for dating, and the discrepancy may be as large as 200 years. For the sake of clarity, therefore, archaeologists refer to carbon-14 age determinations as *radiocarbon years*, to differentiate them from *calendar years*. Fortunately, the dendrochronology date/radiocarbon date correlation that allows us to measure the magnitude of radiocarbon deviation also allows us to calculate correction factors that enable the archaeologist to adjust his radiocarbon years to calendar years (Suess 1970; Ralph 1971) (see Table 8).

The Preparation and Dating of Samples

Each kind of material poses special problems with regard to preparation for dating. Several of the more widely dated materials are discussed separately later on in this chapter. In general, however, the archaeologist must recover enough material to provide carbon in sufficient quantity that reliable results can be expected. Upon arrival at the radiocarbon dating laboratory the material (bone, charcoal, wood, iron, etc.) is examined, and obvious contaminants are mechanically and chemically removed. The material then is converted into a gas form—carbon dioxide, methane, acetylene, or benzene—by burning or by other means. The gas, however, contains radioactive and electronegative impurities derived from the original material. These are removed in an elaborate vacuum system, through which the sample passes (Figure 44). The purified sample, which contains impurities of less than one part in 1×10^5, is then piped into a *proportional counter*.

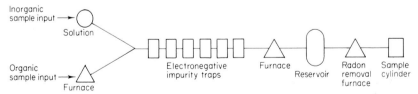

Figure 44. *Schematic drawing of carbon dioxide combustion and purification train. (Adapted from Ralph 1971.)*

TABLE 8 *MASCA Correction Factors*[a,b]

Time period represented by radiocarbon dates	Average deviation of ^{14}C dates (+ = younger, – = older)	Calendric period represented by precisely dated tree-ring samples	Number of samples
A.D. 1525 – 1879	+50	A.D. 1500 – 1829 (329 years)	12
A.D. 1250 – 1524	0	A.D. 1250 – 1499	7
A.D. 975 – 1249	0	A.D. 1000 – 1249	8
A.D. 700 – 974	–50	A.D. 750 – 999	4
A.D. 450 – 699	–50	A.D. 500 – 749	11
A.D. 200 – 449	–50	A.D. 250 – 499	9
A.D. 25 – 200 A.D.	–50	A.D. 1 – 249	7
B.C. 225 – 26 B.C.	0	249 – 1 B.C.	7
450 – 226 B.C.	+50	499 – 250 B.C.	7
675 – 451 B.C.	+50	749 – 500 B.C.	7
900 – 676 B.C.	+100	999 – 750 B.C.	8
1125 – 901 B.C.	+100	1249 – 1000 B.C.	10
1325 – 1126 B.C.	+150	1499 – 1250 B.C.	4
1550 – 1326 B.C.	+200	1749 – 1500 B.C.	9
1750 – 1551 B.C.	+200	1999 – 1750 B.C.	6
1900 – 1751 B.C.	+300	2249 – 2000 B.C.	12
2050 – 1900 B.C.	+400	2499 – 2250 B.C.	4
2225 – 2051 B.C.	+500	2749 – 2500 B.C.	6
2450 – 2226 B.C.	+550	2999 – 2750 B.C.	6
2650 – 2451 B.C.	+550	3249 – 3000 B.C.	7
2850 – 2651 B.C.	+650	3499 – 3250 B.C.	5
[3700 – 2951 B.C.]	+700	[4395 – 3645 B.C.] (750 years)	11
[4366 – 4060 B.C.]	+750	[5116 – 4810 B.C.] (306 years)	9
			Total 176

[a]From Ralph (1971: Table 1.5).

[b]Suggested method of adjustment of radiocarbon dates to calendric dates based on the determination of average deviations for 250-year periods in the A.D. and B.C. eras except for the first and last two periods which span longer intervals of years. The ^{14}C dates are calculated with the 5,730 year half-life.

153

The Proportional Counter

A proportional counter operates on the principle that the size of electrical pulses originating in it is proportional to the energy of the beta particle initiating each pulse. The beta particles from carbon-14 have energies ranging from zero up to 150,000 electron volts (150 keV). An electric pulse analyzer is used to reject pulses corresponding to a beta-particle energy of greater than 160 keV in order to discriminate against interfering high-energy background. The proportional counter also must be shielded from background radiation coming from the earth, such as uranium, thorium, and potassium. The shield consists of about 8 inches of iron.

Cosmic rays, however, consisting largely of μ-mesons (or muons), easily penetrate the thick iron shield. The count rate of background radiation without a shield is about 1500 counts per minute, and is decreased to about 400 counts per minute by the iron shield. The remaining activity, due largely to μ-mesons, is removed by surrounding the proportional counter (with the carbon dating sample inside it) with a complete layer of Geiger counters (Figure 45). The Geiger counters are in tangential contact with one another and wired so that when any one of them counts, the central proportional counter with the dating sample is turned off for about one-thousandth of a second. In this way the μ-mesons are eliminated from the record, and background radiation is reduced to something between 1 and 8 counts per minute.

The sample is counted for 1000-min intervals and each sample is counted at least twice, preferably with at least a week intervening

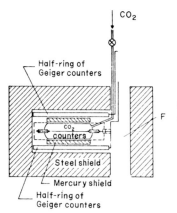

Figure 45. *Block diagram of a carbon dioxide counter and surrounding cosmic ray counters. (After Ralph 1971: Fig. 15.)*

between the two counts. The net activity of the sample (gross counts per minute minus background counts per minute) then is compared with the activity of a *modern standard*, and an age determination is computed together with a statistical limit of accuracy. The modern standard is prepared by the National Bureau of Standards to simulate the atmosphere carbon-14 activity of the year 1950, as it should have been without the effects of nuclear explosions and industrial coal burning. At the Fifth Radiocarbon Dating Conference, it was agreed to use A.D. 1950 as the standard for computing dates B.P. (before present).

Calculation of a Radiocarbon Date

The procedure for calculating a radiocarbon date has recently been summarized by Ralph (1971). The applicable equation, according to Ralph is:

$$I = I_0 e^{-\lambda t}, \tag{1}$$

where

I = the activity of the sample when measured;
I_0 = the original activity of the sample (as reflected by a modern standard);
λ = the decay constant = $0.693/T_{1/2}$ with $T_{1/2}$ the half-life;
t = time elapsed.

If $T_{1/2}$ = 5568 years, then we can write the equation for a routine calculation as

$$t = \log \frac{I_0}{I} \times 18.5 \times 10^3 \text{ years.} \tag{2}$$

Isotopic Fractionation

Under certain circumstances it is desirable to apply a correction factor to the final measurement in order to control for possible isotopic fractionation. By *fractionation* is meant a change in the natural carbon-14–carbon-12 ratio by causes other than radiocarbon decay. Peculiarities of different specimen materials and in processing can cause fractionation. The fractionation effect can be determined indirectly by measuring carbon-13–carbon-12 ratios. This is done with the aid of a mass spectrograph. Isotopic fractionation is often a significant factor in the comparative dating of inorganic and organic samples.

Isotopic Enrichment

The level of the counter background sets a practical limit of about 50,000 years to the age that can be determined. The limit can be extended by artificial enrichment of the carbon-14 relative to the carbon-12 with the aid of a thermal diffusion column. Work along this line has already indicated that an enrichment factor of 12, corresponding to an increase of 20,000 years in the limiting age, can be achieved. Thus, at the present time, the technique of radiocarbon dating has an operational limit of 70,000 years (Haring *et al.* 1958).

How to Interpret a Radiocarbon Date

Each radiocarbon date calculated has an associated *standard deviation*. This is a measure of the natural statistical dispersion of a series of readings or observations about a mean value. In dating samples of carbon, the standard deviation emphasizes the random nature of radioactive decay. The carbon-14 date is directly related to the level of radioactivity and it must permit some allowance for random decay. For example, a date of 1200 ± 100 B.C. does not mean that the sample material dates to exactly 1200 B.C., but only that there are approximately two chances out of three that the true age of the sample falls somewhere within the range given, that is, between 1300 and 1100 B.C. If we had two contemporaneous samples, it would only be by the purest chance that both would produce the exact date 1200 ± 100 B.C. All that we are permitted to expect is that the total ranges of the two dates in question overlap.

A tightly knit stratigraphic sequence for which we have a sample from each level is not likely to be represented by a series of mean radiocarbon values that seriate perfectly. There will be a general trend from older to younger, which corresponds roughly to the stratigraphy, lower to upper, but the correspondence very likely will exhibit disturbing exceptions. By plotting the calculated standard deviation the overlap of the ranges of time for dating the samples from successive strata is likely to produce a more plausible time sequence with every date in the series fitting the stratigraphy.

Radiocarbon dates obtained from different kinds of materials are fully comparable, as is illustrated by the recent dating of the skin tissue, bone collagen, and vegetal clothing of a well preserved Nevada mummy by Orr and Berger (1965). The mummy, commonly referred to as *Whiskey Lil*, was discovered in 1955 in Chimney Cave, Lake Winnemucca, Nevada. The good preservation was due to the extremely dry desert air. The mummy is that of an adult female who had been buried in a tightly flexed position. Apart from the face, most of the skin was intact. The body was wrapped in a mountain sheep hide and was covered with a loosely woven blanket or mat of cedar bark.

A section of the rib weighing 50 gm was removed from the upper thorax, freed of dust and connective tissue, and treated with hydrochloric acid to destroy the mineral matrix. The collagen, thus isolated, was washed, dried, and burned to carbon dioxide. After being purified, the carbon dioxide was admitted into a proportional counter of the radiocarbon laboratory at the University of California at Los Angeles. In repeated counting for 1000-min intervals, it yielded a radiocarbon date of 2500 ± 80 years.

A second measurement was made from skin tissue. Twelve grams of skin, similarly cleaned and converted to carbon dioxide, produced an average date of 2510 ± 80 years from several counts. Finally, a sample of the cedar bark mat was dated. After treatment with hydrochloric acid to remove calcium carbonate dust and rat excrement, about 15 gm of mat was burned to carbon dioxide and then purified. The sample yielded a date of 2590 ± 80 years. All three dates overlap extensively when their standard deviations are considered.

Radiocarbon Date Reporting

The growing number of laboratories publishing radiocarbon dates and the resulting rapid increase in the number of dates being reported annually are indicators of the general acceptance of the validity of the radiocarbon dating technique by archaeologists. In 1959, 10 years after the first determinations were published, the first volume of the *Radiocarbon Supplement* of the *American Journal of Science* carried a roster of 36 laboratories and published the date lists of 14. The 1966 edition of *Radiocarbon* (Volume 8) listed 70 active laboratories and published the date lists of 33. To most users of radiocarbon dates, it has become apparent that an efficient means of reporting and locating the thousands of available dates is needed.

At present, probably the most comprehensive retrieval system for radiocarbon dates is the file of McBee edge-punched cards prepared for Radiocarbon Dates Association, Inc., Massachusetts. This card file is an important index source; however, it has difficulty keeping up with the volume of new dates being published. Also, some critics point to the tedious and time-consuming operation of retrieval using the needle-point technique. The need for a more flexible index for radiocarbon dates with shorter retrieval times has led to experiments with electronic data-processing systems of storage and retrieval for radiocarbon dates. A suggested format for coding radiocarbon data on IBM punch cards and techniques for the rapid retrieval of desired information are provided by Taylor *et al.* (1968: 180–184). They provide for coding such information as archaeological and geographical provenience, counting technique, material, statistical error, published references, and the name of the dating laboratory.

An index of radiocarbon dates associated with cultural materials for the period 1949–1962 has been completed by Jelinek (1962), and contains nearly 2500 dates. These were brought together from approximately 115 separate documentary sources.

Radiocarbon Dating of Charcoal

Charcoal has acquired primary importance as a source of radioactive carbon for the purposes of dating. Cook (1964), however, has observed a tendency on the part of the archaeologist to assume that any black, crumbly, amorphous substance found on or excavated from the earth is charcoal, and further, that being charcoal, it consists almost exclusively of elementary carbon. These assumptions, according to Cook, are not always justified. He points out that the sources of elementary or fixed carbon in any soil are two in number. One consists of carbonized or charred organic matter produced by fire of either human or natural origin. This is the component upon which archaeologists have focused attention.

The other consists of organic compounds manufactured initially by local vegetation or deposited as a result of those human activities that do not concern burning. Normal plant residues, together with all kinds of detritus caused by human occupation, undergo a long series of transformations. The general consequence is the formation and accumulation of a highly variable substance known as *humus*. The mature product of humification has a color, form, and consistency very similar to that of the charcoal derived from other sources and may very easily be mistaken for it. Humus is the final product of reactions that have been going on for a very long time. During that time the original substance may have been reworked repeatedly, with the consequent addition of new carbon compounds and the loss of old. The resulting humus therefore cannot automatically be assigned to a specific time in the past.

The debris from fires is a different category. During the high-temperature combustion of wood, much of the organic matter undergoes rapid oxidation to carbon dioxide, often leaving the mineral behind as a light-colored ash. However, more or less incomplete combustion occurs in most outdoor fires. Black material (charcoal) remains and consists of some pure carbon but also much condensed organic matter.

Thus, according to Cook, the first task of the archaeologist is to take the sample from an excavation and determine by chemical means its probable origin and its composition in terms of elemental or fixed carbon. He should be able to state whether his sample has been derived from prolonged humification, or from fire, or from both.

When it has been determined that the sample is charcoal, it is submitted to the dating laboratory, where it is first treated for removal of contaminants. Rootlets, often microscopic in size, are a source of modern carbon in such samples and are mechanically and chemically eliminated. Carbonates and humic acids, introduced to the sample by groundwater, are decomposed by alternately leaching the sample with dilute hydrochloric acid and sodium hydroxide and washing it with distilled water. Next, the sample is converted into carbon dioxide, methane, acetylene, or benzene for measurement in the counting equipment described earlier.

Radiocarbon Dating of Wood

When animal remnants are radiocarbon dated, every part of the body gives approximately the same age because carbon in the body is derived directly or indirectly from plants. Usually the plant parts used for animal food are leaves, herbaceous stems, or seeds, that is, parts of plants that have only recently incorporated atmospheric carbon dioxide through photosynthesis. Also, animal cells lack the rather thick cell walls, made up of various carbohydrates, so characteristic of plant cells, and most cells that make up the body of an animal continue their metabolism as long as the body stays alive. There is thus a continuous elimination and intake of elements in an animal body, including carbon and carbon-14. As a result, when the animal's metabolism ceases at death, most of its carbon will be modern carbon.

In plants, particularly woody plants, the situation is very different. The bulk of a tree consists of wood. The wood of conifers consists of tracheids, wood parenchyma, and resinferous ducts. That of broad-leaved trees consists of vessels, tracheid fibers, wood parenchyma, and, in certain cases, lacticiferous or gummiferous ducts. The tracheids and vessels function as conducting tubes for water and dissolved minerals. They consist of cells devoid of living protoplasm and are thus incapable of metabolism. The same can be said of fibers, the walls of which are even thicker. The wood parenchyma and the secretory cells of ducts are living cells, but their life span is relatively short.

In a stem, the wood is arranged in concentric growth rings, each of which represents one year's growth. The more central rings are the oldest and the peripheral rings are the youngest. Thus, the age of wood decreases from the center of the stem to the periphery. The vessels and tracheids in the older growth rings eventually cease even their water conducting activities. This more central, nonfunctioning, portion of the tree stem is called *heartwood,* while the more external part of the stem is known as *sapwood.*

It thus can happen that if various sections of a tree are radiocarbon dated, they could give off different dates—each corresponding to the cessation of metabolic activity in that particular section. Furthermore, if many growth rings are included in the sample, the age obtained will not be that of any particular ring but will represent the average for the rings included.

The implications for the archaeologist are clear according to Kovar (1966). The dating of construction timbers involves an additional error factor that must be taken into consideration. This is especially true for timbers or beams that have been burned. The burning removes the outer rings, which disperse in the form of ash. Only the carbonized central part remains compact. Dating this central part or heartwood will consistently yield dates that are older than dates obtained by other means, and cannot possibly indicate the time when the tree was cut for use in construction.

Radiocarbon Dating of Bone and Shell

Dry modern bone is composed approximately of 50% calcium phosphate (containing inorganic carbon), 10% calcium carbonate (also containing inorganic carbon), 25% collagen (an organic protein constituent), and 5–10% bone fat. There have been attempts to use the carbonate portion of bones for radiocarbon dating by generating carbon dioxide by means of hydrochloric acid. Efforts also have been made to extract inorganic carbon from calcium phosphate. Error, however, is a serious problem in both cases because of the incidence of groundwater contamination, as groundwater contains atmospheric carbon dioxide of modern carbon-14 age.

This has led to the dating of bones from their collagen, since collagen does not suffer from *exchange* phenomena (Berger *et al.* 1964). There is no known natural mechanism by which collagen may be altered to yield a false age. A problem does arise, however, because the collagen content of bone decreases with age to such low concentrations that isolation of sufficient collagen for radiocarbon dating becomes difficult with the oldest bones. The oldest specimen that has been dated in this way had a collagen content of about 0.16%; it was approximately 9000 years old (UCLA-630). Unfortunately, collagen does not decrease uniformly with age. Bones of the same age have a different collagen content in different environmental conditions in which they were buried. This is due to such factors as groundwater erosion, collagenase activity in the bone, and invasion of saprophytes, which feed on the organic material.

In preparation for dating, bones must be checked microscopically for bore canals that contain foreign protein. After thorough cleaning, the bone is treated in hydrochloric acid at room temperature. This dissolves the mineral matter but leaves behind about 95% of the collagen as insoluble material. The collagen then is filtered off and allowed to dry. After drying, it is converted to carbon dioxide.

Radiocarbon laboratories have reported many shell dates from the carbonate of the shell as the sample. Recently, there has been a growing lack of confidence in the reliability of the dates from river shells and land snail shells because of the varying and unknown amounts of *dead* carbonate from limestone that are incorporated by the living organisms.

This problem is not encountered with marine shells, but when marine shells are dead and buried, they may be subjected—like bones—to various groundwater environments. Investigators have attempted to circumvent possible errors arising from carbonate exchange by removing the outer layer of shells with hydrochloric acid and using only the central portion for dating.

Similar to bones, shells also contain an organic protein constituent, conchiolin, which is present in 1–2% amounts in modern shells. Its solubility characteristics are similar to those of collagen. Thus, conchiolin can be relied on for dating to the same extent as collagen in bones. Good-sized quantities of both bone and shell are needed for dating. Kilogram amounts of raw materials of shells are required and decagram amounts for bones (10 gm of collagen yield 5 gm of carbon).

Radiocarbon Dating of Iron

Iron, when reduced from its ores by man, contains carbon; if it did not, it would be too soft to be of any use in the fashioning of tools and weapons. The basic alloys of iron—wrought iron, steel, and cast iron—are distinguished from one another by differences in carbon content (steel 0.1–2.0%; wrought iron less than 0.06%; cast iron 1.5–5.0%). The carbon in iron alloys derives from the fuel used in smelting. When the smelting fuel involved is charcoal or wood (nearly exclusively the case until 1709), a carbon-14 activity measurement of the carbon in an iron specimen can provide a date for its manufacture (Van de Merwe 1968).

To date iron, one follows the same procedures as with organic samples: (1) the sample is treated against possible contaminants; (2) the carbon is extracted in a form in which its carbon-14 activity can be measured. The carbon in an iron sample that has been buried in the ground is not subject to the contamination by rootlets, carbonates, and humic acid; it is in fact sealed in a sterile environment at the time of manufacture. Iron, however, corrodes easily when sufficient moisture and oxygen are present; most ancient iron specimens have at least a layer of iron oxide. The corrosion layer is porous and may entrap small quantities of organic materials, especially at the surface. A further problem may result from the fact that a corroded surface absorbs more atmospheric carbon dioxide than does a clean iron surface. Specimens must therefore be treated to remove at least the surface corrosion layer.

Carbon can be extracted from iron either by dissolving the iron in an acid that does not attack carbon, or by burning the carbon from the iron at high temperatures. The latter technique, which extracts carbon from the alloy in the form of carbon dioxide, is used at the Yale Radiocarbon Laboratory, where the most extensive research in this application of the technique has taken place.

A carbon-14 date obtained from an iron specimen gives consistently accurate results for two reasons according to Van de Merwe (1968). First, the fuel used to smelt the iron ore is derived from trees felled while they are still green, thus excluding the possibility of a time lag between the felling of the tree and the inclusion of its organic material in the iron alloy. Second, the probability of contamination of the carbon in the specimen is low.

Cast iron is by far the best material for dating purposes; a specimen of 30 gm or more may well be datable, whereas wrought-iron specimens should weigh at least 500 gm. At present, no radiocarbon laboratories are routinely dating iron samples, and it is hoped that this particular application will be made generally available to archaeologists in the very near future.

Other Materials Suitable for Radiocarbon Dating

Nearly any material containing carbon is potentially suitable for radiocarbon dating. Organic materials with high carbon content are, of course, the most reliable. In addition to the materials already discussed, radiocarbon dating laboratories are prepared to date the following materials: (1) peat, (2) paper, (3) parchment, (4) cloth, (5) animal tissue, (6) leaves, (7) pollen, (8) nuts, (9) carbonaceous soils, (10) the organic temper in pottery sherds, (11) wattle-and-daub contruction material, and (12) prehistoric soot from the ceiling of caves.

For materials with low carbon content, large quantities must be used to obtain a reliable date; for materials with high carbon content, smaller quantities are needed. Table 9 gives the sample size desired for a number of common archaeological materials.

Collection and Storage of Samples for Dating

When it is determined that a sample may be used for radiocarbon dating, care must be exercised in obtaining the sample from its original environment. If possible, only metal or glass should come in contact

TABLE 9

Sample Size Desired for Common Archaeological Materials[a]

Material	Weight desired (gm)[b]		Minimum Weight
Charcoal	8 –	12	1
Wood	10 –	30	3
Shell (carbonate date)	30 –	100	5
Shell (conchiolin date)	500 –	2500	200
Bone (carbonate date)	100 –	500	50
Bone (collagen date, less than 5,000 years old)	200 –	500	100
Bone (collagen date, more than 5,000 years old)	400 –	1000	250
Iron (cast iron)	100 –	150	30
Iron (steel)	300 –	500	150
Iron (wrought iron)	1000 –	2500	500
Peat	10 –	25	3

[a]From J. Buckley, Teledyne Isotopes, Inc.
[b]These refer to dry samples which possess average carbon contents.

with the sample. The tools and containers should be clean and free from all organic material, greases, lubricants, preservatives, etc. Samples should be removed with clean metal trowels or spatulas, and placed directly in new aluminum foil. After being wrapped in foil, the sample should be placed in a glass or metal container. If the sample has to be cut from a larger piece of material, again clean metal tools should be used. The cuttings should be caught directly on aluminum foil and wrapped tightly. If a piece of the sample drops on the ground, it should be discarded. Many dating laboratories have some routine decontamination or cleansing procedures. By making the laboratory aware of possible sources of contamination, one can avoid needless error in dating.

READINGS

Aitken, M. J.
  1961 *Physics and archaeology.* New York: Wiley (Interscience).
Benington, F., C. Melton, and P. J. Watson
  1962 Carbon dating prehistoric soot from Salts Cave, Kentucky. *American Antiquity* **28**, No. 2: 238–243.
Berger, R.
  1970 The potential and limitations of radiocarbon dating in the Middle Ages: The radiochronologist's view. In *Scientific methods in Mediaeval Archaeology*, edited by R. Berger. Berkeley: University of California Press.

Berger, R., A. G. Horney, and W. F. Libby
  1964 Radiocarbon dating of bone and shell from their organic components. *Science* **144**: 999–1001.
Bray, J.R.
  1967 Variation in atmospheric carbon-14 activity relative to a sunspot–auroral solar index *Science* **156**: 640–642.
Broecker, W. S., and J. L. Kulp
  1956 The radiocarbon method of age determination. *American Antiquity* **22**: 1–11.
Bucha, V.
  1970 Influence of the earth's magnetic field on radiocarbon dating. In *Radiocarbon variations and absolute chronology, Proceedings of the Twelfth Nobel Symposium, Uppsala*, edited by I. U. Olsson. New York: Wiley.
  1971 Archaeomagnetic Dating. In "Dating Techniques for the Archaeologist," edited by H. N. Michael and E. K. Ralph. Cambridge, Mass: MIT Press.
Bucha, V., and E. Neustupny
  1967 Changes of the earth's magnetic field and radiocarbon dating. *Nature* **215**: 261–263.
Burke, W. H., Jr., and W. G. Meinschein
  1955 Carbon-14 dating with a methane proportional counter. *Review of Scientific Instruments* **26**: 1137–1140.
Cook, S. F.
  1964 The nature of charcoal excavated at archaeological sites. *American Antiquity* **29**, No. 4: 514–517.
Craig, H.
  1957 The natural distribution of radiocarbon and the exchange time of carbon dioxide between atmosphere and sea. *Tellus* **9**: 1–17.
Damon, P. E.
  1970 Climatic versus magnetic perturbation of the atmospheric carbon-14 reservoir. In *Radiocarbon variations and absolute chronology*, edited by I. U. Olsson. New York: Wiley.
Damon, P. E., A. Lang, and D. C. Grey
  1966 Fluctuations in atmospheric carbon-14 during the last six millennia. *Journal of Geophysical Research* **71**: 1055–1063.
de Vries, H., and G. W. Barendsen
  1953 Radiocarbon dating by a proportional counter filled with carbon dioxide. *Physica* **19**: 987–1003.
Dyck, W.
  1967 Recent developments in radiocarbon dating: Their implications for geochronology and archaeology. *Current Anthropology* **8**, No. 4: 349–351.
Evans, C., and B. J. Meggers
  1962 Use of organic temper for carbon-14 dating in lowland South America. *American Antiquity* **28**, No. 2: 243–245.
Haring, A., A. E. de Vries, and H. de Vries
  1958 Radiocarbon dating up to 70,000 years by isotopic enrichment. *Science* **128**: 472–473.
Haynes, C. V., Jr.
  1966 Radiocarbon samples: Chemical removal of plant contaminants. *Science* **151**: 1391–1392.
  1968 Radiocarbon: Analysis of inorganic carbon of fossil bone and enamel. *Science* **161**, No. 3842: 688–689.

Hole, F., and R. F. Heizer
  1965   *An Introduction to Prehistoric Archaeology.* New York: Holt.
Houtermans, J., H. R. Suess, and W. Munk
  1967   Effect of industrial fuel combustion on the carbon-14 level of atmospheric
         CO_2. In *Radioactive dating and methods of low-level counting,* pp. 57–68. Vienna:
         International Atomic Energy Agency.
Jelinek, A. J.
  1962   An index of radiocarbon dates associated with cultural materials. *Current
         Anthropology* **3**, No. 5: 451–477.
Johnson, F.
  1959   A bibliography of radiocarbon dating. *American Journal of Science Radiocarbon
         Supplement* 1, 199–214.
  1965   Half-life of radiocarbon. *Science* **149**: 1326.
  1967   Radiocarbon dating and archaeology in North America. *Science* **155**: 165–169.
Karlen, I., I. U. Olsson, P. Kallberg, and S. Kilicci
  1966   Absolute determination of the activity of two carbon-14 dating standards.
         Arkiv Geofysik **6**: 465–471.
Kim, S. M., R. R. Ruch, and J. P. Kempton
  1969   Radiocarbon dating at the Illinois State Geological Survey. *Environmental
         Geology Notes, Illinois State Geological Survey,* No. 28: 1–19.
Kovar, A. J.
  1966   Problems in radiocarbon dating at Teotihuacán. *American Antiquity* **31**, No.
         3: 427–430.
Krueger, H. W.
  n.d.   *Sampling Rules for Radiocarbon Age Determination.* Cambridge, Massachusetts:
         Geochron Laboratories, Inc.
Lal, D., and Rama
  1966   Characteristics of global tropospheric mixing based on man-made C^{14}, H^3,
         and Sr^{90}. *Journal of Geophysical Research* **71**: 2865–2874.
Libby, W. F.
  1955   *Radiocarbon dating.* Chicago: University of Chicago Press.
  1961   Radiocarbon dating. *Science* **133**: 621–629.
Michael, H. N., and E. K. Ralph
  1970   Correction factors applied to Egyptian radiocarbon dates from the B.C. Era.
         In *Radiocarbon variations and absolute chronology,* edited by I. U. Olsson. New
         York: Wiley.
Noakes, J. E., S. M. Kim, and J. J. Stipp
  1965   Chemical and counting advances in liquid scintillation age dating. *6th Interna-
         tional Conference on Radiocarbon and Tritium Dating Proceedings,* U.S. Atomic
         Energy Commission CONF-650652: 68–92.
Noakes, J. E., S. M. Kim and L. K. Askers
  1967   Recent Improvement in Benzene Chemistry for Radiocarbon Dating. *Geochim.
         et Cosmochim. Acta* **31**: 1094–1096.
Olson, E. A., and R. M. Chatters
  1965   Carbon-14 and tritium dating. *Science* **150**: 1488–1492.
Olsson, I. U., and D. G. Eriksson
  1965   Remarks on C^{14} dating of shell material in sea sediments. *Progress in Oceano-
         graphy* **3**: 253–266.

Olsson, I. U. (Editor)
1970 *Radiocarbon variations and absolute chronology, Proceedings of the twelfth Nobel Symposium, Uppsala, Sweden, August 11–15, 1969*. Stockholm: Almquist and Widsell. New York: Wiley (Interscience).

Olsson, I. U., and D. G. Eriksson
1965 Polach, H. A., and J. J. Stipp
1967 Improved synthesis techniques for methane and benzene radiocarbon dating. *International Journal of Applied Radiation and Isotopes* **18**: 359–364.

Orr, P. C., and R. Berger
1965 Radiocarbon age of a Nevada mummy. *Science* **148**: 1466–1467.

Ralph, E. K.
1971 Carbon 14 Dating. In *Dating techniques for the archaeologist*, edited by H. N. Michael and E. K. Ralph. Cambridge, Massachusetts: M.I.T. Press.

Ralph, E. K., and H. N. Michael
1967 Problems of the radiocarbon calendar. *Archaeometry* **10**: 3–11.

Robbins, M.
1965 *The amateur archaeologist's handbook*. New York: Crowell-Collier.

Rubin, M., R. C. Likins, and E. G. Berry
1963 On the validity of radiocarbon dates from snail shells. *The Journal of Geology* **71**: 84–89.

Stuiver, M.
1970 Long-term C^{14} variations. In *Radiocarbon variations and absolute chronology*, edited by I. U. Olsson. New York: Wiley.

Suess, H. E.
1954 Natural radiocarbon measurements by acetylene counting. *Science* **120**: 5–7.
1970 Bristlecone pine calibration of the radiocarbon time scale 5200 B.C. to the present. In *Radiocarbon variations and absolute chronology*, edited by I. U. Olsson. New York: Wiley.

Tauber, H.
1958 Difficulties in the application of C-14 results in archaeology. *Archaeologia Austriaca* **24**: 59–69.

Taylor, R. E., and R. Berger
1968 Radiocarbon dating of the organic portion of ceramic and wattle-and-daub house construction materials of low carbon content. *American Antiquity* **33**, No. 3: 363–366.

Taylor, R. E., R. Berger, and B. Dimsdale
1968 Electronic Data Processing for Radiocarbon Dates. *American Antiquity* **33**: 180–184.

Van de Merwe, N. J.
1969 *The Carbon-14 Dating of Iron* Chicago: University of Chicago Press.

Van de Merwe, N. J. and M. Stuiver
1968 Dating Iron by the Carbon-14 Method. *Current Anthropology* **9**, No. 1: 48–53.

Willis, E. H.
1970 Radiocarbon dating. In *Science in archaeology*, edited by D. Brothwell and E. Higgs pp. 35–46. New York: Praeger.

CHAPTER TEN

Potassium–Argon Dating

Introduction

The potassium–argon (K–Ar) dating method covers nearly the whole range of the time scale, with published dates extending from 4.5 billion years ago to 2500 years ago (Evernden and Curtis 1965: 349). This impressive range is due in part to the extremely long half-life (1.3 billion years ± 40 million years) of the radioactive isotope of potassium, potassium-40 (^{40}K), and in part to the availability of suitable procedures by which its decay product, argon-40 (^{40}Ar) can be detected.

The potassium–argon dating method can only be used in situations where new rock has been formed. Although most rock-forming events antedate the periods of archaeological interest, the widespread distribution of localities that have recently (in the last half-million years) experienced volcanic activity is sufficient to suggest reasonable success in locating useful juxtapositions between strata resulting from this activity and culture-bearing deposits. Potassium–argon (K–Ar) dating has been accomplished on lavas, tuffs, and pumice found as overlying strata at localities that contained culture-bearing deposits in such diverse areas as Italy, East Africa, and Java (Evernden and Curtis 1965). Like other chronometric techniques developed during the 1960s, K–Ar dating has yet to develop a substantial corpus of dates upon which the archaeologist can base his confidence. Once this confidence is achieved, it seems very likely that opportunities to make use of this technique will be energetically sought out.

The one important exception to this is the field of Early Hominid research. Already, there is substantial agreement among human paleontologists about the accuracy of K–Ar determinations as applied to the Olduvai Gorge sequence of hominid fossils (Evernden and Curtis 1965) (see Table 10). High confidence in these dates rests upon the large number of determinations made, compatibility with stratigraphic studies, and the independent verification provided by the new fission-track technique of dating when applied to the same strata (Everndon and Curtis 1965).

Underlying Principles of the Method

Potassium (K) is one of the elements that occurs in great abundance in the earth's crust. It is present in nearly every mineral, either as a principal constituent or as a trace element. In its natural form, potassium contains 93.2% ^{39}K, 6.8% ^{41}K and 0.0118% radioactive ^{40}K. For each 100 ^{40}K atoms that decay, 89% become ^{40}Ca and 11% become ^{40}Ar, one of the rare gases. Figure 46 gives the decay scheme of ^{40}K as it is presently understood.

Figure 46. *Decay scheme of ^{40}K (γ, energy, 1.46 ± 0.02 MeV; β^-, threshold energy, 1.33 ± 0.01 MeV). (From Gentner, W. and Lippolt, H. J. Potassium-argon dating of Upper Tertiary and Pleistocene deposits. In "Science in Archaeology," edited by D. Brothwell and E. Higgs. New York: Praeger, 1970.)*

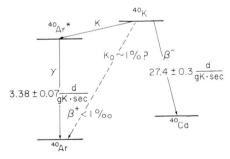

TABLE 10

Potassium–Argon Dates from Olduvai Gorge[a]

Sample	Mineral	Weight (gm)	K (%)	Ar⁴⁰ (%)	HF	Age (10^6 years)	Stratigraphic position[b]
KA 405A	Anorthoclase	10.56	5.01	70	No	0.502	Overlies Chellean II
KA 664R	Biotite	5.98	6.96	82	No	1.13	Middle or Lower Bed II
KA 1062	Plagioclase	9.16	0.837	49	Yes	1.57 ± 0.06	"Marker Bed A"
KA 1050	Anorthoclase	10.39	0.924	37	Yes	1.66 ± 0.05	Equivalent to Marker Bed A
KA 1045	Plagioclase	9.33	0.717	26	Yes	1.64 ± 0.06	15 inches below "Marker Bed A"
KA 1179	Anorthoclase	4.41	3.30	17	Yes	1.70	*Nuee ardente* overlying hominid site at DK site
KA 1057	Anorthoclase	8.71	3.28	16	Yes	1.75	Same stratum, different locale
KA 1058	Anorthoclase	9.63	3.56	11	Yes	1.76	Same stratum, different locale
KA 1053	Anorthoclase	8.07	3.24	23	Yes	1.76	Same stratum, different locale
KA 1043	Anorthoclase	9.67	3.43	7	Yes	1.76	Same stratum, different locale
KA 1047	Anorthoclase	9.16	0.670	36	Yes	1.86 ± 0.06	12 inches above Zinjanthropus floor
KA 850	Anorthoclase	8.16	3.94	41	No	1.78	1 inch above Zinjanthropus floor
KA 1037	Anorthoclase/Plag	9.85	1.41	17	Yes	1.79	50 inches below Zinjanthropus floor
KA 1040	Anorthoclase	7.76	2.56	9	Yes	1.65	65 inches below Zinjanthropus floor
KA 1180	Anorthoclase	7.86	3.25	9	Yes	1.85	81 inches below Zinjanthropus floor
KA 1100	Plagioclase/Augite	9.37	0.967	70	Yes	1.92 ± 0.06	Basalt
KA 1080	Anorthoclase	2.50	3.96	28	Yes	1.85	Few feet below basalt
KA 1088	Plagioclase	3.95	2.51	60	Yes	1.91 ± 0.04	Few feet below basalt

[a] Adapted from Tables 5 and 6 of Evernden and Curtis (1965).

[b] See Hay (1963) for full discussion of the stratigraphy of Olduvai Gorge, Tanganyika.

Argon-40 is classified as an inactive gas—one which by means of diffusion can easily escape from its parent material under certain conditions. The processes associated with the production of igneous rock provide such conditions. During rock formation, virtually all ^{40}Ar that had accumulated in the parent material will escape. As the rock or mineral crystalizes, the concentration of ^{40}Ar drops off to practically zero. The process of radioactive decay of ^{40}K continues, but the concentration of ^{40}Ar that develops over time will now, when dated, denote the moment of rock formation.

History of the Potassium–Argon Method

Houtermans (1966) provides us with a concise history of the potassium–argon method. He observes that during the late 1930s C. F. V. Weizsacker was studying the excessive amount of ^{40}Ar in the earth's atmosphere and postulated that the total radioactivity of potassium is due to ^{40}K. He went further, and asserted that the entire excess of ^{40}Ar in the earth's atmosphere is due to ^{40}K decay by electron capture. Ultimately, he suggested that the measurement of ^{40}Ar in minerals and rocks would be a means of dating these objects.

Houtermans points out that not until the 1950s did reliable dates begin to be computed. These were the work of W. Gentner and his associates, and their success was primarily due to the selection of appropriate samples. Sampling is of extreme importance in geochronology, and it took years to choose the right samples for the potassium–argon method. However, success was not due only to sampling; it was also the result of the development of a reliable method for the extraction of argon. The 1950s witnessed a steady increase in popularity of potassium–argon dating as a tool of geochronology. During this period, minerals that have a high retention capability for argon were identified. It was shown that geochronologists could apply the technique to a wide range of potassium-bearing minerals.

It was the 1960s, however, that witnessed the application of potassium–argon dating to archaeological problems. In 1961 Evernden and Curtis, in collaboration with Leakey, published the first series of dates for volcanic-derived sediments of Pleistocene age at Olduvai Gorge, Tanzania, which suggests the startling conclusion that man and his culture were almost a million years older than previously believed

(Leakey *et al.* 1961). By 1965 Evernden and Curtis were reporting that useful potassium–argon dates are obtainable on certain kinds of samples as young as 30,000 years (Evernden and Curtis 1965). Currently, there is continuing interest in procedural and instrumentation developments that will increase the precision and reliability of the technique in connection with dating young samples (Miller 1970).

Datable Materials

Potassium–argon dates have been determined for such igneous minerals as muscovite, biotite, phlogopite, orthoclase, sanidine, microcline, and leucite, for volcanic glass (obsidian), and for the sedimentary minerals glauconite, illite, carnallite, and sylvite (Gentner and Lippolt 1970). Because a number of these minerals are easily altered by metamorphism or can lose argon through diffusion, Gentner and Lippolt (1970) recommend restricting dating to biotite, muscovite, and sanidine. Other minerals are also datable although they only have trace amounts of potassium. These are anorthoclase, oligoclase, augite, calcite, and hornblende.

There are a number of processes which alter the $^{40}Ar/^{40}K$ ratio in dated material. These include recrystallization, devitrification, and chloritization. Changes resulting from these processes can sometimes be recognized microscopically, and samples exhibiting any of them should be rejected.

Whole-rock samples often contain many minerals. Some of these minerals, such as large biotite and sanidine crystals, are excellent for dating. Other minerals, however, may be unable to retain argon, and if not excluded from the sample will produce erroneous results. For this reason, it is not advisable to use whole-rock samples when complicated strata are being dated.

In the course of their extensive program of dating at Olduvai Gorge, Tanzania, Evernden and Curtis have developed the following set of criteria for interpreting the significance of dates from a sequence of samples (Evernden and Curtis 1965).

Dates are acceptable if

(1) two different crystal types from the same tuff yield essentially the same age;
(2) if the sample is a volcanic flow (basalt, trachyte, etc.) and the problem of argon loss is not insurmountable;

(3) if several samples from the same horizon at scattered localities yield the same age;

(4) if the primary nature of a tuff can be established.

Dates should be rejected if

(1) there is any possibility of the deposit having been reworked;

(2) if there is any possibility of there being admixed detrital components of different age;

(3) if different concentrates of the same mineral from the same tuff yield markedly different ages.

Sample Preparation

Sample preparation involves first, crushing of the rock sample; second, concentrating it to high purity; third, washing it on screens to remove fines; and fourth, treating it with hydrofluoric acid.

The last step relates to one of the main problems in potassium–argon dating, that is, the elimination of atmospheric argon from the sample to be run. This is especially true of very young samples. Treatment of samples with hydrofluoric acid has proved to be very effective in reducing the amount of atmospheric argon in the sample since atmospheric argon is not found uniformly distributed throughout the sample, but is concentrated near the surface. By removing the outer layer of the sample, most of the atmospheric argon also is removed. A 20–30-min treatment in 7–10% hydrofluoric acid (50°C) is a recommended procedure in the preparation of the sample. Treatment with hydrofluoric acid also aids in the removal of adhering grains of the matrix materials from the sample. Immediately after sample preparation and drying it should be put into the extraction line and placed under vacuum.

Potassium–Argon Analysis: Conventional Procedures

Potassium–argon dates are calculated from measurements of the sample content of argon-40 and potassium-40. The amount of potassium in a sample fraction can be determined by a flame photometer, although for small concentrations, isotopic dilution analysis and even neutron activation analysis can be used (Gentner and Lippolt 1970).

The determination of potassium content by these procedures is reliable, although its comparability to the argon-40 values determined with a second sample fraction can be questioned due to the inhomogeneity of potassium distribution in the samples (Miller 1970).

The determination of the concentration of argon involves three steps. First, the gases have to be completely extracted from the sample. Then the rare or *noble* gases, including argon, must be separated from the other gases by means of a purification procedure. Finally, the amount of argon and the contribution of atmospheric contamination have to be determined by mass spectrometric analysis. What follows is a somewhat detailed description of the procedures involved.

The following description is drawn primarily from the excellent paper on this subject by Kirsten (1966), with some references to the description by Evernden and Curtis (1965).

The extraction of the gases involves melting the sample at temperatures up to 2000°C in a vacuum system. The extraction procedure must insure that all the argon is extracted, but that contamination by atmospheric argon be minimal.

The apparatus used for extraction consists of a *furnace* located within a vacuum system, and a vacuum line with provision for the trapping and preliminary separation of the released gases. The furnace consists of a molybdenum crucible (in which the sample is positioned) surrounded by a quartz container. Beneath the crucible a quartz dish is placed that contains *getter* materials. Gettering refers to a property of heated metals of combining selectively with and/or adsorbing various gases. The getter dish contains titanium chips that, when heated, adsorb many of the active gases released during the melting of the sample. Heating is effected by an induction coil around the furnace. The entire furnace assembly with the exception of the heating coil is housed in a vacuum-tight Pyrex tube.

The extraction apparatus is connected with the furnace by a glass tube. The vacuum established for both the furnace and the other components of the extraction apparatus is produced by means of a mechanical fore pump and two mercury diffusion pumps.

A glass sleeve connected to the apparatus serves as a holding device for samples to be dated. Ten or twenty samples can be stored at one time so that cutting and resealing of the apparatus can be kept to a minimum.

The sample is melted slowly. Normally, complete degassing of the sample is accomplished when the melting has lasted about 20 min.

The crucible used may vary in size. Commonly used crucibles as reported by Kirsten (1966) are 3 cm high with a capacity of not more than 6 cubic centimeters (6 cm³) of material. Evernden and Curtis (1965) report that their crucibles permit a maximum sample size of 15–20 gm of crystal concentrate or 30–35 gm of solid rock.

Argon must be separated from the other gases released during the extraction process. This is done in the purification part of the apparatus which is connected to the extraction part by a valve. The principal components of the purification system are the furnaces that contain metals with which many of the nonnoble gases react (a gettering process).

Evernden and Curtis recommend the use of two furnaces. In the first furnace, copper oxide powder and fine copper chips are heated to temperatures between 450 and 550°C, thus trapping hydrogen and oxygen in the form of water vapor. Next, the gases are exposed to a titanium furnace. At about 850°C titanium granules react with them, trapping such nonnoble gases as oxygen, nitrogen, carbon dioxide and carbon monoxide. The remaining noble gases, including argon, then are adsorbed onto charcoal previously cooled with liquified air or liquid nitrogen.

Normally, the extraction and purification systems are independent of the mass spectrometer. It is therefore possible to carry out argon separations using several independent extraction systems. The number of analyses that can be done by a laboratory with only one mass spectrometer is thereby increased. One man can operate two extraction lines, completing two argon extractions and reassemblies within 6–7 hours (6–7 hr) (Evernden and Curtis 1965).

The argon, awaiting measurement, is usually stored in small glass bottles or "fingers" that can be closed off and then separated from the purification apparatus. The sample containers are attached to the gas inlet system of the mass spectrometer. A steel ball inside the tube can be moved magnetically and dropped onto the glass seal, thereby releasing the argon from the cold finger and allowing it to enter the mass spectrometer (Figure 47).

The initial step in mass spectrometer analysis is the ionization of the argon gas. This takes place in an ionization chamber. Electrons are emitted from a tungsten cathode. The electrons are focused with electric lenses to a narrow beam and collected at a trap anode. Between the cathode and the anode the electrons pass through a metal housing (the ionization chamber) where the argon gas is ionized. The produc-

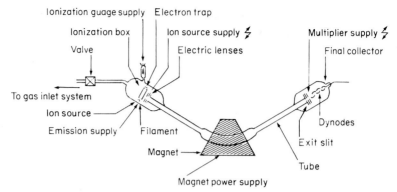

Figure 47. *The mass spectrometer. (After Kirsten 1966: Fig. 7.)*

tion of ions varies with each specific argon isotope. With a potential of a few volts the ions are extracted in a direction perpendicular to the electron beam, and then enter an electric lens system, where they are focused to a narrow beam and accelerated. The ion beam then enters the mass spectrometer tube and passes through a magnetic field. The magnetic field deflects the ions in the ion beam, and the deflection radius of the ions is a function of their respective masses. A spectrum of variable ion currents is thereby produced, the strength of each current being proportional to the number of atoms of each isotope in the argon gas. By changing the magnetic field or the accelera-tion voltage, it is possible to bring into focus at the *exit slits* the current of any given isotope. The current is amplified and the signal then goes into a chart recorder.

In order to determine the amount of ^{40}Ar, it is also necessary to determine the amount of ^{36}Ar (in order to compute the amount of argon contamination from the air) and ^{39}Ar (by which the purity of the gas is determined). The procedure of recording the various masses is usually repeated at least 10 times.

Calculation of Potassium–Argon Dates

The ^{40}Ar and ^{40}K contents are used to calculate the potassium–argon date of a sample. The primary assumption, required to assure a correct age, is that the initial concentration of ^{40}Ar was zero, and that no diffusion losses took place.

Kirsten (1966: 31–32) describes in detail the formula used to calculate potassium–argon age t, and the way in which this initial formula is reduced to a more operational form without significant increase in error as follows. The equation for calculating t, based on the law of radioactive decay, is

$$t = \frac{1}{\lambda} \ln \left\{ 1 + \frac{1 + R}{R} \times \frac{(^{40}Ar_{rad})}{(^{40}K)} \right\}, \tag{1}$$

where

$(^{40}Ar_{rad})$ and (^{40}K) are given in number of atoms;
λ = the total decay constant of ^{40}K;
R = the banding ratio of the double decay of ^{40}K.

By substituting the values $\lambda = 5.32 \times 10^{-10}$ y^{-1} and $R = 0.123$ (the most reliable decay constants), replacing ^{40}K by K_{total} (using the isotopic abundance of ^{40}K), converting the ratio $(^{40}Ar_{rad})/(K)$ into the units

$$\frac{cm^3 \; STP}{gm} \times \frac{^{40}Ar_{rad}}{K}$$

and using the common logarithm instead of the natural logarithm, Equation (1) can be reduced to the form

$$t = 4320 \log_{10} \left\{ 1 + 134.7 \; \frac{^{40}Ar_{rad}}{K} \right\}, \tag{2}$$

where t is given in millions of years.

Consideration of the linearity of this function for small t will further reduce this equation to the form

$$t = 2.53 \times 10^5 \times \frac{^{40}Ar_{rad}}{K} . \tag{3}$$

This equation is a useful approximation for ages up to 30 million years.

It can be shown that the errors introduced with the substitutions to reduce the initial equation to the more practical form, Equation (2), are negligible, and are generally decreased with increasing age of the sample.

The Argon-40–Argon-39 Method

The conventional techniques for determining argon-40 and potassium-40 amounts in a sample (just described) present several problems. Among the most crucial are, first, that potassium may be distributed inhomogeneously through the sample so that the amount of potassium-40 determined with one fraction may not accurately reflect the amount present in the fraction undergoing argon-40 determination. Second, procedures used to remove all atmospheric argon-40 can cause some loss of radiogenic argon-40.

The argon-40–argon-39 method (Miller 1970) is designed to resolve these and other problems. Essentially, the method involves the intentional irradiation of a sample (together with appropriate standards) in a nuclear reactor. The isotope potassium-39 is thereby converted into argon-39. The sample then is introduced into a standard argon extractor line (as described previously) and heated up in stages, beginning with very gentle heat and ending with complete fusion. After each heating stage the ratios of argon-39 to argon-40, or argon-36 to argon-40, and of argon-39 to argon-36 are measured in the mass spectrometer.

When the ratio of $^{40}Ar/^{36}Ar$ is plotted against the $^{39}Ar/^{36}Ar$ ratio, the result will be a line, the slope of which will be related to the age of the specimen (Miller 1970).

Conclusion

Miller (1970) has recently reviewed some advances in technique that contribute to the success with which young samples can be dated. He gives special attention to the argon-40–argon-39 method, and to the use of Omegatron-type mass spectrometers for accurate detection of the relative abundance of argon isotopes. Miller exhibits a cautious optimism that echoes an earlier evaluation by Evernden and Curtis (1965). In the latter case, the technical breakthrough was the treatment of feldspar with hydrofluoric acid.

A number of universities throughout the world have potassium–argon dating laboratories where samples might be submitted for dating. These would include various campuses of the University of California, Massachusetts Institute of Technology, Oxford, Cambridge, Arizona, Columbia, Minnesota, Hawaii, British Columbia, Heidelberg, and Australia, to name only a few. Unfortunately, none of the above-named institutions perform this service on a commercial basis. Instead, they seek samples for dating that fit into their general research schemes. Many laboratories seek samples of exclusively geological interest. For archaeologists unable to locate a university laboratory willing to perform the analysis, there are commercial dating laboratories available. Most laboratories will recommend that a trained geologist collect the sample, and will insist that all phases of the analysis be performed under their supervision.

READINGS

Curtis, G. H.
  1966 The problem of contamination in obtaining accurate dates of young geologic rocks. In *Potassium–argon dating*, compiled by O.A. Schaeffer and J. Zahringer. New York: Springer Publ.

Dalrymple, G., and M. A. Lanphere
  1969 *Potassium–argon dating*. San Francisco: Freeman.

Evernden, J. F., and G. H. Curtis
  1965 The potassium–argon dating of Late Cenozoic rocks in East Africa and Italy. *Current Anthropology* 6: 343–385.

Evernden, J. F., and J. R. Richards
  1962 Potassium–argon dates in eastern Australia. *Journal of the Geological Society of Australia* 9: 1–50.

Evernden, J. F., G. H. Curtis, and R. Kistler
  1957 Potassium–argon dating of Pleistocene volcanics. *Quarternaria* 4: 1–5.

Evernden, J. F., G. H. Curtis, R. W. Kistler, and J. Obradovich
  1960 Argon diffusion in glauconite, microline, sanidine, leucite, and phlogopite. *American Journal of Science* 258: 583–604.

Evernden, J. F., D. E. Savage, G. H. Curtis, and G. T. James
  1964 Potassium–argon dates and the Cenozoic mammalian chronology of North America. *American Journal of Science* 262: 145–198.

Faul, H.
  1971 Potassium–argon dating. In *Dating techniques for the archaeologist*, edited by H. N. Michael and E. K. Ralph. Cambridge, Massachusetts: M.I.T. Press.

Gentner, W., and H. J. Lippolt
  1970 The potassium–argon dating of Upper Tertiary and Pleistocene deposits. In *Science in archaeology*, edited by D. Brothwell, and E. Higgs. New York: Praeger.

Hay, R. L.
  1963 Stratigraphy of Beds I through IV, Olduvai Gorge, Tanganyika. *Science* 139: 829–833.

Houtermans, F. G.
  1966 History of the K–Ar method of geochronology. In *Potassium–argon dating*, compiled by O. A. Schaeffer and J. Zahringer. New York: Springer Publ.

Howell, F.
  1962 Potassium–argon dating at Olduvai Gorge. *Current Anthropology* 3, No. 3: 306–308.

Kalbitzer, S.
   1966   The diffusion of argon in potassium-bearing solids. In Potassium–argon dat-
           ings, compiled by O. A. Schaeffer and J. Zahringer. New York: Springer Publ.
Kirsten, T.
   1966   Determination of radiogenic argon. In *Potassium–argon dating*, compiled by
           O. A. Schaeffer and J. Zahringer. New York: Springer Publ.
Leakey, L. S. B., J. F. Evernden, and G. H. Curtis
   1961   Age of Bed I, Olduvai Gorge, Tanganyika. *Nature* **191**: 478–479.
McDougall, I.
   1964   Potassium–argon ages from lavas of the Hawaiian Islands. *Bulletin of the Geologi-
           cal Society of America* **75**: 107–128.
Miller, J. A.
   1967   Problems of dating East African Tertiary and Quarternary volcanics by the
           potassium–argon method. In *Background to Evolution in Africa*, edited by W. W.
           Bishop and J. D. Clark. Chicago: University of Chicago Press.
   1970   Dating by the potassium–argon method—some advances in technique. In
           Science in Archaeology, edited by D. Brothwell and E. Higgs. New York: Praeger.
Muller, O.
   1966   Potassium analysis. In *Potassium–argon dating*, compiled by O. A. Schaeffer
           and J. Zahringer. New York: Springer Publ.

CHAPTER ELEVEN

O

Fission-Track Dating

Introduction

Fission-track dating is another new technique of geochronology that promises to have important archaeological applications in the future. Thus far, the method has been tested and shown to be applicable for dating a wide variety of minerological materials over a time range that can extend from historic times to a billion years and more into the past. Figure 48 shows a comparison of fission-track dates and dates known by other chronometric methods. It can be seen that dates obtained by the fission-track method are generally in accord with ages determined by other methods, and that even for very old periods there are enough cases of agreement to establish the basic validity of the method (Fleischer et al. 1956b). From the standpoint of archaeological applications, however, the effective limits for typical samples are 100,000 years to 1,000,000 years B.P. (Walker et al. 1971).

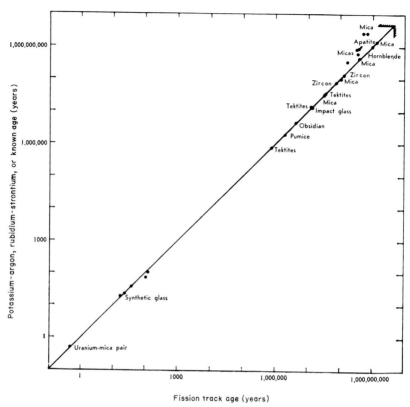

Figure 48. *Comparison of ages found by fission-track dating with those established by other means. The samples less than 200 years old are man-made; the older ones are geological. (From Fleischer, R. L. et al. Tracks of charged particles in solids.* Science, **149**: 383–393, Fig. 13. *Copyright 1965 by the American Association for the Advancement of Science.)*

Like potassium–argon dating, fission-track dating is customarily applied to newly formed rock. Archaeological application of this technique is thus generally contingent upon having a site that underwent inundation by minerological by-products of a geological event (such as a volcanic eruption) just before, during, or shortly after human occupation. Applying the principle of superposition, an investigator can establish an *upward age ceiling* to a site by dating the overlying geological stratum, and a *lower age limit* by dating the underlying geological stratum.

What is being dated is, with some exceptions, the *time of origin* of the rocks, not the time of their utilization (as in the case of obsidian dating). However, when we consider how many regions of the world have experienced volcanic activity during the Pleistocene Epoch, there is a good possibility that numerous settlements will come to light that are susceptible to dating by this technique.

Principle of the Technique

Many minerals and natural glasses (obsidian, tektites, etc.) contain very small quantities of uranium. Through time, the uranium undergoes a slow spontaneous process of decay. Most uranium atoms decay by alpha particle emission, but about one in every two million atoms decays by spontaneous fission. The fission-decay constant is 10^{-16} per year.

In fission decay, massive, energy-charged particles produce narrow trails of damage in the material—called *tracks*—that can be seen under high magnification (Fleischer *et al.* 1965b). The tracks are visible because the light diffraction contrast has been altered by the presence of damaged areas around the paths of the bombarding fission frag- ments (Fleischer *et al.* 1965b). Fleischer, Price, and Walker, scientists affiliated with the General Electric Research Laboratory who played a key role in the discovery and development of this technique, have proposed a model of fission-track formation which they call the ion- explosion spike (Fleischer *et al.* 1965b). A continuous, cylindrical region of damage is created in the material by the violent repulsion of the positive ions remaining after the scattering away of electrons by a charged particle. Figure 49 illustrates the model schematically.

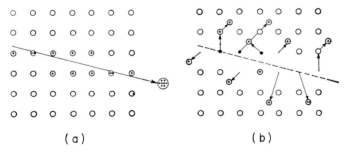

(a)   (b)

Figure 49. *Ion-explosion spike model: (a) the atoms have been ionized by the massive charged particle that has just passed; (b) the mutual repulsion of the ions has separated them and forced them into the lattice. (From Fleischer, R. L. et al. Tracks of charged particles in solids. Science, **149**: 383–393, Fig. 5. Copyright 1965 by the American Association for the Advancement of Science.)*

The density of these spontaneous-fission tracks increases with the uranium concentration and the age of the sample. By counting the tracks and measuring the uranium content, it is possible to calculate the age of the sample. The age A is found from the equation

$$\rho_s/\rho_i = \left[\exp(\lambda_D A) - 1\right](\lambda_F/\lambda_D f),$$

where
ρ_s = the density of spontaneous fission tracks;
λ_F and λ_D = the spontaneous-fission and total-decay constants of uranium-238;
f = part of the total uranium fissioned in the reactor irradiation that was used to measure the uranium content;
ρ_i = the new density of tracks induced by this irradiation (Fleischer et al. 1965b).

Dating Procedure

It is necessary to obtain two counts of the fission tracks: first, to determine the density of tracks that has been achieved through natural fission-decay, and second, after artificial irradiation, to determine the new density of tracks induced by this irradiation. The counts are made with the aid of an optical microscope. To prepare samples for microscope observation it is necessary to etch the tracks with hydrofluoric acid. Since the acid works more quickly on the damaged trails made by charged particles than on normal, undamaged regions of a sample, controlled hydrofluoric acid etching will attack the tracks specifically. The acid penetrates the full length of the tracks, replacing the linear trails of damaged material with fine hollow tubes, some 50 angstrom units (50 Å) in diameter (Fleischer et al. 1965b). These tubes become permanent features of the sample. The etching will have increased the diameter of the hollow tubes to a point where they are visible in the optical microscope; appearing black in normal bright-field illumination, and white when viewed in dark field (Fleisher et al. 1965b) (see Figure 50).

As mentioned, the second count of fission tracks is necessary to calculate the uranium content in the sample. This is done by inducing fission of uranium-235 through neutron irradiation. The age of the material then is a function of the ratio of the number of observed tracks resulting from natural fission to those resulting from the induced fission.

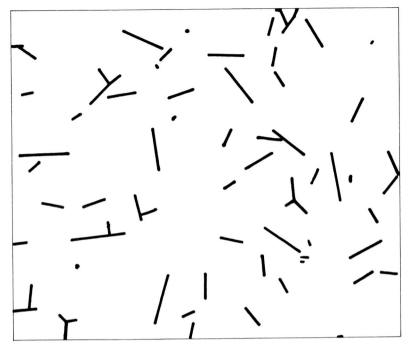

Figure 50. *Fission tracks in mica. The tracks are about 10 μm long and have a fairly uniform, diamond-shaped cross section. The revelation of tracks is accomplished by etching in concentrated hydrogen fluoride. (From Walker* et al. *1971: Fig. 21.1)*

Applications of Fission-Track Dating

The critical factor that determines if a given sample can be dated is the uranium content. A concentration of 1 part per million gives a fission track density of 0.3 square centimeters (0.3 cm²) per 1000 years. It is difficult to work with samples having too few tracks per square centimeter, and for this reason samples with typical uranium concentrations must fall within the time range 100,000–1,000,000 years ago to be suitable for dating by this method (Walker *et al.* 1971). For man-made objects in which high concentrations of uranium are present, such as some kinds of artificial glass, the technique can be used to date historic artifacts. One such object, dated by R. H. Brill of the Corning Museum of Glass, is a 19th century candlestick (Brill 1964).

One of the most famous and scientifically significant applications of fission-track dating to archaeology is the dating of volcanic obsidian from Bed I of the Olduvai Gorge, Tanzania. This is the source of two varieties of hominid remains, Zinjanthropus and *Homo habilis* discovered by the Leakeys. Leakey *et al.* (1961) dated anorthoclase from Bed I at 1.8 million years by means of potassium–argon dating. Since the implications of the date for the study of human biological and cultural evolution were important, it was appropriate to verify the date by means of some other chronometric method. Fleischer, Price, and Walker, in collaboration with Leakey (1965a), measured the age of the volcanic pumice in Bed I of Olduvai Gorge with the fission-track method. The result was a value of 2.03 ± 0.28 million years. When the standard deviation is considered, the two dates are very much in agreement.

In the context of the above example, it is important to note that the possible sources of error in the potassium–argon and fission-track methods are different. For example, the presence of inherited argon in the anorthoclase, which, with the potassium–argon method, would lead to too high a date, would not affect fission-track dating at all. On the other hand, dates obtained by the fission-track method more often deviate from true dates as a result of heating episodes, which make the apparent date too low. The fact that dates obtained by the two methods agree is strong support for the validity of both techniques.

Annealing

Fission tracks are stable in most materials as long as they are kept at moderate temperatures. If, however, the temperature is raised, a point is reached when the electrons and ions in the material become unstable, thus altering their positions. The phenomenon is called *annealing*, and if prolonged, all fission tracks will disappear. Annealing temperatures vary among materials. For example, annealing occurs in zircon at 700°C if exposed 100 min, whereas apatite anneals at 335°C if exposed for the same amount of time (Faul and Wagner 1971).

The implications of the phenomenon for archaeology relate to the effects of man-made fires. Lithic artifact materials that were in contact with the heat of such fires might lose their original fission tracks, and subsequent track accumulation would date from the time of burning. Thus hearth stones, boiling stones, burnt clay, fired ceramics, and a host of other potentially annealed mineral-bearing materials would be susceptible to fission-track dating (Faul and Wagner 1971).

Future Developments in Track Dating: Alpha-Recoil Dating

Although track dating has been shown to be a valid chronometric technique, its applications, especially in archaeology, have been few owing to the recentness of its discovery and development. There are indications, however, that the technique will witness further refinement and will emerge as a very high-precision dating method. The study of all forms of radioactive dating was the subject of a symposium, organized by the International Atomic Energy Authority in conjunction with the Joint Commission for Applied Radioactivity (ICSU), and held at the Palais des Congres, Monte Carlo, in March of 1967. The highlight of the symposium was a report by R. M. Walker, the originator of the fission-track method. He reported the presence of small etch pits, some 3000 times more numerous than the normal fission tracks, on a carefully prepared cleavage of mica. These tracks, caused by a series of alpha-particle recoil events, are of the order of 100 angstrom units (100 $\overset{\circ}{A}$) in length, and require observation by an electron microscope or a scanning electron probe. By making track counts on these phenomena, a higher degree of precision in measurement is possible (Switsur 1967). Although alpha-recoil dating has not received sufficient archaeological application with which to determine its full value as a potential dating method, one intriguing application recently reported concerns the dating of potsherds by measuring alpha-recoil tracks, in high uranium inclusions, acquired since the vessel was fired (Zimmerman 1971).

READINGS

Brill, R. H.
  1964 Applications of fission-track dating to historic and prehistoric glasses. *Archaeometry* 7: 51–57.
Faul, H., and G. A. Wagner
  1971 Fission track dating. In *Dating techniques for the archaeologist*. edited by H. N. Michael and E. K. Ralph. Cambridge, Massachusetts: M.I.T. Press.
Fleischer, R. L., L. S. B. Leakey, P. B. Price, and R. M. Walker
  1965 Fission track dating of Bed I, Olduvai Gorge. *Science* **148**: 72–74.   (a)
Fleischer, R. L., P. B. Price, and R. M. Walker
  1965 Tracks of charged particles in solids. *Science* **149**, No. 3682: 383–393.   (b)

Fleischer, R. L., P. B. Price, R. M. Walker and L. S. B. Leakey
  1965   Fission track dating of a mesolithic knife. *Nature* **205**: 1138.   (c)
Fleischer, R. L., P. B. Price, and R. M. Walker
  1969   Nuclear tracks in solids. *Scientific American* **220**: 30–39.
Huang, W., and R. Walker
  1967   Fossil alpha-particle recoil tracks: A new method of age determination. *Science*
         155: 1103.
Leakey, L. S. B., J. F. Everden, and G. H. Curtis
  1961   Age of Bed I, Olduvai Gorge, Tanganyika. *Nature* **191**: 478–479.
Miller, D., and E. Jager
  1968   Fission track ages of some alpine micas. *Earth and Planetary Science Letters*
         4: 375–378.
Naeser, C. W., and F. C. W. Dodge
  1969   Fission track ages of accessory minerals from granitic rocks from the Sierra
         Nevada Batholith. *Bulletin of the Geological Society of America* **80**: 2201–2212.
Rainey, F., and E. K. Ralph
  1966   Archaeology and its new technology. *Science* **153**: 1481–1491.
Switsur, V. R.
  1967   Radioactive dating and low level counting. *Science* **157**: 726–727.
Walker, R., M. Maurette, R. Fleischer, and P. Price
  1971   Applications of solid-state nuclear track detectors to archaeology. In *Science
         and archaeology*, edited by R. H. Brill. Cambridge, Massachusetts: M.I.T. Press.
Watanabe, N., and M. Suzuki
  1969   Fission-track dating of archaeological glass materials from Japan. *Nature* **222**:
         1057–1058.
Zimmerman, D. W.
  1971   Uranium distributions in archaeological ceramics: dating of radioactive inclu-
         sions. *Science* **174**: 818–819.

CHAPTER TWELVE

Thermoluminescence Dating of Pottery

Introduction

The dating of ancient pottery by thermoluminescence measurements was suggested by Farrington Daniels of the University of Wisconsin as early as 1953. During the past 15 years this pottery dating technique has undergone serious investigation and development at the University of California at Los Angeles. The University of Pennsylvania, Oxford, Kyoto University, The University of Berne, and The University of Birmingham. Success at relative dating with the technique came rather early, and this encouraged researchers to continue. By 1968, a concensus among researchers seemed to suggest that the technique was on the verge of becoming fully operational as an absolute dating technique with an accuracy of plus or minus 10% (Aitken *et al.* 1968: 445). As yet, there are no laboratories that have established the technique on a routine basis, although archaeologists can probably look forward to routine thermoluminescence dating services within the very near future.

The Principle of Thermoluminescence

Thermoluminescence is the release in the form of light of stored energy from a substance when it is heated. The phenomenon occurs in a number of different crystalline solids, including pottery. All ceramic material contains certain amounts of radioactive impurities (for example, uranium, thorium, and potassium) in the parts-per-million concentration range. These elements emit alpha, beta, and gamma radiation at a specific rate that will depend only on the impurity content of the sample. This radiation will cause ionization within the sample, and electrons and other charge carriers (called *holes*) will result. Also within the ceramic materials will be crystal imperfections (or *traps*) that were formed during and after crystallization. The released charge carriers will tend to be trapped in this lattice of crystal imperfections at ordinary ambient temperatures. These charge carriers will exist in a metastable state, a few electron volts above the ground state. When the ceramic is heated, the electrons and holes are released from their traps at definite temperatures. Upon their release, electron–hole recombination will occur, returning these charge carriers to their ground state, and effecting the release of their excess voltage as light, measurable in photons. The longer the ceramic has been crystallized, the more ionizing radiation will have resulted and the more trapped electrons and holes will be held in the crystal structure.

The thermoluminescence observed is a measure of the total dose of radiation to which the ceramic has been exposed since the last previous heating. In the case of pottery, the event dated is the firing of the pot during the pottery-making process. The temperature of the firing environment, believed to have been in excess of 750°C was high enough to remove the thermoluminescence that had been acquired by the clays and tempering materials during geological times.

The natural radiation dosage for pottery is derived from uranium, thorium, and potassium. These sources emit the alpha, beta and gamma radiation that makes up the radiation dosage. The dosage, however, is not uniform. The major part of the dosage consists of alpha particles produced by the uranium and thorium impurities carried in fine grain clay. The situation for a typical pottery sherd is shown in Figure 51. The major environmental contribution is the gamma dose from the soil in which the sherd is buried. This is because gamma rays can travel a relatively long range. Beta particles do not

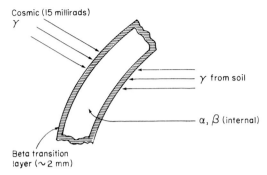

Cosmic (15 millirads)
γ

γ from soil

α, β (internal)

Beta transition
layer (∼2 mm)

Figure 51. *Typical annual radiation dose for fragment of pot buried in soil, both having 3 ppm of uranium, 12 ppm of thorium, and 1% potassium. (From Aitken 1968: Fig. 7.6.).*

travel as far, and such particles originating outside the sherd only affect a transitional layer at the surface of the sherd. However, beta particles originating within the sherd contribute an important share of radiation dosage. The cosmic-ray contribution is estimated for burial 5 feet below the surface. Alpha particles seldom travel more than 50 microns (50 μm), and therefore only alpha particles originating within the sherd affect the radiation dosage of the sherd.

Dating Procedure

In order to obtain accurate chronometric dates, researchers have been forced to take into account the inhomogeneity of the material out of which ancient pottery is fashioned. Generally, pottery consists of a fine-grained clay matrix in which are embedded mineral inclusions, such as quartz or feldspar. These inclusions have dimensions ranging from 1 mm to 1 μm or less. Inclusions have been found to have a much higher thermoluminescent sensitivity than the clay matrix. They are relatively transparent and give off more light than the opaque clay matrix. This difference in sensitivity is important. Since most radiation dosage is in the form of alpha particles originating in the fine-grained clay matrix, and since alpha particles travel such a short range (20–50 μm), their contribution to the dosage of an inclusion is greatly restricted, and is almost nothing in cases where inclusions exceed 100 μm across in size. The result is that the most sensitive thermoluminescent material (mineral inclusions) is shielded from the major component of radiation (alpha particles). Chronometric dates determined in early investigations were grossly in error because no allowance was made for this nonuniformity of natural dosage.

The solution hit upon to cope with this problem has been the segregation of the two components—fine-grained clay and mineral inclusions—and the dating of one or the other, or both, separately.

For *inclusion dating*, grains in the size range 100–200 μm are separated out, and their natural thermoluminescence and their sensitivity to beta and gamma radiation are measured. For this size range the contribution of alpha particles to the dosage is negligible. Only the calculation of the beta-particle contribution from the uranium, thorium, and potassium elements of the sherd itself, the gamma-ray contribution from these same elements within the surrounding soils, and a small contribution from cosmic rays need be undertaken.

For *fine-grain* dating, the thermoluminescence measurements are made on fine grains (both clay and mineral inclusions) in the size range 1–5 μm separated from the crushed pottery fragment by a sedimentation technique. These fine grains will have been exposed to a full alpha-particle dose, and so an alpha-irradiation contribution must enter dosage calculations.

An important consideration for fine-grain dating is the technique used for crushing the pottery fragment, because large mineral inclusions must not be crushed down to the 1–5-μm range. Researchers at the laboratory of archaeology, Oxford University, crush the pottery fragment between the jaws of a vise, taking care not to bring the jaws of the vise to within less than 2 mm of each other. This avoids putting stress directly across an inclusion and allows the sherd to crumble along the weakest paths, which are usually through the clay rather than through the hard mineral inclusions such as quartz. This process produces fragments ranging from about 2 mm to less than 1 μm in size.

After the crushing operation, grains of about 1–5 μm in size are selected by their settling rate in acetone and deposited onto eight 1-cm diameter, 0.254-mm thick aluminum disks. The rest of the material (about 2 gm) is ground with a mortar and pestle and used for the measurement of radioactive contents of the sherd. Each of the eight samples is 1 milligram (1 mg) in weight and is spread about 4 μm thick onto the aluminum disk. It is necessary to prepare these multiple samples from each pottery sherd because the thermoluminescence sensitivities of a sample can be changed during measurement through exposure to heat, and several thermoluminescent observa-

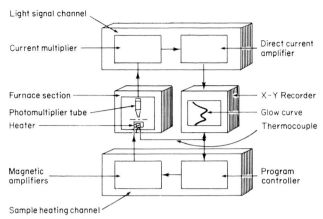

Light signal channel

Current multiplier

Direct current amplifier

Furnace section

X-Y Recorder

Photomultiplier tube

Glow curve

Heater

Thermocouple

Magnetic amplifiers

Program controller

Sample heating channel

Figure 52. *Block diagram of thermoluminescence equipment showing functional interrelation of various sections. (From Lewis et. al., 1959: Fig. 1.)*

tions are required of each sherd. Natural thermoluminescence is measured on a second sample, and alpha-induced artificial thermoluminescence is measured on a third. The alpha and beta radiations are accomplished with plaque sources of polonium-210 and strontium-90, respectively.

The age formula, to be discussed shortly, assumes that the amount of thermoluminescence is linear with dose, but this is not always true. The *linearity* of each sample must be tested. This is accomplished by exposing the fourth and fifth samples to beta and alpha doses of about double the first artificial irradiations. Only very seldom does a nonlinear sample occur.

After the samples have been prepared, the tiny disks of sherd grains are placed individually in special apparatus designed to generate up to 500°C heat rapidly and to record the thermoluminescence emitted by means of a photomultiplier tube (Figure 52). There are several designs now in use. The heating element upon which the sample is placed is heated to 500°C in 25 sec by passing through it a current of approximately 200 amperes (200 A). The rate of heat buildup is kept constant by an attached regulatory mechanism. The glow recorded by the photomultiplier tube is measured with an electrometer, which, in turn, is attached to a recorder that produces a graph of light output versus temperature (glow curve). All glow curves are taken in an atmosphere of nitrogen in order to remove, or at least reduce, the spurious thermoluminescence not associated with radiation-filled traps. Also, all operations are conducted in subdued light in order to avoid optical bleaching of the thermoluminescence.

Because of thermal decay during antiquity, the natural glow curve shows little light below 300°C. In the context of dating, *thermoluminescence* is implicitly assumed to refer to the light emitted in the 400°C region of the glow curve. A glow curve is a plot of the ratio of light intensity versus temperature. A natural glow curve remains at zero until about 250°C, and then rises to a plateau value, usually by 350°C (Figure 53). The onset of the plateau is taken to indicate that the traps responsible for the light in that temperature region are deep enough for decay effects to have been negligible over the thousands of years of burial.

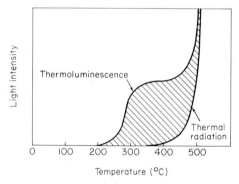

Figure 53. *Typical glow curve from ancient pottery. (From Aitken 1968: Fig. 7.3.)*

The height of the plateau in the natural glow curve is taken as the natural thermoluminescence. As mentioned earlier, thermoluminescence is a measure of the total dose of radiation to which the sherd has been exposed since firing. An evaluation of the total dosage is made in rads (1 rad = 100 ergs of absorbed energy) by measuring the sensitivity of thermoluminescent minerals found in the pottery sherd. This sensitivity of the pottery to radiation-induced thermoluminescence is obtained by measuring the thermoluminescence produced by a standard, artificial dose of alpha and beta rays. The object is to determine the radiation dose that induces thermoluminescence of the same magnitude as the natural thermoluminescence (that is the *equivalent radiation dose*; see Figure 54).

In addition to knowing the natural thermoluminescence of the sherd, and the sensitivity of the thermoluminescent components of the sherd to alpha and beta irradiations, it is also necessary to know

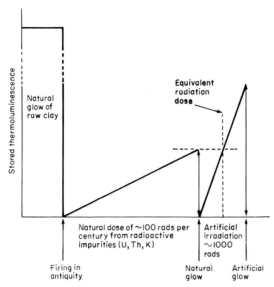

Figure 54. *Simplified illustration of the basis for thermoluminescence dating. (From Aitken 1968: Fig. 7.1.)*

the natural radiation dose received by the sherd each year. Figure 51 illustrates a typical dosage per year for a given sherd, but in the actual process of dating, it is necessary to make this calculation on each sherd to be dated. The calculation is based on measurements of the radioactive contents of the sherd. The total uranium and thorium content is measured in terms of alpha activity using a device called a *scintillation counter*. The potassium-40 content of the sherd is usually determined by means of X-ray fluorescent analysis.

The actual age of the pottery sherd is then given by the relationship

$$\text{age} = \frac{\text{natural TL}}{(\text{TL/rad})_a \times (\text{rads/year})_a + (\text{TL/rad})_{\beta,\gamma} \times (\text{rads/year})_{\beta,\gamma}},$$

in which (TL/rad) denotes thermoluminescent sensitivity and (rads/year) denotes annual dosage of radiation. (Aitken *et al.*, 1968).

Dating Results

The results of one of the most recent test programs, administered by M. J. Aitken, D. W. Zimmerman, and S. J. Fleming of the Research Laboratory for Archaeology at Oxford, are given in Table 11. The

TABLE 11

Fine-Grain Dating Results; Tests with Pottery of Known Age[a,b]

Location	Pottery fragment	Equivalent[c] rads (β)	k^d	U and Th series		Soil + K cosmic rays		TL	Ages (years B.P.)	
				α	β	β	γ		TL	Archaeological
Lezoux	6b1	640	0.190	2.82	0.114	0.155	0.201	640		600 ± 50
	2	925	0.272	3.45	0.141	0.164	0.201	640	635	
	3	720	0.214	2.88	0.119	0.214	0.201	625		
Orton	41a2	1320	0.154	3.22	0.127	0.240	0.077	1400		
Longueville	3	1760	0.134	4.11	0.168	0.247	0.077	1690	1370	1650 ± 150
	6	1000	0.166	3.43	0.106	0.233	0.077	1010		
Portchester	69d1	855	0.157	1.28	0.051	0.233	0.096	1480		
	2	930	0.132	1.76	0.072	0.133	0.096	1750	1615	1650 ± 50
Cambridge	72b1	800	0.184	1.33	0.047	0.150	0.080	1540		
	3	750	0.180	0.97	0.037	0.080	0.080	2020	1780	1750 ± 50
Dragonby	68f1	835	0.218	1.39	0.056	0.144	0.060	1500		
	2	825	0.174	1.68	0.066	0.149	0.060	1460	1430	1750 ± 50
	3	730	0.190	1.28	0.053	0.200	0.060	1320		
Bainbridge	67a1	885	0.215	1.07	0.041	0.128	0.080	1850		
	3	1020	0.182	1.67	0.068	0.238	0.080	1480		
	5	1640	0.250	1.80	0.080	0.220	0.080	1980	1695	1780 ± 20
	6	960	0.151	1.72	0.064	0.243	0.080	1470		
Winchester	70d1	620	0.073	1.07	0.040	0.093	0.052	2350		
	2	835	0.194	1.63	0.066	0.078	0.052	1630	1920	1800 ± 50
	3	1000	0.142	1.29	0.055	0.276	0.052	1770		
Lezoux	6a2	1360	0.124	2.80	0.114	0.164	0.142	1770		
	4	1560	0.097	2.83	0.117	0.213	0.142	2090	1880	1800 ± 10
	5	2100	0.190	3.68	0.153	0.172	0.142	1790		
Cirencester	71a1	775	0.138	1.29	0.058	0.137	0.070	1750		
	2	700	0.118	1.57	0.063	0.104	0.070	1660	1760	1850 ± 30
	3	825	0.152	1.26	0.054	0.128	0.070	1870		

Site	Sample	Equivalent rads (β)[c]	k[d]				[b]	TL age	Average TL age	Archaeologic age
Winchester	70e1	1265	0.168	3.37	0.132	0.252	0.045	1270		
	2	840	0.215	1.14	0.045	0.120	0.045	1850	1470	1770 ± 200
	3	920	0.188	1.82	0.075	0.245	0.045	1300		
Wroxeter	51a1	940	0.106	1.51	0.057	0.275	0.093	1610		
	2	660	0.103	0.88	0.035	0.087	0.093	2150	1780	1900 ± 10
	3	960	0.105	1.58	0.064	0.280	0.093	1600		
Cambridge	72a1	1040	0.173	1.12	0.043	0.233	0.090	1860		
	2	935	0.128	1.05	0.041	0.131	0.090	2360	2070	1900 ± 25
	4	960	0.130	1.25	0.045	0.187	0.090	1980		
Waddon Hill	65b1	1000	0.153	1.22	0.050	0.070	0.140	2230		
	2	620	0.064	1.61	0.074	0.057	0.140	1660	1820	1910 ± 10
	3	540	0.069	1.28	0.058	0.060	0.140	1560		
Fishbourne	77b6	720	0.090	1.41	0.055	0.091	0.110	1880		
	7	840	0.080	1.17	0.050	0.102	0.110	2370	2070	1910 ± 20
	12	1260	0.195	1.63	0.067	0.142	0.110	1970		
Dragonby	68e2	885	0.157	1.05	0.043	0.110	0.074	2250		
	3	560	0.116	0.99	0.041	0.120	0.074	1600		
	5	665	0.175	0.97	0.37	0.091	0.074	1790	1910	1925 ± 25
	6	935	0.180	1.14	0.043	0.144	0.074	2000		
	68c2	965	0.180	0.98	0.041	0.133	0.081	2250		
	3	910	0.147	1.20	0.043	0.101	0.081	2260	2240	1950 ± 50
	4	820	0.135	1.05	0.043	0.108	0.081	2200		
Stephania	5a1	625	0.296	0.38	0.013	0.009	0.035	3700		
	3	574	0.242	0.35	0.010	0.022	0.035	3780	3660	3500 ± 200
	c1	370	0.120	0.22	0.009	0.035	0.035	3510		

[a] From Aitken (1968: Table 1).

[b] Standard deviation of thermoluminescent (TL) ages within a context, 10%. Standard deviation of a single TL age from the Archaeologic age, 15%. Standard deviation of the average TL age of a context from the Archaeologic age, 10%.

[c] Equivalent rads (β) is the beta dose which produces an amount of TL equal to the natural TL.

[d] k is the ratio of TL response for alpha particles to that for beta particles.

scientists summarize the results of this test in an article in *Nature* (Aitken *et al.* 1968: 443). They point out that the relative importance of the different types of ionizing radiation can be seen. Alpha particles, although they contribute about 80% of the dose, produce only about 40% of the natural thermoluminescence, due to their reduced effectiveness relative to beta particles. In addition, they note that uranium and thorium contributed about 60%, potassium 38%, and cosmic rays 2% of the effective dose.

They report that the standard deviation of a single thermoluminescence age from the true archaeological age is 15%. However, they also point out that the average spread of ages within a given archaeological context is 10%, based on the dating of several different pottery types within a single context.

In concluding their summary of these test results, the researchers declare that some error-contribution factors are not serious, and that the technique, even at the present ±10% level of accuracy, is likely to be of considerable importance in prehistoric archaeology. A very recent review of the potential of thermoluminescence dating by Ralph and Han (1971) reflects comparable optimism. Although the dating of prehistoric pottery is just beginning, the technique has received considerable public attention, both professional and amateur, in connection with a series of authentication studies of fine-art ceramic and terra-cotta objects in the possession of several museums.

READINGS

Aitken, M. J.
    1961   *Physics and archaeology*, New York: Wiley (Interscience).
    1968   Thermoluminescent dating in archaeology: Introductory review. In *Thermoluminescence of Geological Materials*, edited by D. J. McDougall, pp. 369–378. New York: Academic Press.
Aitken, M. J., D. W. Zimmerman, and S. J. Fleming
    1968   Thermoluminescent dating of ancient pottery. *Nature* **219**: 442–445.
Aitken, M. J., D. W. Zimmerman, S. J. Fleming, and J. Huxtable
    1970   Thermoluminescent dating of pottery. In *Radiocarbon variations and absolute chronology*, edited by I. U. Olsson. New York: Wiley.
Aitken, M. J., P. R. S. Moorey, and P. J. Ucko
    1971   The authenticity of vessels and figurines in the Hacilar style. *Archaeometry* **13**: 89–142.
Bonfiglioli, G.
    1968   Thermoluminescence: What it can and cannot show. In *Thermoluminescence of geological materials*, edited by D. J. McDougall, pp. 15–24. New York: Academic Press.

Fagg, B. E. B., and S. J. Fleming
1970 Thermoluminescent dating of a terra-cotta of the Nok culture, Nigeria. *Archaeometry* **21**: 53–55.

Fleming, S. J.
1968 Thermoluminescent age studies on mineral inclusions separated from ancient pottery. In *Thermoluminescence of geological materials,* edited by D. J. McDougall, pp. 431–440. New York: Academic Press.
1970 Thermoluminescent dating: Refinement of the quartz inclusion method. *Archaeometry* **12**: 133–145.
1971 Thermoluminescent authenticity testing of ancient ceramics: The effects of sampling by drilling. *Archaeometry* **13**: 59–69.

Fleming, S. J., H. M. Moss, and A. Joseph
1970 Thermoluminescence authenticity testing of some 'Six Dynasties' figures. *Archaeometry* **12**: 57–65.

Fleming, S. J., H. Tucker, and J. Riederer
1971 Etruscan wall-paintings on terra-cotta: A study in authenticity. *Archaeometry* **13**: 143–168.

Fremlin, J. H.
1968 Effects of non-uniformity of material on the thermoluminescent method dating. In *Thermoluminescence of geological materials,* edited by D. J. McDougall, pp. 419–426. New York: Academic Press.

Huang, F. S. W.
1970 Thermoluminescence dating applied to volcanic lava. *Nature* **227**: 940–941.

Kennedy, G., and L. Knopf
1960 Dating by thermoluminescence. *Archaeology* **13**: 137–148.

Lewis, D. R., T. N. Whitaker, and C. W. Chapmen
1959 Thermoluminescence of rocks and minerals, Part I: An apparatus for quantitative measurement. *The American Mineralogist* **44**: 1122.

Mazess, R. B., and D. W. Zimmerman
1968 Thermoluminescence dating of some Peruvian pottery, in *Thermoluminescence of geological materials* edited by D. J. McDougall, pp. 445–450. New York: Academic Press.

Mejdahl, V.
1969 Thermoluminescence dating of ancient Danish ceramics. *Archaeometry* **11**: 99–104.
1970 Measurement of environmental radiation at archaeological excavation sites. *Archaeometry* **12**: 147–159.

Ralph, E. K., and M. C. Han
1968 Progress in thermoluminescent dating of pottery. In *Thermoluminescence of geological materials,* edited by D. J. McDougall, pp. 379–388. New York: Academic Press.
1969 Potential of thermoluminescence in supplementing radiocarbon dating. *World Archaeology* **1**: 157–169.
1971 Potential of thermoluminescence dating. In *Science and archaeology,* edited by R. H. Brill. Cambridge, Massachusetts: M.I.T. Press.

Sampson, E. H., S. J. Fleming, and W. Bray
1972 Thermoluminescent dating of Colombian pottery in the Yotoco style. *Archaeometry* **14**: 119–126.

Tite, M. S.
1968 Some complicating factors in thermoluminescent dating and their implications.

In *Thermoluminescence of geological materials,* edited by D. J. McDougall, pp. 389–406. New York: Academic Press.

Winter, J.
    1971   Thermoluminescent dating of pottery. In *Dating techniques for the archaeologist,* edited by H. N. Michael and E. K. Ralph. Cambridge, Massachusetts: M.I.T. Press.

Zeller, E. J.
    1968   Geologic age determination by thermoluminescence. In *Thermoluminescence of geological materials,* edited by D. J. McDougall, pp. 311–326. New York: Academic Press.

Zimmerman, D. W.
    1967   Thermoluminescence from fine grains from ancient pottery. *Archaeometry* **10**: 26–28.
    1971   Thermoluminescent dating using fine grains from pottery. *Archaeometry* **13**: 29–52. (a)
    1971   Uranium distributions in archaeologic ceramics: Dating of radioactive inclusions. *Science* **174**: 818–819. (b)

Zimmerman, D. W., and J. Huxtable
    1971   Thermoluminescent dating of Upper Palaeolithic fired clay from Dolni Vestonice. *Archaeometry* **13**: 53–57.

CHAPTER THIRTEEN

Obsidian Hydration Dating

Introduction

Obsidian is a natural-glass substance that is often formed as a result of volcanic activity. Prehistoric man undoubtedly was impressed by the naturally sharp edges produced when a piece of obsidian was fractured. With little difficulty, the prehistoric tool maker could fashion a wide range of implements from quarried chunks or river-worn cobbles. Obsidian flakes in most large assemblages will exhibit collectively the whole roster of tool forms with which archaeologists are familiar: knives, scrapers, saws, gravers, drills, punches, and hafted points. Artisans in some cultures produced long, slender, razor-sharp prismatic blades. These are sometimes recovered in large quantities at a site. Occasionally, as in the case of certain sites in Highland Guatemala, the entire chipped-stone industry consists of these prismatic blades.

Quarried obsidian chunks are excellent material for the preparation of bifaces. Often preformed bifaces are the focus of vigorous trade networks, as in the case of central California. The biface *blank*, or preform, can be converted easily into a number of specific implement forms, such as knives, dart tips, drills, denticulates, or it can remain unmodified and function as a *valuable*, signifying wealth and status.

The intrinsic beauty of the lustrous glass, ranging from translucent greens to opaque blacks, inspired Stone Age artisans to fabricate personal ornaments such as nose plugs, ear spools, and pendants. The same aesthetic qualities led to the use of obsidian objects in religious and ceremonial activities: elaborately flaked figurines, nonrepresentational geometrical forms, and mirrors. In Mesoamerica, large obsidian ceremonial blades were used in human sacrifice ceremonies.

Wherever quarry obsidian can be obtained through surface collection or shallow mining, the archaeologist finds evidence of its use by Prehistoric man (Figure 55). Artifacts of this volcanic glass are to be found in the western part of North and South America, East Africa, the Near East, New Zealand, Easter Island, Japan, and certain parts of Central Europe. In these areas, it is often as ubiquitous as pottery, and potentially just as significant for dating (Table 12).

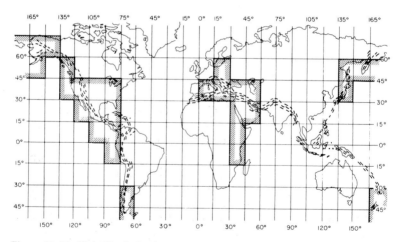

Figure 55. *World obsidian hydration zones: dashed lines, potential sources of obsidian; hatching, zones of origin of cultural obsidian. (After Clark 1964: Fig. 1.)*

TABLE 12

Summary of Obsidian Dating through 1971 (Based on Available Information)[a]

Geographical Area	Artifacts dated (No.)	Sites sampled (No.)
New World		
Alaska	375	18
California	1300	25
Northwestern Plains	1732	134
Southwestern United States	158	16
Ohio	24	5
West Mexico	560	11
Valley of Mexico	2565	47
Guatemala	2288	75
Ecuador	530	17
Africa		
Egypt	18	3
East Africa	29	10
Near East	300	16
Asia		
Japan	65	35
New Zealand	140	14
Europe		
Yugoslavia	15	1

[a] A total of 12,000 artifacts and 500 sites have been dated.

The Hydration Process

The dating of obsidian artifacts is based on the fact that a freshly made surface of obsidian will adsorb water from its surroundings to form a measurable hydration layer. This layer is not visible to the unaided eye and should not be confused with the patina that develops on many materials as a result of chemical weathering. The surface of obsidian has a strong affinity for water as is shown by the fact that the vapor pressure of the adsorption continues until the surface is saturated with a layer of water molecules. These water molecules then slowly diffuse into the body of the obsidian. Most obsidians contain from 0.1 to 0.3% water originally. Hydrated zones, however, contain approximately 3.5% water, representing the saturation point of the sorption of water by obsidian at atmospheric temperatures and pressure. In many substances the diffusion fronts are sloping or gradational. In obsidians this diffusion front is sharp, varying only in the order of plus or minus 0.07 μm in depth. An artifact that has a hydration layer 3 μm thick is "saturated" with about 3.5% water to this depth. Beyond it the nonhydrated mass of obsidian has a water content of only 0.1–0.3%.

The greater water content increases the density of the hydrated layer, and magnifies its volume. The mechanical strains produced as a result throughout the hydrated layer can be recognized under polarized light. The optical phenomenon then appears as a measurable luminescent band (Plate 2).

Each time a freshly fractured surface is prepared on a piece of obsidian, the hydration process begins from scratch. The depth of hydration achieved on any obsidian artifact, therefore, represents the amount of time that has elapsed since the artisan made the object.

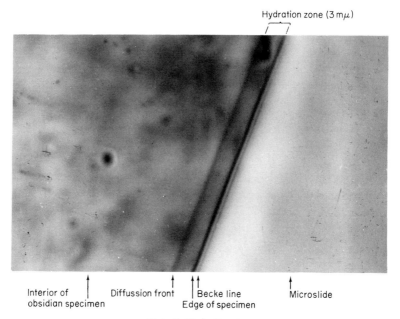

Plate 2. *Hydration rim.*

The Measurement of Hydration

The optical measurements of hydration are carried out on microscope thin sections prepared in the standard petrographic manner from obsidian artifact samples. Using a diamond-embedded continuous rim saw, the investigator makes two parallel cuts about 2 mm apart and 4 mm deep into the artifact. The section between these cuts is removed and ground down to about half of its original thickness. Next the section is cemented to a microscope slide with cooked Canada balsam. The section is ground down further to 0.003 inch to achieve the desired optical qualities under transmitted light. The slide then is washed and dried. Finally, the section is sealed with another application of Canada balsam and a cover slip.

After cooling, the sections are examined in cross-polarized light using a 100× oil-immersion lens and an image-splitting eyepiece. A part of the rim is sought that appears to consist of two parallel lines of minimum thickness, indicating that the outer edge of the sample and the advancing surface of the hydration rim are both perpendicular to the plane of the section. When such a region is found, contrast-enhancing adjustments may be made (some workers have found that various filters improve contrast for their eyes; others prefer to open or stop down aperture diaphragms in the optical path). Measurements then are made using the image-splitting eyepiece, an instrument that depends only on the operator's ability to shear apart and then overlap two identical images. It has been shown that this technique is capable of measuring with a precision of at least an order of magnitude greater than the resolution of the optical system being used, because it does not depend on being able to resolve the measured objects, but rather simply on being able to match intensity variations. The Pennsylvania State University Obsidian Dating Laboratory has reported a measurement error of approximately ± 0.1 μm (standard deviation) using the image-splitting eyepiece.

The procedure has been to make two measurements at each of two widely separated points on each sample. The mean value of the four measurements is calculated, and using the instrument calibration constant, the mean is converted into units of microns. The calibration constant is determined using a carbon replica of a 15,000 line-per-inch diffraction grating as a standard. Calibration constants differ little between operators and introduce an error of no more than ± 0.01 μm.

A second measurement technique also has been developed in an effort to evaluate the image-splitting method. The technique is the same as the one previously described, as far as sample preparation is concerned, except that after final grinding a cover slip is not cemented on. The sample is cleaned in acetone to remove excess Canada balsam, and a temporary cover slip is mounted with an index oil. Again, a good sample area is chosen, the lighting and filters are adjusted for maximum contrast, and a photograph is taken using a contrast process film. The film is developed for maximum contrast, and the negative is put on a *scanning densitometer*. The negative is oriented so that the densitometer slit is parallel to the edge of the sample image; the slit then is stopped down to minimum width, and the sample is scanned. The output of the photometer is recorded on a strip chart. The rim width is determined by measuring the distance on the chart recording between the peaks marking the advancing edge of the hydration rim and the outer surface of the artifact. It has been found that measurements made photographically are very close to measurements made by the image-splitting technique.

Hydration Rate-Controlling Variables

In order for obsidian hydration values to yield chronometric dates, the rate of hydration must be calculated. Physical scientists engaged in research on obsidian hydration have argued on theoretical grounds that the diffusion of water into obsidian should follow the diffusion law

$$M^2 = Kt, \tag{1}$$

where

   M = microns;
   K = the diffusion coefficient
   t = the time in years.

The effect of temperature on the rate of hydration was recognized at an early stage in the research on hydration dating. Using archaeologically dated obsidian specimens from various parts of the world, Friedman and Smith (1960) demonstrated that there were systematic differences in the rate of hydration between different worldwide climatic zones. In order to clarify and further validate the temperature dependence of obsidian hydration, Friedman *et al.* (1966) experimentally induced hydration of obsidian under controlled laboratory conditions. They suspended freshly chipped rhyolitic obsidian in a furnace maintained at a constant temperature of $100 \pm 5°C$ and at 1 atmosphere H_2O of pressure. The samples were removed at intervals over a four-year period, thin sections were cut, and the depth of hydration was measured.

The results of their study confirmed that hydration proceeds according to the law $M^2 = Kt$, and aided in defining the relation between the diffusion coefficient K and the effective hydration temperature T; this relation is given in the following equation

$$K = A \exp(E/RT) \tag{2}$$

where

> K = the diffusion coefficient;
> A = a coefficient which is dependent upon the physical and chemical properties of the glass;
> $\exp$ = 2.71828, the base of the natural logarithms;
> E = activation energy in kilocalories per mole;
> R = the universal gas constant;
> T = the effective hydration temperature.

As this equation makes clear, temperature T is only one of several variables that affect the diffusion coefficient K.

Obsidians of different composition also can have different rates of hydration. This was recognized in the early stages of obsidian hydration research with respect to major compositional classes such as *rhyolitic* versus *trachytic*. Friedman and Smith reported as early as 1960 that evidence from archaeologically dated obsidian artifacts found in Egypt permitted them to argue that trachytic obsidian hydrated at an estimated rate of 14 μm^2 per 1000 years, while rhyolitic obsidians in the same climatic environment hydrated at an estimated rate of 8.1 μm^2 per 1000 years. It was not until more recently, however, that compositional variation within a single class of obsidians was discovered to affect hydration rate just as significantly. This author has discovered that green rhyolitic obsidian hydrates almost three times as fast as grey rhyolitic obsidian in the central Mexican highlands under uniform temperature conditions (11.45 μm^2 per 1000 years versus 4.5 μm^2 per 1000 years) (Michels 1971).

Thus, current knowledge strongly points to temperature and composition as the principal variables that affect the diffusion coefficient K in the diffusion equation $M^2 = Kt$. Special situations may arise when soil chemistry or solar radiation may affect the coefficient. Relative humidity does not appear to function as a variable under any circumstances.

TABLE 13

Chronometric Scale for Valley of Mexico Hydration Measurement[a,b]

Period		Date		Gray obsidian ($4.5\mu^2$/1000 years[c])	Green obsidian ($11.45\mu^2$/1000 years[c])
		A.D.	1821	0.88 micron	1.37
	Late				
Colonial		A.D.	1669	1.08	1.77
				1.23	1.92
	Early				
		A.D.	1519	1.34	2.19
				1.49	2.34
	Aztec				
Post-		A.D.	1200	1.78	2.89
classic				1.93	3.04
	Early				
		A.D.	900	2.12	3.42
				2.27	3.57
Classic					
		A.D.	300	2.66	4.29
				2.81	4.44
	Late				
		600	B.C.	3.32	5.35
				3.47	5.50
Formative	Middle				
		1500	B.C.	3.88	6.23
				4.03	6.37
	Early				
		2500	B.C.	4.41	7.08
				4.56	7.23
Archaic					
		7200	B.C.	6.35	10.17
				6.50	10.32
Paleo-					
Indian					

[a]From Michels (1971: Table 19.3).

[b]The chronometric scale for Valley of Mexico cultural periods is based on that of Sanders and Price (1968). Period boundaries are identified by an 0.14-^{m}m exclusion interval to ensure that assignment of artifacts involves no overlapping of periods as a result of measurement error (standard deviation, $\pm 0.07\mu$m).

[c]Rates of hydration for gray and green obsidian, respectively.

Estimating Rates of Hydration

Although much remains to be learned about the determinants of hydration rate, empirical studies involving hundreds, and sometimes thousands, of obsidian hydration measurements have indicated that broad controls for temperature and composition can provide an adequate basis for hydration value comparisons. Such conditions often can be met by such areas as a river valley, a highland plateau, or a coastal strip. Under these conditions intrasite and intersite chronometric dating can be confidently pursued (Table 13).

Estimating Rates by Averaging

One method for estimating the rate of hydration for an archaeological subregion involves the correlation of hydration rim thickness with an independent chronometric scale such as that provided by radiocarbon dating or dendrochronology. The method can be illustrated by describing the procedures used by Johnson (1969) in calculating a hydration rate for the Klamath basin of California and Oregon. The Klamath basin rate was calculated from data acquired during the excavation of the Nightfire Island site (4SK4) in Siskiyou County, Northern California. A deep, well stratified excavation pit was selected for the rate determination. Radiocarbon samples and obsidian flakes were obtained from ten excavation levels within the pit. Table 14 gives the results of radiocarbon dating and hydration rim measurements for the samples.

TABLE 14

Carbon-14 Dates and Hydration-Layer Measurements for Obsidian Samples from Ten Levels of the Nightfire Island Site (4SK4), California[a]

Years (B.P.)	Sample No.	No. of specimens	Level mean (μm)	Level S.D. (μm)
1540 ± 100	GaK-1841	5	2.4	0.3
2180 ± 80	GaK-1831	5	2.4	.7
2340 ± 100	GaK-1832	8	2.7	.6
2180 ± 90	GaK-1833	5	3.1	.7
3470 ± 80	GaK-1834	11	3.5	.8
3450 ± 90	GaK-1835	15	3.7	.8
4260 ± 100	GaK-1836	18	3.8	.7
4750 ± 110	GaK-1837	14	4.1	.4
4030 ± 90 4500 ± 110[b]	GaK-1838} GaK-1839}	16	4.2	.9
5750 ± 130	GaK-1840	10	4.4	.6

[a]From Johnson, L., Jr. Obsidian hydration rate for the Klamath Basin of California and Oregon. *Science*, **165**: 1354–1356, Table 1. Copyright 1969 by the American Association for the Advancement of Science.

[b]$X_{activity}$ = 4,265 years (B.P.).

He starts with the exponential equation

$$y = a \times x^b, \tag{3}$$

which, by taking logarithms, can be transformed to the linear equation

$$\log y = \log a + b \times \log x. \tag{4}$$

Using the ten data points, with the hydration rim thickness substituted for y, and time in years for x, the regression coefficients are calculated. In Johnson's example, they were found to be a log $a = -1.2679$ (the y-intercept of the regression line) and $b = 0.512$ (the slope of the regression line). These values result in the exponential equation

$$y = 0.054 \times x^{0.512}. \tag{5}$$

Johnson tests whether the value $b = 0.512$ is significantly different from the universally established value of 0.5. He finds that with his data they are not significantly different, and he therefore substitutes the established value of b in the exponential equation

$$y = a \times x^{1/2}, \tag{6}$$

and, using this equation, its logarithmic equivalent

$$\log y = \log a + \tfrac{1}{2} \log x, \tag{7}$$

TABLE 15

Data Set for Hydration Rate Averaging[a,b]

No.	y	x	$a = \dfrac{y}{x^{1/2}}$
1	2.4	1,540	0.061
2	2.4	2,180	0.051
3	2.7	2,340	0.055
4	3.1	2,180	0.068
5	3.5	3,470	0.059
6	3.7	3,450	0.063
7	3.8	4,260	0.058
8	4.1	4,750	0.059
9	4.2	4,265	0.063
10	4.4	5,750	0.058

[a]From Michels and Bebrich (1971: Fig. 7.3).
[b]See Table 14.

and the ten data points, the average value of a now can be found. By substituting the values of y (hydration rim thickness) and x (years) in the equation, ten values for a (Table 15) can be obtained which are averaged to yield the value of $a = 0.059_5$.

The exponential equation now has the form

$$y = 0.059_5 x^{1/2}, \tag{8}$$

and we can solve for the diffusion coefficient K in the hydration equation $M^2 = Kt$:

$$K = a^2 = (0.059_5)^2 = 0.00354. \tag{9}$$

Thus, the hydration rate for Klamath basin was established as 3.54 μm^2 per 1000 years.

Establishing a Rate by Least-Squares Regression

The data used for computation is a set of chronometric dates and the corresponding hydration rim thicknesses together with the standard deviations of both.

As before, we start with the exponential equation

$$y = a \times x^b, \tag{3}$$

which in logarithmic form becomes

$$\log y = \log a + b \log x. \tag{4}$$

A computer program is used to find the regression coefficients $\log a$ and b. The mean values of y and x may yield a b value quite different from the established theoretical value of 0.5. By varying the values of x and y within the range of their standard deviations, new values for the regression coefficients are computed. If the data are reliable, a systematic search will finally yield the value of $b = 0.5$, and the corresponding value of a can be used to solve for the diffusion coefficient K ($K = a^2$). This value of a is a least-squares value, rather than the simple mean.

Rate Approximation

The procedure to follow begins with the arbitrary correlation of a fixed point in time with a specific hydration rim thickness (essentially one point along an imaginary regression line). This is not always so arbitrary, for a particularly good association of obsidian with a cross-datable feature within a site can suggest an especially plausible correlation.

A rate then is calculated using Equation (1)

$$M^2 = Kt, \tag{1}$$

where t is the fixed point in time and M^2 is the hydration rim thickness squared. The resulting rate then is tested by comparing the obsidian dates with archaeological age estimates. If no satisfactory correspondence between obsidian dates calculated with this rate and archaeological estimates of age is observed, another arbitrary point in time and hydration rim thickness are correlated. A second "rate" thus is established, and the obsidian artifacts are assigned new dates based on this second rate. A test of correspondence between these dates and archaeological expectations of age again is undertaken. These procedures are repeated until a rate is calculated that produces obsidian dates that correspond significantly to archaeological age estimates throughout the full chronological range of site occupation.

The rate which is ultimately accepted serves as a working hypothesis. Because of the nature of diffusion, a small error in the rate calculation can produce gross anomalies in age determinations at points over a 3–5-μm dating range. Thus, even though a rate may yield what appears to be an acceptable date when calculated for a hydration rim of 3.9 μm, the archaeologist may discover that it is an invalid rate because it would require that the chronometric value of a hydration rim 1.2 μm thick falls outside the estimated limits of time in which site occupation occurred.

The success of this approach to hydration rate determination rests upon

(1) the extent to which archaeological estimates of age are reliable;
(2) the presence of a significantly large micron range within the obsidian collection dated;
(3) a suitably large sample of dated obsidian that precludes the introduction of error through insufficient sample size.

Relative Dating Applications

Relative dating programs such as seriation of artifacts or site components require large samples of dated materials, a requirement that most other chronometric techniques cannot meet since the cost of such dating is usually so high. Obsidian dating, however, is cheap and fast. For the cost of five commercially processed radiocarbon dates the archaeologist can obtain 100 commercially processed obsidian dates, a sample size that can often yield a reliable profile of occupational intensity through time at a multicomponent site.

Instead of securing two or three obsidian dates from a single site, as is the pattern for radiocarbon dating, the archaeologist now often obtains anywhere from 60 to 500 dates. Originally, sampling from a single site was this massive for the purpose of seriating artifact types. However, many applications of such a large-scale dating sample soon began to emerge.

Relative dating applications of this technique include a study of the history of artifact style at a site. Since each artifact can be assigned a discrete hydration measurement, the investigator can serialize all specimens within an artifact class (such as projectile points) and can observe the behavior of stylistic traits, with time functioning as a fully controlled variable. Similarly, members of a typological set can be arrayed at measurable intervals along a temporal axis on the basis of their hydration measurement, and the investigator can determine the persistence of a type relative to other types of the same artifact class.

Artifact reuse has been identified as a major obstacle in the path of obsidian dating. It has also been a difficult factor to control for in archaeological analysis, generally. Obsidian dating, however, provides several approaches to this problem:

1. the investigator can often detect two hydration rims of different thickness on the same specimen, suggesting a time of original manufacture and a later time of reuse.
2. By measuring the hydration of a sample of associated tools, one can determine the percentages that either are of original manufacture or have been collected from the surface of the ground nearby and reused.
3. By generating a three-dimensional scatter graph showing the distribution of artifact hydration measurements within a stratified site deposit, one can ascertain the presence or absence of a cultural pattern of artifact reuse by determining whether a period of time can be isolated during which there is marked intrusion of older artifacts into younger strata that correlates with a period of negligible artifact manufacture.

This latter approach to determination of reuse is connected with another very important application of the dating technique—the testing of site stratigraphy. Hitherto, we have had no economical way of determining the degree to which an archaeological deposit conforms with the geologic principle of superposition; we all take conformity for granted, unless there is conspicuous evidence of systematic disturbance at the site. With this new technique one can observe the nature and extent of disturbance, and mixing of artifacts, by plotting the distribution of hydration measurements on a three-dimensional scattergraph. Thus, the archaeologist can segregate geological stratigraphy from archaeological or cultural stratigraphy. In the application of this test, instances have been studied in which physical stratigraphy is conspicuously present, whereas cultural stratigraphy obtains only in a statistically significant sense; that is, the disposition of the dated cultural materials indicates merely a tendency toward superposition, since large numbers of artifacts at all levels were very much out of place. This application of the technique is of great benefit in permitting the archaeologist to evaluate the integrity of the association between a radiocarbon sample and the cultural matrix of the site that it is intended to date. (See Chapter Three for more discussion of this application.)

Another very useful application of this technique to relative dating is for determination of the relative intensity of occupation of the site through time. This one can do by graphing the frequency distribution, through time, of a large sample of artifacts postulated to be of primarily domestic utility. The resultant graph yields something analogous to a demographic curve for that site locality.

A related application has to do with the discovery of a commercial focus within a lithic industry. If a site became the locus of commercially motivated manufacture of artifacts, the graph of frequency distribution for that particular class of lithic artifacts exhibits a curve that does not conform with those for other classes of artifacts; it shows a conspicuous rise in the production of artifacts of that class along a specific segment of the curve. The isolation of periods of commercially motivated production of artifacts at a site allows the archaeologist to sketch, in broad outline, the temporal and geographic parameters of a trading network.

Perhaps the most fundamental contribution of the technique is its use by archaeologists to associate artifacts with each other for the purpose of forming artifact complexes in the absence of reliable stratigraphy. For the first time, we have a perfectly unbiased procedure for segregating surface materials, and materials from poorly stratified or unstratified sites, into analytically useful units of association. Segregation is accomplished by establishing arbitrary micron ranges and treating all artifacts having hydration values falling within the established range as in some sense being associated. Artifacts having hydration values falling outside the range then belong to other similarly constituted units of association. For artifact samples that are very large, an added advantage is achieved by constituting *dead spaces* between micron-range units. All artifacts having hydration values falling within these dead spaces are excluded from analysis; this has the effect of artificially creating what can be figuratively described as sterile layers between deposits of cultural refuse, so that the absence of all contamination is ensured.

Source Identification Studies

Obsidian flows are so limited in number in any given archaeological provenience that it is feasible to attempt to identify them through analysis of chemical composition. In recent years this has become an important archaeological objective, for it permits us to control precisely the chemical comparability of obsidian artifacts which we seek to date.

Using neutron activation analysis, x-ray fluorescence, and optical emission spectroscopy, investigators have begun to characterize discrete obsidian flows in many parts of the world. In order to accomplish this, some investigators concentrate upon minor or trace elements such as beryllium, calcium, manganese, and zirconium, whereas others focus on combinations of such minor elements with major elements, such as sodium. In all cases the investigators are looking for element sets the relative concentrations of which are uniquely characteristic of a particular obsidian flow. Once all obsidian flows for a particular archaeological region have been "fingerprinted" in terms of characteristic concentrations of chemical constitutents archaeological specimens of obsidian can be classified by origin.

READINGS

Clark, D. L.
    1961   The application of the obsidian dating method to the archaeology of Central California. Doctoral dissertation, Stanford University. (a)
    1961   The obsidian dating method. *Current Anthropology* 2: 111–114. (b)
    1964   Archaeological chronology in California and the obsidian hydration method. *Annual Report of the Archaeological Survey, Department of Anthropology, University of California, Los Angeles*: 143–211.
Davis, L. B.
    1966   Cooperative obsidian dating research in the Northwestern Plains: A status report. *Montana Archaeological Society*, University of Montana, Missula, 7, No. 2: 3–5.
Dixon, K. A.
    1966   Obsidian dates from Temesco, Valley of Mexico. *American Antiquity* 31, No. 5, Part 1: 640–643.
    1970   A brief report on radiocarbon and obsidian hydration measurements from

ORA-58, Orange County, California. *Pacific Coast Archaeological Society Quarterly* **6**: 61–67.

Dixon, L. E.
1969   *Catalog of obsidian hydration measurement data for Mexico.* Washington, D.C.: Smithsonian Institution.

Dyson, J.
1960   Precise measurement by image-splitting. *Journal of the Optical Society of America* **50**, No. 8: 754–759.
1961   The precise measurement of small objects. *Associated Electrical Industries (Rugby) Ltd. Engineering* **1**: 1–5.

Duffy, F. C. H.
1960   Optical methods of helix measurement for the XV.4164 traveling wave tube. *Associated Electrical Industries (Rugby) Ltd. Research Laboratory Report* No. L4758.

Evans, C.
1965   The dating of Easter Island archaeological obsidian specimens. *Reports of the Norwegian Archaeological Expedition to Easter Island and the East Pacific* **2**, No. 18: 469–495. (Published as a monograph of the School of American Research and the Kon-Tiki Museum No. 24, Part 2.)

Evans, C., and B. J. Meggers
1960   A new dating method using obsidian: Part II, An archaeological evaluation of the method. *American Antiquity* **25**, No. 4: 523–537.

Friedman, I.
1968   Hydration rind dates rhyolite flows. *Science* **159**: 878–880.

Friedman, I., and N. Peterson
1971   Obsidian hydration dating applied to dating of basaltic volcanic activity. *Science* **172**: 1028–1029.

Friedman, I., and R. L. Smith
1958   The Deuterium Content of Water in Some Volcanic Glasses. *Geochimica et Cosmochimica Acta* **15**: 218–228.
1960   A new dating method using obsidian: Part I. The development of the technique. *American Antiquity* **25**, No. 4: 476–522.

Friedman, I., W. D. Long, and R. L. Smith
1963   Viscosity and water content of rhyolite glass. *Journal of Geophysical Research* **68**: 6523–6535.

Friedman, I., R. L. Smith, and W. D. Long
1966   The hydration of natural glass and the formation of perlite. *Bulletin of the Geological Society of America* **77**: 323–330.

Friedman, I., D. Clark, and R. L. Smith
1970   Obsidian dating. In *Science in archaeology,* edited by D. Brothwell and E. Higgs. New York: Praeger.

Gibbon, D. L., and J. W. Michels
1967   Electron microscope and optical observations of obsidian hydration. *Proceedings of the Electron Microscopy Society of America* edited by C. J. Arceneaux. Baton Rouge: Claitor's Book Store.

Gordus, A. A., W. C. Fink, M. E. Hill, J. C. Purdy, and T. R. Wilcox
1967   Identification of the geologic origins of archaeological artifacts: An automated method of Na and Mn neutron activation analysis. *Archaeometry* **10**: 87–96.

Green, R. C.
1964   Sources, ages and exploitation of New Zealand obsidian. *New Zealand Archaeological Association Newsletter* **7**, No. 3: 134–143.

Green, R. C., R. R. Brooks, and R. D. Reeves
  1967 Characterization of New Zealand obsidians by emission spectroscopy. *New Zealand Journal of Science* **10**: 675–682.
Haller, W.
  1960 Kinetics of the transport of water through silicate glasses at ambient temperatures. *Physics and Chemistry of Glasses* **1**, No. 2: 46–51.
  1963 Concentration-dependent diffusion coefficient of water in glass. *Physics and Chemistry of Glasses* **4**, No. 6: 217–220.
Johnson, L.
  1969 Obsidian hydration rate for the Klamath basin of California and Oregon. *Science* **165**: 1354–1356.
Katsui, Y, and Y. Kondo
  1965 Dating of stone implements by using hydration layer of obsidian. *Japanese Journal of Geology and Geography* **46**, No. 2–4: pp. 45–60.
Marshall, R. R.
  1961 Devitrification of natural glass. *Geological Society of America Bulletin* No. 72: 1493–1520.
Meggers, B. J., C. Evans, and E. Estrada
  1965 Early Formative period of coastal Ecuador: The Valdivia and Machalilla phases. *Smithsonian Contributions to Anthropology* Vol. 1. Washington, D. C.: Smithsonian Institution.
Meighan, C. W., L. J. Foote, and P. V. Aiello
  1968 Obsidian dating in West Mexican archaeology. *Science* **160**, No. 3832: 1069–1075.
Meighan, C. W. and C. V. Haynes
  1970 The Borax Lake site revisited. *Science* **167**: 1213–1221.
Michels, J. W.
  1965 Lithic serial chronology through obsidian hydartion dating. Doctoral dissertation, University of California, Los Angeles.
  1965 A progress report on the UCLA obsidian hydration dating laboratory. *Annual Report of the Archaeological Survey, department of Anthropology,* University of California, Los Angeles: 377–387.
  1967 Archaeology and dating by hydration of obsidian. *Science* **158**, No. 3798: 211–214.
  1969 Testing stratigraphy and artifact re-use through obsidian hydration dating. *American Antiquity* **34**: 15–22.
  1971 The Colonial obsidian industry of the Valley of Mexico. In *Science and archaeology,* edited by R. H. Brill. Cambridge, Massachusetts: M.I.T. Press.
Michels, J. W., and C. Bebrich
  1971 Obsidian hydration dating. In *Dating techniques for the archaeologist,* edited by H. N. Michael and E. K. Ralph. Cambridge, Massachusetts: M.I.T. Press.
Morland, R. E.
  1967 Chronometric dating in Japan. *Arctic Anthropology* **4**, No. 2: 180–211.
Renfrew, C., J. E. Dixon, and J. R. Cann
  1966 Obsidian and early cultural contact in the Near East. *Proceedings of the Prehistoric Society for 1966* **XXXII**: 30–72.
Rose, C. S., and R. L. Smith
  1955 Water and other volatiles in volcanic glasses. *American Mineralogist* **40**: 1071–1089.
Sanders, W. T., and B. J. Price
  1968 *Mesoamerica: The evolution of a civilization.* New York: Random House.

Weaver, J. R., and F. J. Stross
  1965   Analysis by X-ray fluorescence of some American obsidians. *Contributions of the University of California Archaeological Research Facility:* 89–93.

Subject Index

N

O

C 5
D 6
E 7
F 8
G 9
H 0
I 1
J 2
  3